ILLEGAL IMMIGRATION

A Reference Handbook

Other Titles in ABC-CLIO's
CONTEMPORARY
WORLD ISSUES
Series

Books in the Contemporary World Issues series address vital issues in today's society such as genetic engineering, pollution, and biodiversity. Written by professional writers, scholars, and nonacademic experts, these books are authoritative, clearly written, up-to-date, and objective. They provide a good starting point for research by high school and college students, scholars, and general readers as well as by legislators, businesspeople, activists, and others.

Each book, carefully organized and easy to use, contains an overview of the subject, a detailed chronology, biographical sketches, facts and data and/or documents and other primary-source material, a directory of organizations and agencies, annotated lists of print and nonprint resources, and an index.

Readers of books in the Contemporary World Issues series will find the information they need in order to have a better understanding of the social, political, environmental, and economic issues facing the world today.

ILLEGAL IMMIGRATION

A Reference Handbook

Michael C. LeMay

**CONTEMPORARY
WORLD ISSUES**

A B C ☷ C L I O

Santa Barbara, California
Denver, Colorado
Oxford, England

Library of Congress Cataloging-in-Publication Data

LeMay, Michael C., 1941–
    Illegal immigration : a reference handbook / Michael C. LeMay.
        p.   cm. —(ABC-CLIO's contemporary world issues series)
    Includes bibliographical references and index.
    ISBN-10: 1-59884-039-8 (hard cover : alk. paper)
    ISBN-10: 1-59884-040-1 (ebook)
    ISBN-13: 978-1-59884-039-1 (hard cover : alk. paper)
    ISBN-13: 978-1-59884-040-7 (ebook)
    1. Illegal aliens—United States.   2. Illegal aliens—Government policy—United States.   3. United States—Emigration and immigration—Government policy.   I. Title.
JV6483.L46 2007
325.73—dc22

                                                        2006032617

10   09   08   07   10 9 8 7 6 5 4 3 2 1

This book is also available on the World Wide Web as an eBook. Visit abc-clio.com for details.

ABC-CLIO, Inc.
130 Cremona Drive, P.O. Box 1911
Santa Barbara, California 93116–1911

This book is printed on acid-free paper. ∞
Manufactured in the United States of America.

Contents

Tables and Figures

Preface

Illegal Immigration: A Reference Handbook examines the flow of unauthorized immigration to the United States, largely since 1970, and the policy attempts to grapple with this vexing political issue. It documents the unanticipated consequences of legal immigration policy and shows how gaps and failures in those laws and in policy implementation have fed the unauthorized immigration flood. It discusses how immigration policy both influences and reacts to the flow of immigration, whether legal or unauthorized. It emphasizes the struggle among competing interests in U.S. politics and society to determine the nature and content of illegal immigration policy. Finally, it examines the issue within the context of increasing globalization: how worldwide events, agreements, and organizations and the effects of policy enacted by other nations influence the illegal immigration problem for U.S. domestic policy-making.

Since 1970, concern over the flow of unauthorized immigration has remained on the national agenda. It is a political policy issue that is substantive in its importance and ever timely in its impact on U.S. culture, economy, politics, society, and sense of national identity (that is, of our collective "peoplehood"). Most recently, it has become an important element in our sense of homeland security and defense against international terrorism.

The United States is unique among the nations of the world in the scope and degree to which it has absorbed immigrants from other nations. As a "nation of nations" the United States has permanent residents among its population who have come from more than 170 countries of origin. It has welcomed some 70 million legal immigrants. In addition, it has experienced the influx of an estimated 11 million illegal immigrants.

How these vastly differing groups of newcomers have mixed and mingled and ultimately incorporated into U.S. society is a story of compelling human interest. Immigration policy is intended to control the flow of newcomers. The unauthorized flow is a perennially vexing issue in U.S. politics and policy-making. Immigration policy-making, whether directed at legal or illegal immigration flow, is a blend of four major elements: (1) the effect that immigration has on the economy, and the question of whether illegal immigration is an economic burden or a blessing; (2) how the flow of immigrants, both legal and illegal, affects the very nature of the mix of race and ethnicity that makes up the American people; (3) how that flow affects the composite sense of "peoplehood"; and (4) considerations of national defense, homeland security, and foreign policy. Sometimes these four elements reinforce one another, defining or characterizing an "era" of immigration policy lasting several decades; at other times, they work against one another. Then, contending forces, competing interest groups in U.S. politics, seek to influence immigration policy, sometimes precipitating a major shift in immigration policy and ushering in a new era. In all cases and periods, however, these four elements are key to an understanding of policy aimed at illegal immigration.

The 1970s have been described as a decade of *stagflation,* an unprecedented mixture of double-digit unemployment and inflation. Those unsettling economic conditions, coupled with a shift in the national origin of both legal and, increasingly, illegal immigrants away from northwestern Europe and toward Latin America and Asia, led to calls for sweeping changes in immigration law. One such dramatic shift in policy aimed at illegal immigration was the enactment of employer sanctions as the "new" approach to discouraging it, embodied in the Immigration Reform and Control Act of 1986 (IRCA). The policy issues and battles associated with the decade-long struggle to enact IRCA have continued on and characterize much of the debate over the issue today. Proposals before the Congress in 2006 were remarkably similar to the issues and proposals of the mid-1980s.

Politics today struggles with heightened fears that illegal immigration overburdens governmental education, health care, prison, and welfare systems, particularly at the state and local levels—as well as the presumed harm done by illegal immigration to the national economy and culture. The attacks of September 11, 2001, on the New York World Trade Center Twin Towers and on the Pentagon led to serious proposals involving major overhauls of U.S. immigration policy to cope with the threat that international terrorism poses through the possibility of terrorist cells infiltrating the country through illegal immigration. The U.S. Immigration and Naturalization Service was dissolved into the new Department of Homeland Security. As of this writing, Congress is again involved in considering a guest-worker program, the problems of human trafficking, and the dual nationality aspects of a new world order with its increasingly multiple allegiances. Such developments suggest that we are entering a new era of immigration policy-making—one that we refer to as the "storm-door era."

Chapter One discusses the background and history of the illegal immigration issue, beginning with the seeds planted in the Bracero Program of 1942 to 1964, and covering all of the major laws and developments since the Immigration and Naturalization Act of 1965 established the present basis of U.S. immigration policy.

Chapter Two covers the problems and controversies raised by illegal immigration and discusses numerous proposed solutions. It covers the major laws and court cases that implement policy aimed at control of the unauthorized immigration flow, and shows how gaps in or unanticipated consequences of those policies have affected the issue.

Chapter Three presents a worldwide perspective on the issue. It discusses major international agreements and organizations that are involved in international migration, both legal and illegal. It touches on how other nations are grappling with the issue of illegal immigration, and how failures in national policy in other nations contribute to emigration that swells the illegal migration flow.

Chapter Four lists a chronology of the major events, court cases, laws, and policies concerning the issue of illegal immigration.

Chapter Five offers brief biographical sketches of the major actors involved in illegal immigration policy matters. These include governmental officials and the leaders of numerous nongovernmental organizations.

Chapter Six offers graphs and tables that illuminate the issue of illegal immigration. The chapter also presents summary excerpts from the key laws and court cases that determine or implement immigration policy.

Chapter Seven presents a directory of the organizations, both governmental and nongovernmental, engaged in the arena of immigration policy-making.

Chapter Eight contains an annotated list of print and non-print resources, including books, government reports, journals, and videos, that collectively provide the basis for a firm grasp of this complex and controversial public policy issue.

The book closes with a detailed glossary of key terms one needs to grasp in order to understand the topic.

1

Background and History

Introduction:
The Nature of Unauthorized Immigration

Since the United States began keeping count of the number of legal immigrants who have entered the nation, approximately 70
million have arrived as authorized immigrants. Throughout that
history, a number of illegal—or better said, unauthorized—immigrants have also entered the country to stay more or less permanently. The flow of unauthorized entrants became especially
heavy after 1970, and estimates now place the flow at its heaviest
ever. Today there are an estimated 10.5 to 11 million unauthorized immigrants residing in the United States (Pew Hispanic
Center, 2005). More commonly known as illegal aliens, their
presence here in such massive numbers has once again brought
the issue of illegal immigration to the forefront of the U.S. political scene, to the halls of the U.S. Congress, and to the public policy agenda of virtually all levels of government.

In order to address the nature and scope of this vexing political problem, several terms must be clarified. A person may become an illegal alien or immigrant in one of several ways. Unauthorized immigration primarily includes two types of migration
to the United States that qualify as illegal: (1) the undocumented,
more popularly known as the "illegal immigrant," who comes
into the country without paperwork or authorization, typically
crossing the southern border with Mexico. In reference to their
coming across the Rio Grande, such unauthorized immigrants
are often called "wetbacks." And (2), the visa overstayer, or the
migrant who enters the country with a valid but temporary visa

1

(for example, for tourism or as a student), who then simply goes underground and stays beyond the terms of the visa, thereby becoming illegal—an unauthorized immigrant rather than a temporary visitor. Since visa overstayers first enter the country with valid paperwork, they do so from the north—from Canada—and at the various ports of entry (airports and seaports) all over the nation. In many respects, the "Ellis Island" of today's immigration to the United States is LAX airport in Los Angeles, or Kennedy Airport in New York City, or any of the other major international airports. A third way in which someone may become an illegal resident is by entering the country with fraudulent documents. Finally, an illegal alien may be a person who, as a legal permanent resident, committed a crime after entry, became subject to deportation, but then failed to depart (Information Plus, 2006: 73). Of the estimated 10.5 to 11 million unauthorized immigrants in the United States today, approximately 60 percent are undocumented immigrants, and 40 percent are overstayers, fraudulent entrants, or persons failing to depart. This analytical distinction is necessary for any discussion of immigration policy and its reform, as the nature and effectiveness of the policy options used to cope with each type of unauthorized immigration vary considerably.

Another important distinction to be made that likewise has serious public policy implications concerns two terms that refer to the question of why someone becomes an international migrant intending to permanently reside in another country. These two terms have been called the "factors" of immigration. Push factors are those reasons, trends, or events that compel people to emigrate—that is, to leave their country of birth and nation of origin. Push factors may be defined simply as those reasons that compel individuals to emigrate from their country of origin and seek permanent resettlement elsewhere (LeMay, 2004: 269). A worldwide population explosion, coupled with enormous poverty, extremely high levels of unemployment, and the political turmoil experienced by so much of the Third World have all added to ethnic and religious tensions and natural disasters as powerful push factors driving international migration to an unprecedented scale. The United Nations has estimated that there are more than 15 million refugees worldwide. Many millions more are not displaced as refugees but leave their nation of birth to escape grinding poverty, epidemic disease of humans or crops, mass starvation, and the like. U.S.

policy-makers can do little in making public policy that will directly affect push factors. Such factors must be addressed by policy-makers in the nation of origin and by multinational organizations, such as the United Nations, the World Health Organization, UNICEF, the World Bank, the World Trade Organization, and so on. Since the United States is nearly unique in being an advanced First World economy that shares nearly 2,000 miles of border with a Third World country, it experiences enormous immigration pressures caused by push factors (LeMay, 1994: 18).

Pull factors may be defined as those characteristics of a country that attract immigrants for permanent settlement (LeMay, 2004: 269). There is, of course, a direct link between the two factors. The United States, having by far the world's largest economy, draws to itself those migrants seeking relief from poverty or simply hoping for a better economic future for themselves and their children. The United States, being among the most stable political democracies in the world, draws, as does a magnet, those seeking stability, safety, and freedom—both freedom to participate in public affairs and freedom from cultural, ethnic, political, racial, or religious persecution.

This chapter will discuss the background and history of the issue, stressing particularly the trend toward increasing numbers of illegal entries and their greater dispersion in recent years throughout the United States. Illegal immigration is no longer a "border-states problem." It is truly a national problem. This discussion will summarize and explain the trend, cover differing points of view as to the nature and impact of the massive unauthorized immigration, and touch upon some possible solutions—some tried with little success so far, and others proposed but not yet enacted.

The Roots of the Problem

Ultimately, unauthorized immigration arises out of problems in the legal immigration system and policy enacted for its implementation. Legal immigration policy for the United States today is established by the Act of October 3, 1965: Immigration and Naturalization Act of 1965 (Re: Amending the Act of June 27, 1952), 79 Stat. 911. Gaps, flaws, and unanticipated consequences associated with that fundamental law establishing current legal immigration policy, and with its several amendments over the years since its passage, form the basis for the nature and scope of the illegal flow. In a very real sense, however, one cannot fully grasp the development of the unauthorized immigration flow without first understanding the impact of the Bracero Program and its demise in 1964.

The illegal influx increased dramatically after 1970, reflecting unanticipated consequences associated with ending the Bracero Program. A type of guest-worker program (more specifically, a temporary-worker program), the Bracero Program allowed U.S. employers to import workers from Mexico on a temporary basis—for nine months of a given year. It began in 1942, during World War II, as a measure to cope with the severe labor shortages in agriculture created when millions of workers left the farms for the high-wage wartime production jobs in the nation's metropolitan areas. Workers also left to serve in the U.S. military, which grew to millions in uniform. The expanding U.S. economy after the war continued the need for—and even the expansion of—the Bracero Program. Congress enacted the Agricultural Act of 1949, which codified prior laws and provisions for temporary workers—that is, the Bracero Program (63 Stat. 1051), which peaked in the mid-1960s. It is estimated that more than 5 million Mexicans participated in the program over its twenty-two years. The program ended in 1964, when it was stopped as part of an agreement to garner support for passage of what became the Immigration Act of 1965 (LeMay, 2004: 266; see also Calavita, 1992; Craig, 1971, and Information Plus, 2006). Organized labor and various patriotic and other restrictionist groups argued that the program was getting out of hand, and their political agitation resulted in the program's termination in 1964. Its controlled entry of temporary farm workers was thus replaced by the flow of illegal immigrants, particularly from Mexico. These were essentially the same workers who had participated in the Bracero Program (Muller and Espanshade, 1985: 13; LeMay and Barkan, 1999: 252).

Numerous studies and scholars have noted the importance of the Mexican immigration patterns to the United States established during the Bracero period, which essentially set up chain-migration patterns that have persisted long after the end of the Bracero Program— indeed, these patterns even influence today's undocumented immigration flows (see, for example, Andreas, 2000; Bustamente, 1981; Calavita, 1992; Chiswick,

1988; Crockroft, 1986; Conover, 1987; Craig, 1971; Kiser and Kiser, 1979; Kirstein, 1977; Massey et al., 1987; and Nevins, 2002). The Bracero Program workers filled an "economic wage" niche. Their jobs paid wages low enough to allow the employer to make a profit. Faced with the loss of such cheap labor, employers had but few options. They could move their operations overseas or across the border, replace their workers with machines, hire illegal immigrants, or simply go out of business. When the Bracero Program ended in California, only the lettuce and citrus growers raised wages in an attempt to attract domestic workers. The tomato growers began using mechanical harvesters, the asparagus growers moved to Mexico, and marginal growers in all crops simply closed down and sold their farms. When the 1965 law imposed a 20,000 per country limit on legal immigration and the guest-worker Bracero Program was closed down, hundreds of thousands of Mexican immigrants who had been coming regularly and annually to the United States to work for nine months simply continued to come without authorization, and their numbers gradually grew to an estimated half-million per year. These workers knew where to find places to live and work, and former Bracero Program workers passed on that knowledge to their kinfolk and their village compatriots.

Likewise, the employers who had legally hired workers in the Bracero Program continued to hire them after it ended. From 1965 until enactment of the Immigration Reform and Control Act of 1986 (IRCA), it was illegal for workers to come to the United States without documents, but it was not illegal for employers to hire the undocumented worker. A provision known as the "Texas Proviso," included in the 1952 McCarran-Walter Act, exempted employers of illegal aliens from the harboring provisions of the law. Under this provision, essential to securing support for the McCarran-Walter Act among Southwestern growers, "No employer could be found to have violated federal law for hiring illegal aliens" (Glazer, 1985: 52–53; LeMay, 1994: 10). Employers knew and valued the former Bracero Program workers and accepted their recommendation to hire their compatriots. The illegal immigration flow simply replaced those who had been entering under the guest-worker provision, except that they did not return to Mexico after nine months of seasonal work in the United States. Increasingly, after the 1970s, they came and remained permanently in the

United States as unauthorized immigrants (LeMay, 1994: 26–27).

The consistency of the flow of immigrants from Mexico to specific states within the United States, termed "gateway states," can be seen in Table 6.1 in Chapter Six, showing the distribution of Mexican immigrants by state of residence from 1940 to 2000. A clear pattern of such immigrants residing primarily in those gateway states is evident, as is their gradual dispersion to non–gateway states after enactment of IRCA, 1986.

This flow of illegal immigrants exacerbated the job and income problems of blacks, legal residents of Hispanic origin, and other secondary job market workers by reducing the number of such jobs available to them, depressing wages for those jobs they did hold, and generally undercutting working conditions (Papademetrious and Miller, 1984: 88; Phillips and Massey, 1999: 233; Zuniga and Hernandez-Leon, 2005: 11–12).

During the late 1970s and throughout the 1980s, push factors propelled the rising flow. As the *Final Report* of the U.S. President's Select Commission on Immigration and Refugee Policy (SCIRP) noted:

> One of the greatest pressures for international migration is and will be world population growth. Projections of this growth show more than a 50 percent increase from 1975 to the year 2,000, from 4 billion to 6.35 billion. It has been estimated that 92 percent of this growth will take place in countries whose resources are least able to accommodate the needs of new population. . . . World economic and political instability would be threatened by the sudden, large-scale population moves which could result from widespread political or economic chaos in developing nations. (1981: 19–20)

Rising push factors induced waves of immigration that had significant long-term impact and were more powerful than any other factor.

What resulted from the changing flow of legal and unauthorized immigration into the United States was a growing sense of crisis. There was widespread dissatisfaction registered in the news media, in public opinion polls, and within government over the inadequacy of immigration laws to meet the new challenge. A pervasive sense that the nation's immigration policy was out of control and that the nation had lost control of the borders resulted (see SCIRP, 1981: 10; Bean and Sullivan, 1985: 67–73; LeMay, 1989: 8–10).

Indeed, more immigrants—legal and unauthorized—entered the United States between 2000 and 2005 than during any other five-year period in U.S. history. An estimated 8 million immigrants entered during this time, and nearly half of those—about 3.7 million—entered illegally, according to Census Bureau data reviewed by the Center for Immigration Studies (CIS) in Washington, D.C. Arizona and New Mexico in 2005 declared states of emergency in an effort to cope with problems of crime and financial exigencies that their respective governors (both Democrats) linked to massive illegal immigration. The nation's immigrant population set a record at 35.2 million in March 2005, greater than the number of immigrants at the peak of the "new" immigrant wave of 1910. Today, immigrants, legal and unauthorized, make up 12.1 percent of the entire U.S. population. For a detailed look at their pattern of residency, see Table 6.2 in Chapter Six, which presents the number of immigrants by state, ranked by their share of the population of that state, and the numbers that arrived from January 2000 to March 2005.

The Change in Legal Immigration: Setting the Stage for Illegal Immigration

The Immigration and Naturalization Act of 1965, also known as the Kennedy Immigration Act, changed legal immigration policy from the quota system to a preference system. Whereas the quota system reflected the racism of the 1920s, when the quota policy approach was enacted, the 1965 act reflected a changed attitude that was more open to immigration. National policymakers were reevaluating the racial bias inherent in many of the nation's laws, and immigration law was no exception. The post–World War II need to tinker with the quota system, exemplified in special acts, nonquota immigration policies, and refugee/escapee laws, demonstrated the need to comprehensively revise the quota system of immigration policy. The healthy nature of the national economy prevalent throughout the early to mid-1960s enabled even organized labor to favor a more liberal immigration policy. The 1965 Immigration Act tried to balance five goals: to preserve the family unit and to reunite separated families; to meet the need for highly skilled workers; to ease population problems created by emergencies, such as political upheavals, Communist country aggression (enhancing U.S. foreign policy goals), and natural disasters; to better the understanding of people through cross-cultural, national exchange programs; and to bar from the United States those aliens who were likely to represent adjustment problems because of their physical or mental health, criminal history, or dependency, or for national security reasons. The 1965 act replaced the quota system with a preference system that allocated immigrant visas within each foreign state, with a cap of 20,000 visas being issued per nation per year on a first-come, first-served basis, within each foreign state as follows:

1. First preference: unmarried sons and daughters of U.S. citizens
2. Second preference: spouses and unmarried sons and daughters of permanent resident aliens
3. Third preference: members of the professions and scientists and artists of exceptional ability
4. Fourth preference: married sons and daughters of U.S. citizens
5. Fifth preference: brothers and sisters of U.S. citizens
6. Sixth preference: skilled and unskilled workers in short supply
7. Seventh preference: refugees

Worldwide events soon outstripped the law's ability to accommodate refugees, and its annual limit of 20,000 visas per country was applied to immigrants from the Western Hemisphere nations, which previously had been without such limits. These provisions soon resulted in enormous pressures for immigrants to arrive in the United States "through the back-door"—that is, illegally—because the waiting lists for legal visas began to backlog into scores of years.

The number of persons crossing without authorization began, by the 1970s, to swell to a veritable flood. In 1970 the INS apprehended about a quarter-million undocumented aliens attempting to cross the nation's borders, mostly along the 2,000 miles of porous border to the nation's south. By 1986 that number had risen to nearly 2 million. In 1978, SCIRP put the total illegal immigrant population in the United States at between 3.5 million and 6 million. Hispanics, especially those from Mexico, and then from Central America, composed the bulk of those who entered "without papers." Roughly two-thirds of undocumented aliens were Mexicans driven north by grinding poverty and enormous unemployment at home. Many who came had themselves been temporary workers during the Bracero Program years or were relatives of those who had come at that time (1942–1964).

Mexican immigrants, who made up more than 60 percent of Hispanic immigrants, especially the undocumented ones, tended to come from rural and small-town areas, fleeing dire poverty. They often exhibited a "sojourner" attitude: since in their new country they resided close to their native areas, they often returned to their place of origin, thereby keeping family, social, and cultural ties strong. They came from near-feudal societies. Whereas earlier immigrant waves had been eager to become U.S. citizens, having come here expecting to remain permanently and often having cut off formal ties with their sending nations, Mexicans—especially the undocumented—considered the border merely a nuisance rather than a barrier. They often moved back and forth, retaining strong Mexican ties and slowing their rate of naturalization.

Estimates of the number of illegal immigrants here vary considerably and are best viewed as educated "guestimates," since persons here illegally do not identify themselves for fear of deportation. Figures also vary between seasons of the year, in part reflecting the availability of seasonal agricultural work. Figure 6.1 shows the estimated number of illegal immigrants living in the United States from 1986 to 2002, based on estimates from several sources. The figure indicates that the total number of illegal immigrants rose from about 3.2 million in 1986 to 9.3 million in 2002, when nearly two-thirds of all such illegal aliens resided in six states: California (with 27 percent), Texas (13 percent), New York (8 percent), Florida (7 percent), Illinois (6 percent), and New Jersey (4 percent) (Information Plus, 2006: 73). The Pew Center for Hispanic Studies estimates that by 2005 the total number had risen to 10.5 to 11 million.

The Crisis of Border Control: Illegal Immigration and the Enactment of IRCA

These trends led to a growing sense that the nation had simply lost control of its borders. Widespread dissatisfaction with the ability of the INS to control the borders was soon registered in the news media, general public opinion polls, and within government. During the Iranian hostage crisis, which lasted nearly two years during the administration of President Jimmy Carter, the nation was shocked to learn that the INS did not even know how many Iranian students were living here, let alone how many were doing so illegally. Many Iranians whom the INS was able to identify as being subject to deportation simply failed to attend deportation hearings or to leave when told to do so. Several hundreds of thousands were estimated to overstay their visas annually (SCIRP, 1981: 8–9).

Organized labor moved to deal with what they then saw as the threat from illegal aliens during the mid- to late 1970s, a period when the U.S. economy was plagued by stagflation: increasing unemployment, rising cost of living, and a recession that hit lower-wage jobs particularly hard. They convinced Rep. Peter Rodino (D-NJ), from one of the states experiencing high levels of the illegal-alien influx, that illegal aliens were taking jobs that rightfully belonged to U.S. citizens. Led by such influential labor organizations as the AFL-CIO and the International Ladies Garment Workers Union, and assisted by the National Association for the Advancement of Colored People (NAACP), which viewed illegal immigration as especially threatening to the status and jobs of poor urban blacks, they moved Rodino to propose an employer-sanctions amendment to the Immigration and Naturalization Act of 1965, essentially eliminating the "Texas Proviso" (Perotti, 1989: 83–84). This provision had favored growers and other employers of unauthorized immigrants by exempting them from criminal action for hiring undocumented workers, although it was still illegal for the workers themselves to immigrate without documents.

Sen. Edward Kennedy (D-MA), Rep. Rodino, and Rep. Joshua Eilberg (D-PA) linked employer sanctions with limited legalization (amnesty) and antidiscrimination provisions. Sen.

James Eastland (D-MS), a friend of the growers who opposed the employer-sanctions approach, with support of such groups as the National Council of Agricultural Employers and the American Farm Bureau Federation, insisted that any reform of immigration law that did not have a foreign-workers (also known as "guest-workers") program would make it unacceptable to growers and other employers. They wanted to replace the illegal immigrant labor force they prospered by employing with such guest-workers in an expanded H-2 temporary workers program acceptable to Sen. Eastland. At the time, he was chairman of both the Judiciary Committee and its Subcommittee on Immigration and Naturalization. He effectively killed the bill by stalling it in committee.

In 1977, the administration of President Jimmy Carter became involved. President Carter appointed as his new secretary of labor F. Ray Marshall, an economist at the University of Texas. Marshall had long been interested in the question. The administration, however, was split on the issue, as was the U.S. Congress. Secretary Marshall and Attorney General Griffin Bell favored limited amnesty and a tamperproof worker-eligibility card. The commissioner of the INS, Leonel J. Castillo, and various White House aides led the campaign for a generous amnesty program and deplored the civil-liberty implications of a worker-eligibility card.

Rep. Rodino was long frustrated that, despite the fact that two presidential commissions (one appointed by President Ford, the other by President Carter) had recommended approaches similar to his (that is, blending employer sanctions, legalization, and strong border enforcement measures), nothing would pass the Senate over the opposition of Sen. Eastland, who was intransigent on the issue. President Carter and Congress, prompted by Sen. Kennedy and Rep. Eilberg, established a joint presidential-congressional commission, the Select Commission on Immigration and Refugee Policy (SCIRP). Sen. Kennedy, then made chair of the judiciary committee, viewed SCIRP as a way to carve out for himself a pivotal role in any legislation on immigration reform or employer sanctions. SCIRP studied the issue thoroughly and issued its final report in 1981. The report ran to more than 450 pages and the supplemental staff report in excess of 900 pages. SCIRP recommendations covered the full spectrum of issues involving the illegal immigration debates.

SCIRP recommended closing the "back door" to undocumented immigration while slightly opening the front door to accommodate more legal immigration. It stressed the need to define immigration goals more sharply, to provide for a more effective structure to implement those goals, and to set forth procedures to ensure fair and efficient adjudication and administration of U.S. immigration law aimed at both legal and illegal immigration. In its final report, SCIRP maintained that immigration unquestionably served humanitarian needs and that continued immigration was in the best national interests of the United States. It noted that immigration entailed many benefits to U.S. society, but it recognized the nation's limited ability to absorb large numbers effectively. It stressed that the nation's first priority was to bring illegal immigration under control. It advocated establishing a rational system of legal immigration, recommending modest increases to expedite the clearance of the huge backlogs and ease family reunification pressures. It advocated an increase in legal immigration from 270,000 to 350,000 annually. It emphasized the enforcement of existing laws by imposing employer sanctions, an increase in law enforcement (mostly by increasing the Border Patrol), and coupled those with an amnesty program and a restructuring of the immigration bureaucracy and procedures of legal immigration. Although each of these ideas had been articulated before, SCIRP linked them together and legitimized the duality of the employer-sanctions/legalization approaches, saying, in essence, that one could not work without the other. Legalization would allow the INS to concentrate its efforts on border apprehension, while employer sanctions would "demagnetize" the pull of the U.S. economy, which was drawing the continued influx of undocumented workers into the United States. SCIRP's final report set the agenda for all subsequent discussions of and proposals to reform immigration law. It gave its weight to proposals and ideas that previously had been stymied in committee.

SCIRP's emphasis on the problem of undocumented immigration as "the most pressing problem" associated with immigration shaped and limited the debates in Congress and much of the news media over immigration policy reform. In its words, "Most U.S. citizens believe that the half-open door of undocumented/illegal immigration should be closed" (SCIRP, 1981: 104).

The Reagan administration, which had just come into office, responded to the SCIRP findings by establishing its own Task Force on Immigration and Refugee Policy in March 1981. The task force was headed by Attorney General William French Smith. It soon made several recommendations to the new president:

1. *Amnesty.* It recommended that aliens living here illegally since January 1, 1980, be permitted to remain, becoming eligible for resident-alien status after having been here for ten years, and they could then seek naturalization. It estimated the number of such at 5 million persons.
2. *Guest-worker Program.* It recommended allowing 50,000 Mexicans to enter the United States annually to work temporarily, and over the course of several years to increase that number gradually up to hundreds of thousands annually.
3. *Employer sanctions.* It recommended that employers hiring more than four employees who "knowingly hire" illegal aliens be fined up to $1,000 per violation.
4. *Enforcement.* It recommended a 50 percent increase in the INS budget and the addition of 1,500 new officers to the Border Patrol to enhance enforcement of immigration and labor laws.
5. *Boat People.* In response to a wave of "economic refugees" flooding in from Haiti, it recommended that boats carrying Haitians be intercepted, and that detention camps be set up to hold as many as 6,000 people pending their deportation hearings.
6. *Legal immigration limits.* It recommended increasing the annual limit for legal immigration to 610,000, with special preference to persons from Canada and Mexico (LeMay, 2004: 14–15)

By the fall of 1981 the House and Senate Judiciary Subcommittees on Immigration, chaired, respectively, by Rep. Romano Mazzoli (D-KY) and Sen. Alan Simpson (R-WY) had crafted the recommendations of the SCIRP Report and the Reagan administration's task force into legislative proposals that they considered essential as incentives to cooperation among the many groups competing over the illegal immigration reform issue. They introduced their measures into their respective chambers in March

1982. After committee hearings, the bills were reported out in mid-May. The Senate passed the Simpson bill by a vote of 81 to 19 in August 1982. The House bill, saddled with several critical amendments, required introduction of a clean version, sponsored by Rep. Mazzoli and Rep. Hamilton Fish Jr. (R-NY). After passage of the Senate version, the full Judiciary Committee finally approved the Mazzoli-Fish version in mid-September.

Because of the differences between the House and Senate versions, and overlapping jurisdictions, the Speaker of the House, Tip O'Neill (D-MA), referred the House bill sequentially to four committees: Education and Labor, Agriculture, Ways and Means, and Energy and Commerce. After each had considered the bill, it finally reached the Rules Committee in December, during the lame-duck session of the Ninety-Seventh Congress. By the time the bill reached the House floor, more than 300 amendments had been filed, showing strong opposition to the measure. It died on the floor.

In 1983, Simpson and Mazzoli renewed their efforts to craft compromises, reintroducing versions of their bills nearly identical to those passed in 1982. Agricultural interests, headed by the Farm Labor Alliance and advocated by Rep. Fish, developed a proposal for a guest-worker program. Rep. Edward Roybal (D-CA), a leader of the congressional Hispanic Caucus, proposed an alternative bill emphasizing tough enforcement of existing labor laws and minimum-wage laws to clamp down on the hiring aspects of illegal immigration as a substitute for the employer-sanctions approach.

The bills moved through their respective chambers, and, once again, the Senate progressed more rapidly toward passage, with Sens. Simpson and Kennedy working out compromises on key provisions. In the House, the Mazzoli bill again moved sequentially through four committee referrals. Reps. Mazzoli and Rodino, with the backing of the Reagan administration and the House Republican leadership, pressed for quick floor action. Political complications arising from the pending 1984 elections, however, led to obstructive amendments; the bill did not pass until June 1984, and then by a slim margin (216–211). Since it had provisions that differed from the Senate version, the bills were sent to a House-Senate conference committee, where it failed to achieve an acceptable compromise and died in committee.

In May 1985, Sen. Simpson introduced a new version of his bill, without the cosponsorship of Rep. Mazzoli. In the House,

Rep. Rodino introduced a measure similar to the version that had died in conference committee. Again, the two chambers passed differing versions of the bill. The Reagan White House, naturally, supported the Senate version sponsored by Sen. Simpson. The Senate Judiciary Committee rejected all attempts by Senate Democrats to make the Senate version more like the House version. After the conference committee again seemed unable to reach a compromise, and the bill seemed to be a corpse going to the morgue, a small group of legislators long committed to passage of illegal immigration reform refused to let it die. In October 1986 they fashioned some key compromises enabling passage in that same year. Rep. Charles Schumer (D-NY) met with Reps. Fish and Hamilton, Rep. Howard Berman (D-CA), Rep. Leon Panetta (D-CA), and Rep. Dan Lungren (R-CA). Their fine-tuning of the bill's provisions led House members to agree on a package of provisions, including numerous points designed to protect the rights of temporary workers. They secured Sen. Simpson's approval of the compromises, and after a decade of dealing with the proposals to reform illegal immigration policy, Congress finally passed the measure. Further deterioration of the Mexican economy led to 1.8 million INS border apprehensions— a historical high. With the midterm elections over, and in view of the growing conservative political mood of the country, opponents of the measure concluded that continued resistance might lead to an even more restrictive bill in 1987. The Hispanic Caucus split on the bill, five favoring and six opposing passage. That split by the Hispanic Caucus enabled the Congressional Black Caucus to split on the bill as well: ten for and eight opposed.

The House passed the compromise conference bill by a vote of 238 to 172 on October 15, 1986. The Senate approved it 63 to 24 on October 17, 1986. The president signed it into law on November 6, 1986, as the Immigration Reform and Control Act of 1986 (IRCA). The long and bumpy road to enactment was followed by an equally bumpy road to implementation of a complex law whose very compromises ensured that its passage led to complications and unintended consequences. Employer sanctions proved ineffective in demagnetizing the draw of the U.S. economy. The bill allowed for some fourteen documents to be accepted as valid demonstrations of a person's eligibility to work. Those provisions simply fueled a phony-document industry enabling illegal aliens to continue coming and employers to hire them without fear of legal penalty for "knowingly hiring" undocumented workers. Enforcement problems by the INS coupled with the massive use of counterfeit documents resulted in a decline of undocumented aliens successfully crossing the border that lasted for only a very brief period. Within a year, illegal immigration was back up to pre-IRCA levels.

While IRCA authorized a 50 percent increase in Border Patrol staff, actual staff increases fell far short of that level because of difficulties in recruiting and expanding training staff and facilities. As Border Patrol staffing increased in size, so did its duties. After 1986, the interdiction of illicit drug traffic across the borders became a prime focus (in response to the 1986 Omnibus Anti-Drug Law). Border Patrol agents shifted their emphasis from alien apprehension and smuggling to work with the Drug Enforcement Agency on Operation Alliance. The Border Patrol also expanded the number of staff being used to guard refugee camps and to identify, prosecute, and deport alien criminals (Bean, Vernez, and Keely, 1989: 44).

Annual apprehensions at the U.S. borders by the Border Patrol agents of the INS climbed from the tens of thousands in the 1960s to nearly a half-million by 1970, to three-quarters of a million by 1985, to nearly 1.5 million by 1985. By the time IRCA was passed, in 1986, the number was approaching 2 million (see Figures 6.1 and 6.2 in Chapter Six). The volume of legal immigration also rose dramatically in the 1970s, to nearly 4.5 million for the decade. That was the highest level since the 1910–1920 decade and the fourth highest level for any decade in the nation's history. Moreover, the 1980 census enumerated 5.6 million foreign-born persons who had entered during the 1970s—a number that included legal and illegal entrants who had been counted as entering during that decade. That number, of course, does not include those foreign-born who came but were *not counted* in the census. Although no firm data are available for those uncounted, estimates of 1 million or more are quite realistic. If so, then net immigration during the decade of the 1970s totaled about 6.6 million, which exceeded the total immigration for the decade beginning in 1910, which had only been about 4.3 million. Thus it is likely that the net flow into the country during the 1970s and 1980s was at the highest level for any period in the twentieth century (LeMay, 1994: 22–23).

As the tide of illegal aliens increased once again to what was perceived of as a "flood-level," traditionally involved as well as some new interest groups entered the battle over policy to restrict illegal immigration. State governments entered the arena as well, placing new pressures on Congress to respond to "fix the problem" of illegal immigration and border control, which so adversely impacted the states receiving the vast bulk of illegal immigrants (Arizona, California, Colorado, Florida, Illinois, New Jersey, New Mexico, New York, and Texas). California, Florida, and Texas sued the federal government in their respective federal district courts for the estimated billions of dollars that the states had to bear for costs related to illegal immigrants and their children. States claimed enormous expenditures in education, health care, prisons, and welfare caused by illegal immigrant residents. States argued that unauthorized workers may have paid income taxes and Social Security taxes that flowed to the federal government's coffers, but that the state and local levels of government bore increased costs and far less additional revenue from the illegal immigrant population. These states argued that the federal government, by failing to control the nation's borders adequately, was thereby responsible for the increased costs borne by the states as a result of its failure. In 1994, California attempted legislatively to reduce the draw of its economy and services to illegal immigrants, and simultaneously to send a message to Congress by passing an anti-immigration measure known as Proposition 187. Using the initiative process, California's voters passed the measure—officially entitled the "Save Our State Initiative," by 60 percent. The measure required state and local agencies to report to the INS any persons "suspected of being illegal," and to prevent illegal aliens from receiving benefits or public services in the state of California.

The authors of Proposition 187 anticipated a federal court challenge as to the law's constitutionality. They were correct in their anticipation. It was immediately brought to court by the League of United Latin American Citizens (LULAC), and the federal district court did rule that most of the law was indeed unconstitutional (see *LULAC et al. v. Wilson et al.*, 908 F. Supp. 755 C.D. Cal. 1995: 787–791).

The federal district court ruled many of Proposition 187's provisions unconstitutional, inasmuch as they constituted state infringement on the national government's sole authority to enact immigration law or were state actions preempted by existing federal law. Despite many of its provisions being thus overturned, Congress got the message sent by Proposition 187. It addressed yet again the "illegal immigration problem."

In 1996, Congress passed and President Bill Clinton signed into law two measures that essentially enacted into national law and policy the major provisions of Proposition 187. Congress enacted a welfare reform act that contained several provisions aimed at illegal immigrants. Still other provisions were folded into the omnibus fiscal 1987 spending bill (Illegal Immigration Reform and Immigrant Responsibility Act of 1996, the IIRIRA, H.R. 3610, P.L. 104–208), which President Clinton signed into law on September 30, 1996 (both laws are discussed more fully in Chapter Two, and excerpts summarizing major provisions are included in Chapter Six).

As noted, the number of illegal aliens entering the United States dipped slightly immediately after passage of IRCA in 1986 but then climbed once again to reach and eventually exceed pre-IRCA levels. Various estimates from reputable sources show that between 1986 and 2002, the number of unauthorized immigrants residing in the United States rose from an estimated 3.2 million in 1986 to 9.3 million by 2002 (see Figure 6.3 in Chapter Six). The region of origin of these unauthorized immigrant residents shifted in significant ways during this period as well. In 1986 a Congressional Research Service study found that among the estimated 3.2 million unauthorized residents, approximately 69 percent were from Mexico, 23 percent were from Canada and South America, 6 percent were from Asia, and 2 percent from Europe (these estimated numbers include both unauthorized entrants and visa overstayers). By 2002, the 9.3 million estimated unauthorized alien residents comprised an estimated 57 percent from Mexico, 23 percent from other Latin American countries, 10 percent from Asia, 5 percent from Canada and Europe, and another 5 percent from all other sources (See Figure 6.4 in Chapter Six).

The Pew Hispanic Center estimated that, between 2000 and 2004, another 3.1 million immigrants arrived, bringing the estimated total of unauthorized in the United States to 10.3 million. These data are shown in Figure 6.5, which graphically presents the number of unauthorized immigrants arriving in the United States during the 1980s, then from 1990 to 1994, from 1995 to 1999, and finally, from 2000 to 2004. Another trend of note for the post-2000 period is their dispersal within the United States. The Pew Hispanic Center estimates that in 1990, 88 percent of all illegal aliens resided in the big six settlement states: California (which had 45 percent of the total), New York (with 15 percent), Texas (with 11 percent), Florida (with 9 percent), Illinois (4 percent), and New Jersey (4 percent). Among the unauthorized immigrants, the remaining 12 percent of the total (some 400,000) resided in all the other states. By 2004, the estimated 10.3 million were far more dispersed. Only 61 percent resided in the big six states: California had 24 percent, New York had 7 percent, Texas had 14 percent, Florida had 9 percent, and Illinois and New Jersey each had 4 percent, while the remaining other states had 3.9 million, or 39 percent of the estimated total of unauthorized immigrants. By 2005 that total is estimated at 11 million. Figure 6.6 in Chapter Six presents the legal status of immigrants in the United States. Of the estimated 35.7 million foreign-born residents of the United States as of the end of 2004, 10.4 million, or 29 percent, were legal permanent resident (LPR) aliens, while 11.3 million, or 32 percent, were naturalized citizens. Temporary legal residents were estimated at 1.2 million, or 3 percent of the total, and refugee arrivals were 2.4 million, or 7 percent of the total. The previously mentioned estimated unauthorized immigrants were 10.3 million, or 29 percent of the total (see Figure 6.6). That number confirms a November 2004 report issued by the Center for Immigration Studies, in Washington, D.C., which also estimated the number of illegal aliens at about 10 million (Camarota, 2005). Other scholars dispute those estimates as being low.

A report by Robert Justich and Betty Ng argues that estimates based on the census data account for only half of the illegal alien population. They projected an unauthorized immigrant population as high as 20 million, basing their projections on such sources as increases in school enrollments, foreign remittances (that is, money sent by foreign workers to their families back home), border crossings, and housing permits. Justich and Ng suggest that more small businesses take advantage of illegal workers, moving what they estimate as 4 to 6 million jobs into the underground market. They also noted that many such employers of illegal immigrants resorted to unrecorded revenue receipts (that is, paying the workers "under the table" or "off the books," by cash). Justich and Ng estimate that as many as 5 million workers were being paid off the books, constituting a sort of "stealth workforce" that distorted official government economic statistics and government projections by understating job growth, inflating U.S. productivity, and shortchanging tax revenues by what they estimated as $35 billion per year (see Information Plus, 2006: 74).

In June 2000, Congress passed the Immigration and Naturalization Service Data Management Improvement Act (PL. 206–215). This act amended Section 110 of the Illegal Immigration Reform and Immigrant Responsibility Act of 1996, which had charged the INS to develop an automated system to track the entry and exit of all noncitizens—nonimmigrants and immigrants entering or leaving any port of entry, including land borders, seaports, and airports. The 2000 amendment required the INS to develop an electronic system to integrate and provide access to the data on all arrivals and departures, and using such available data to identify lawfully admitted nonimmigrants who might have overstayed their visits. A deadline of December 31, 2003, was set for all airports and seaports to have the system in place. Fifty land border ports, selected by the attorney general as having the highest number of arrivals and departures, were given until December 31, 2004, to have the system operating. All remaining land ports of entry were to have such systems operating by December 31, 2005 (ibid.: 75).

Border Security and Anti-Terrorism Concerns

The attacks on the World Trade Center in New York City and the Pentagon in Washington, D.C., on September 11, 2001, resulted in sweeping changes in the law, changes aimed at combating international and domestic terrorism but with significant implications for immigration policy directed at the illegal immigration problem. Indeed, it is the enactment of these laws that demarcate what we might call the "storm-door era" of U.S. immigration policy and signal the erection of what has been called "Fortress America." In part, the disarray at the INS made so apparent by the attacks of 9/11 sped up the process. Attorney General John Ashcroft issued an order to strictly enforce the rule requiring foreign visitors to file change of address forms that the national government was supposedly using to keep track of visitors. The INS had an existing backlog of some 2 million documents piled up in boxes and shipped to its warehouse in Kansas City. After the attorney general's directive, the INS began receiving 30,000 such change of address forms per day, and the backlog quickly rose to 4 million documents. An INS report indicated that an estimated 4 million foreigners were in the country with expired visas. Adding to its misery and reputation for ineptitude, it was then revealed that the INS had sent a letter to a Florida flight school approving the student visas for two of the 9/11 attackers, six months after the attacks! A government report on overall management in the Government Executive's 2002 Federal Performance Report, which had ranked the Coast Guard at an A, gave the INS a D. Border Patrol officers at the INS were quitting faster than they could be replaced. INS investigators were rated as undertrained, overworked, and overstressed, and its information management was assessed as abysmal. Drastic restructuring was needed.

Less than a month after the attacks, President Bush issued Executive Order 13228 of October 8, 2001. It established the Office of Homeland Security and the Homeland Security Council within the Executive Office of the President (Relyea, 2003: 613). In Congress, Sen. Joseph Lieberman (D-CT) introduced a bill (S. 1534) to establish a Department of Homeland Security as a cabinet-level department. He and Rep. Mac Thornberry (R-TX) later introduced a more elaborate version, in early May 2002 (S. 2452 and H.B. 4660). While at first opposing the idea of creating a new department, President Bush responded to political pressure to do more than what E.O. 13228 could accomplish. He had a team from his administration secretly begin drafting an alternative to Sen. Lieberman's bill. Mitchell Daniels Jr., director of the OMB, Tom Ridge, appointed to head the OHS, Andrew Card Jr., the White House chief of staff, and Alberto Gonzales, the White House counsel, met and drafted the president's departmental plan in late April. It was formally introduced as H.R. 5005 on June 24, 2002 (ibid.: 617).

More than any other actions, however, the USA Patriot Act and the law to establish the Department of Homeland Security (DHS) most characterize the period of the "storm-door era" of immigration policy and symbolize "Fortress America." Within six weeks of the 9/11 terrorist attacks, a jittery Congress, then virtually exiled from their offices by an anthrax contamination incident and confronted by warnings of more terrorist attacks soon to come, responded to the Bush administration's demands for a new arsenal of antiterrorism weapons, some at least directly linked to illegal immigration, which many feared was an avenue for international terrorist cells to infiltrate into the United States. For some three weeks, from the initial outbreak of anthrax contamination on October 4, 2001, Congress and the public were unable to obtain clear information about the attack from the Centers for Disease Control (CDC). The fear and threat exceeded actual damage. Despite vigorous objections from various civil liberties organizations at both ends of the political spectrum, Congress overwhelmingly approved the USA Patriot Act by a vote of 356 to 66 in the House and by a vote of 98 to 1 in the Senate. The hastily drafted, complex, and far-reaching legislation spans 342 pages but was passed with virtually no public hearing or debate, and was accompanied by neither a conference committee nor a committee report. On October 26, 2001, the act was signed into law by a triumphant President George W. Bush (Torr, 2004: 43–44).

The USA Patriot Act (which stands for the Uniting and Strengthening America by Providing Appropriate Tools Required to Intercept and Obstruct Terrorism Act), granted powers to the attorney general and the Justice Department that restricted the civil liberties of U.S. citizens, broadened the terrorism-related definitions in the 1965 Immigration and Naturalization Act, expanded the grounds of inadmissibility to include aliens who publicly endorse terrorist activity, and gave the national government broad powers to monitor students and resident aliens and to detain and expedite the removal of noncitizens suspected even of links to terrorist organizations—that is, those whom the attorney general simply certifies as being threats to national security on whatever grounds. Critics charged that the act legalized the racial profiling of Middle Easterners. Parts of the act are reprinted in Chapter Six.

Proponents of the act argued that it was essential to catch terrorists and deter further acts of terrorism. Its advocates called for coercive interrogation of suspected terrorists to find and control "enemy cells" in our midst. They argued that its sweeping new powers were essential to penetrate al-Qaeda. These included expanded surveillance, the use of informants, revisions of the search and seizure procedures, the use of secret wiretaps, and arrests and detention of suspected terrorists, uninhibited by the prior web of laws, judicial precedents, and administrative rules that its proponents argued had hamstrung law enforcement officials in dealing with the new terrorist threat. Soon after its enactment, the Department of Justice

(DOJ) announced that it had broken up terrorist cells in Portland, Detroit, and Buffalo, and charged seventeen individuals with terrorism-related activities. The DOJ also targeted terrorist financing (ibid.: 29).

Critics of the USA Patriot Act, however, argued that the law was too sweeping and too dangerous an intrusion on civil liberty protections. They saw it as a threat to constitutional checks and balances, to open government, and to the rule of law. Those threats they viewed as being greater than any posed by terrorists. "Not since the World War II internment of Japanese Americans have we locked up so many people for so long with so little explanation" (Nancy Chang, cited in ibid.: 16). Its critics maintain that the Patriot Act evades the Fourth Amendment by letting federal officials conduct "sneak and peek" searches—covert searches of a person's home or office that are conducted without notice to the person. Mass arrests accomplished with secrecy and a lack of judicial oversight outraged many civil libertarians. The exercise of unilateral authority by the executive, establishing secret tribunals, and breaching attorney-client communications without court order were, in their eyes, a threat to patriotic dissent, a threat to liberty, and a threat to equality. And, in point of fact, nonterrorists who have been affected by the act have mostly been immigrants. In the months immediately after 9/11, some 1,200 mostly Muslim immigrants were rounded up by the police and the INS across the nation. Many were held for months without access to lawyers or even without having charges brought against them before an immigration judge. Some were deported for visa violations. Only a few were subsequently charged with any crime, and most were released as totally innocent, swept up in the postattack hysteria. The Patriot Act makes aliens deportable for wholly innocent association with a terrorist organization because it defines a "terrorist organization" in such broad terms that any group that used or threatened to use violence could be so construed. The proscription on political association potentially encompasses every organization that has been involved in a civil war or a crime of violence, from a prolife group that once threatened workers at abortion clinics to the African National Congress, the Irish Republican Army, or the Northern Alliance in Afghanistan (our allies against the Taliban there). An estimated 1,500 to 2,000 persons were apprehended under the act, their identities still secret. Indeed, their numbers can only be guessed at, as the government stopped issuing a daily number after November 2001, when it was at 1,182. No one of those detained was ever charged with any involvement in the 9/11 attacks. Most were cleared by the FBI of any involvement in terrorism (Etzioni and Marsch, 2003: 37–38).

Creating the Department of Homeland Security: Dissolving the INS

Roughly a year later, on November 19, 2002, Congress passed the Homeland Security Act, establishing the Department of Homeland Security (DHS). This act abolished the INS, restructuring its jurisdiction and functions into the new behemoth department composed of twenty-two agencies subsumed into it. Many of its provisions dramatically changed the way in which immigration policy was implemented. Highlights of these provisions of the law are discussed and reprinted in Chapter Six (see LeMay, 2004: 27–28).

At about the same time, the DHS launched the National Security Entry-Exit Registration System (NSEERS). The system was made up of three components: point-of-entry registration, special registration, and exit/departure controls. It is aimed at preventing future terrorist attacks like those of 9/11. The special registration component created a national registry for temporary foreign visitors (that is, nonimmigrant aliens) coming from twenty-five designated countries (which the attorney general listed as supporters and exporters of international terrorism) and others who met a combination of intelligence-based criteria that identified them as potential security risks.

NSEERS addressed a variety of security-related deficiencies in immigration policy and procedures. Beginning in January 2003, for example, all commercial carriers (air or sea) were required to submit detailed passenger lists electronically before an aircraft or vessel arrived in or departed from the United States. Certain of its provisions were suspended in December 2003, such as the need for aliens residing in the United States to register each year (the government had millions of such forms backlogged and stored, unprocessed in warehouses in Kansas, and simply could not keep up with the paperwork). Other provisions of NSEERS remained in place, however, including requiring foreign nationals from Iran, Iraq, Libya, Syria, and the Sudan to go through special registration at ports of entry and to report to immigration officials before departing the country; foreign nationals from other countries were registered if Customs and Border Protection officers (a new bureau within the DHS) warranted it necessary based upon initial questioning upon arrival in the United States. Individuals from more than 160 countries had been registered in the NSEERS program by January 2005. The system provides detailed information about the background and purpose of the individual's visit to the United States as well as departure confirmation (Information Plus, 2006: 75).

In April 2002 the Justice Department issued a report on visa overstays substantiating the fact that between 40 and 50 percent of unauthorized immigrants were not persons who had crossed the borders without papers but rather were persons who entered with proper documents as temporary visitors who then failed to depart when required to do so. According to the report, such nonimmigrant overstayer population was growing by at least 125,000 per year (Department of Justice, 2002).

The U.S. Immigration and Customs Enforcement (ICE) bureau of the DHS is responsible for collecting documents from incoming travelers, but airline and shipping lines are responsible for collecting departure forms and for sending such forms to the ICE. Departure forms may have gone unrecorded, however, because they were not collected, or they were collected by the airlines or shipping lines but not sent to the ICE, or the forms were sent to the ICE but were incorrectly recorded. These problems make an accurate assessment of the number of overstays difficult. A 2004 General Accounting Office (GAO) report stated that the DHS estimated the number of visa overstays in the United States to be 2.3 million as of the year 2000. The GAO noted that this figure did not account for an unknown number of short- and long-term overstays from Mexico and Canada, inasmuch as citizens of Canada admitted for up to six months and Mexican citizens with border-crossing cards entering at a border in the Southwest for a stay of less than seventy-two hours are exempt from the visa admissions procedure. The GAO also faulted the tracking system that identified those who entered the country on visas but that did not accurately track when, or if, those persons actually left the country.

In 2001 the INS had reported nearly 33 million arrivals at U.S. ports of entry. Those did not include Mexican and Canadian business or pleasure visitors. Of those nearly 33 million, an estimated 79 percent departed before their authorized stay had expired. While there were no departure records for nearly 15 percent of all persons who arrived by land or sea, departure records were missing for 71 percent of all persons who arrived by land and sea (Information Plus, 2006: 76). In the post-9/11 investigations, the GAO, in a report in May 2004, noted that of the six hijackers who actually flew the planes involved in the 9/11 attacks, two were overstays and one had violated a student visa by not attending school. In response to those investigations, the DHS began an ongoing, multiagency effort it called Operation Tarmac, designed to identify unauthorized foreign nationals working in places vulnerable to terrorism, such as the security areas of airports.

The GAO report, *Overstay Tracking,* found that as of April 2004, a total of 195 airports had been investigated and nearly 6,000 businesses had been audited. In checks on employment eligibility forms (known as I-9 forms) of some 385,000 workers around the country, the DHS found nearly 5,000 unauthorized workers. Of more than 600 unauthorized workers arrested, 30 percent were overstays. Perhaps not surprisingly, but certainly ironically, one of the busiest ports of entry for such unauthorized workers was Houston's Bush Intercontinental Airport. Ten unauthorized workers were from countries identified as "of special interest" under the NSEERS program, and five of those were overstays, according to the GAO report.

Alarmingly, the GAO report noted that many unauthorized workers had access to supposedly secured areas and were employed by the airports themselves, by airlines, or by support service companies in jobs such as aircraft maintenance, airline cabin service attendant, airplane fueler, baggage handler, and predeparture screener. One was even working in the airport badging office. Such individuals had used phony Social Security numbers and identity documents to obtain airport jobs and security badges. Operation Tarmac found unauthorized employees at critical infrastructure sites, such as nuclear plants, sensitive national landmarks, military installations, and the Alaska pipeline, at the 2002 Olympics in Salt Lake City, and at the Super Bowl game. Seventy-nine unauthorized workers were arrested at the 2003 Super Bowl in San Diego, according to the GAO report. Of those, eight were visa overstays and twelve came from countries that were included in NSEERS' "special registration" category (ibid., 78).

Conclusion

This chapter has provided an overview of illegal immigration background and history, including references to several laws and court cases. The next chapter will discuss more fully the problems, controversies, and proposed solutions to this vexing political problem. It will discuss some of those laws and cases again, with an emphasis on why they failed to stem the tide of illegal immigration. Factual data, graphically presented, and summary excerpts from those laws will be presented in Chapter Six.

References

Andreas, Peter. 2000. *Border Games: Policing the U.S.-Mexico Divide.* Ithaca, NY: Cornell University Press.

Bean, Frank D., and Teresa A. Sullivan. 1985. "Immigration and Its Consequences: Confronting the Problem." *Society* 22 (May/June): 67–73.

Bean, Frank D., Georges Vernez, and Charles B. Keely. 1989. *Opening and Closing the Doors.* Santa Monica, CA: Rand Corporation; Washington, DC: Urban Institute.

Bustamente, Antonio Rios, ed. 1981. *Mexican Immigrant Workers in the United States.* Los Angeles: UCLA, Chicano Studies Research Center.

Calavita, Kitty. 1992. *Inside the State: The Bracero Program, Immigration, and the INS.* New York: Routledge.

Camarota, Steven A. 2005. *Economy Slowed, But Immigration Didn't: The Foreign-Born Population, 2000–2004.* Washington, DC: Center for Immigration Studies.

Chiswick, Barry R., ed. 1988. *The Gateway: U.S. Immigration Issues and Policies.* Washington, DC: American Enterprise Institute.

Conover, Ted. 1987. *Coyotes: A Journey through the Secret World of America's Illegal Aliens.* New York: Vintage.

Craig, Richard B. 1971. *The Bracero Program: Interest Groups and Foreign Policy.* Austin: University of Texas Press.

Crockroft, James D. 1986. *Outlaws in the Promised Land: Mexican Immigrant Workers and America's Future.* New York: Grove.

Department of Justice. 2002. *Follow-up Report on INS Efforts to Improve the Control of Nonimmigrant Overstays, Report No. 1-2002-006.* Washington, DC: U.S. Government Printing Office.

Etzioni, Amatai, and Jason H. Marsch, eds. 2003. *Rights v. Public Safety after 9/ll: America in the Age of Terrorism.* Lanham, MD: Rowman and Littlefield.

General Accounting Office. 2004. *Overstay Tracking: A Key Component of Homeland Security and a Layered Defense. GAO-04-82.* Washington, DC: U.S. Government Printing Office.

Glazer, Nathan, ed. 1985. *Clamor at the Gates: The New American Immigration.* San Francisco: ICS.

Hamermesh, Daniel S., and Frank D. Bean, eds. 1998. *Help or Hindrance? The Economic Implications of Immigration for African Americans.* New York: Russell Sage.

Information Plus. 2006. *Immigration and Illegal Aliens: Burden or Blessing?* Farmington Hills, MI: Thomson/Gale.

Kirstein, Peter N. 1977. *Anglo over Bracero: A History of the Mexican Worker in the United States from Roosevelt to Nixon.* San Francisco: R. and E.

Kiser, George C., and Martha W. 1979. *Mexican Workers in the United States.* Albuquerque: University of New Mexico Press.

LeMay, Michael. 1987. *From Open Door to Dutch Door: An Analysis of U.S. Immigration Policy since 1820.* New York: Praeger.

———. 1989. *The Gatekeepers: Comparative Immigration Policies.* New York: Praeger.

———. 1994. *Anatomy of a Public Policy.* New York: Praeger.

———. 2004. *U.S. Immigration: A Reference Handbook.* Santa Barbara, CA: ABC-CLIO.

LeMay, Michael, and Elliott Barkan, eds. 1999. *U.S. Immigration and Naturalization Laws and Issues.* Westport, CT: Greenwood.

Massey, Douglas S., et al. 1987. *Return to Aztlan: The Social Process of International Migration from Western Mexico.* Berkeley: University of California Press.

Muller, Thomas, and Thomas Espanshade. 1985. *The Fourth Wave.* Washington, DC: Urban Institute.

Nevins, Joseph. 2002. *Operation Gatekeeper: The Rise of the "Illegal Alien" and the Making of the U.S.-Mexico Boundary.* New York: Routledge.

Papademetriou, Demetrious, and Mark Miller, eds. 1984. *The Unavoidable Issue.* Philadelphia: Institute for the Study of Human Issues.

Perotti, Rosanna. 1989. "Beyond Logrolling: Integrative Bargaining in Congressional Policymaking." Paper presented at the American Political Science Association Meeting, August 31–September 3, Atlanta, GA.

Pew Hispanic Center. 2005. *Immigration and the States.* A presentation by Roberto Suro, director, Pew Hispanic Center, to the NCSL Regional Conference on Immigration and the States, Denver, CO, December 12, 2005.

Phillips, Julia A., and Douglas S. Massey, 1999. "The New Labor Market: Immigrants and Wages after IRCA." *Demography* 36, no. 2: 233–246.

Relyea, Harold. 2003. "Organizing for Homeland Security." *Presidential Studies Quarterly* 33, no. 3 (September): 602–624.

Select Commission on Immigration and Refugee Policy (SCIRP). 1981. *Final Report.* Washington, DC: U.S. Government Printing Office.

Torr, James D. 2004. *Homeland Security.* San Diego: Greenhaven.

Zuniga, Victor, and Ruben Hernandez-Leon. 2005. *New Destinations: Mexican Immigration to the United States.* New York: Russell Sage.

2

Problems, Controversies, and Solutions

Introduction

Interest groups and legislators involved in the illegal immigration reform issue struggle over particular bills, often describing the conflict as a battle to solve, once and for all, the immigration problem, or arguing that passage of a bill would result in a national calamity. Conflict over illegal immigration reform, however, is never really over, never finally won or lost, and never without unanticipated consequences.

Why is there a continuing struggle to achieve an illegal immigration policy that satisfies national needs and effectively "resolves" what is viewed as the most pressing "immigration problem"? Why is a true resolution an illusion? The answer lies in the very nature of illegal immigration-related policy. Conditions in the policy environment change. No sooner are some international problems or foreign policy considerations dealt with than the world system changes. National policy-makers cannot resolve the world's international conflict or set policy for other nations. In the global environment, what other nations chose to do, or fail to do, affects the dynamics of illegal immigration and worldwide migration flows. Failure to achieve a sound economy in other nations pushes citizens to emigrate. Foreign civil wars and domestic strife renew mass refugee movements. Natural disasters and epidemics compel hundreds of thousands to migrate elsewhere. Conditions change globally and affect both legal and unauthorized immigration flows, changing them in overall size and origin.

31

Domestic conditions are in constant flux. Any balance achieved can quickly tip out of balance as citizens reassess the value they place on one or another of the four elements. Some groups decline in their political influence while others rise. This process renews pressure to readdress the balance. New problems are perceived. Old problems are viewed in new ways. Demands for a change in the balance are registered in the public policy-making arena.

This chapter reviews current issues arising from illegal immigration in the domestic policy arena. Soon after an immigration reform bill is passed one hears calls for another new law. The implementation of yesterday's law generates demands for some new permutation. What, then, are the present concerns? This chapter examines several policy issues of domestic concern regarding the current illegal immigration problem. Chapter Three will review several from the global perspective.

Current Domestic-Policy Concerns

Amnesty or Legalization Issues of Current Unauthorized Immigrants

The constant arrival of illegal aliens renews calls for an amnesty or legalization program. Many see the proposals to enact a guest-worker program as nothing more than a thinly disguised amnesty. They adamantly oppose the Bush administration's call to establish a guest-worker program that would allow many among the 11 million unauthorized immigrants to legalize their status as an unacceptable amnesty program that rewards law-breakers. According to a poll taken in 2005, 54 percent of those polled disapproved of how President Bush was handling illegal immigration, yet 51 percent rated the illegal immigration issue as a top priority, and 39 percent rated it as an issue of some priority ("Bush Touts Border Plan," 2005). Both Republicans and Democrats split their vote for the last large-scale amnesty program, a provision of the Immigration Reform and Control Act (IRCA) that legalized more than 3 million previously illegal aliens. Democrats voted 196 (55 percent) in favor of IRCA, to 88 (45 percent) opposed. Republicans voted 105 (49 percent) in favor to 109 (51 percent) opposed (LeMay, 1994: 53). Today, Democratic legislators are more likely to sponsor legalization measures. Republicans are more divided over the issue. Republican legislators favoring big business see a guest-worker program as essential to supplying needed, and cheaper, labor. Socially conservative Republicans are more likely to advocate restrictionist immigration reform and object to any guest-worker program.

Democratic sponsors of legalization argue that it will bring undocumented immigrants out of the shadows of an underground economy and into the light of accountability and greater cooperation in our fight against terrorism. They argue that legalization would decrease illegal immigration and aid the homeland security effort by allowing law enforcement agencies to concentrate on border security and tracking down criminals and potential terrorists instead of chasing after millions of ordinary undocumented aliens, especially Hispanics, who are here simply to find work. Proponents contend that there are millions of illegal immigrants residing in the United States who have done what has been asked of them: they work hard, stay out of trouble, obey our laws (other than the immigration laws, of course), help their families, and desire the opportunity to legalize their status. They point to studies which show that illegal immigrants are a net asset to the country, taking menial jobs that U.S. workers will not and paying taxes. When they work illegally, they are subject to exploitation by unscrupulous employers. Democrats refer to it as "earned legalization" and not an incentive for new immigration. Interest groups supporting the proposal include LaRaza, the United Farm Workers, MECHA, and LULAC. Supporters note that it would help improve our foreign policy relations with Mexico. The millions of Mexicans here send billions of dollars back home, but, they say, it all comes back to the U.S. economy. These remittances totaled more than $19 billion in 2005, surpassing foreign investment as the second most important source of revenue for Mexico after oil. All such remittances return to the United States every year, plus a few billion more as these monies contribute to an increase in the economic well-being of Mexico's poor and working classes, thereby enabling them to purchase consumer goods produced in the United States.

Opponents of legalization contend it will spark increased illegal immigration, spur population growth, and place further stress on development, on already overcrowded schools, and on water shortage problems in the Southwest. They view illegal immigrants as coming here to exploit our welfare and public health care systems. As one critic notes: "We pick up the tab in many ways for the undocumented—from burying their dead, to delivery of their babies, to emergency medical and surgical care. There are 300,000 babies born to undocumented mothers annually at a cost of $5,000 a baby." Medicaid costs for such babies born in Colorado alone totaled $30 million annually, in California $79 million, in Texas $74 million, in Arizona $31 million, and in New Mexico $6 million. Some hospitals and emergency rooms have closed after being overrun by the uninsured and the undocumented (Kamau, 2005: B-7).

Others, like the Minutemen group, see illegal immigrants as criminals—for disobeying our legal immigration procedures, and often as criminals from their nation of origin who essentially import increased levels of crime here and overcrowd our jails and prisons. Public opinion, especially since 9/11, opposes legalization and fears unauthorized immigration as an international terrorist threat to the United States. House Judiciary chairman Rep. Jim Sensenbrenner (R-WI) sponsored a law that bars states from giving driver's licenses to illegal aliens. He argued that because some of the September 11 terrorists gained access to aircraft using driver's licenses as identification, all illegal aliens should be denied them. The measure, often called the Real ID Act, included a provision to build a fence along the U.S.-Mexican border south of San Diego by waiving environmental hurdles. At present, ten states do not require proof of citizenship or legal residency by license applicants: Hawaii, Maryland, Michigan, Montana, New Mexico, North Carolina, Oregon, Washington, Wisconsin, and Utah. Tennessee issues "driving certificates" to persons who cannot prove that they are legal residents. The Bush administration supported the Sensenbrenner bill. Many Democrats viewed the measure as a "back-door" effort to impose immigration restriction. Proponents countered that the act addresses recommendations of the 9/11 commission and implements commonsense reforms to strengthen border security. They maintain that it will better protect the homeland because the law contains important border and document security provisions crucial to interrupting terrorist travel by implementing much needed driver's license reforms and closing loopholes in the asylum system ("House of Cards," 2005).

Opponents charge that the law has serious constitutional issues, that it raises the bar for persons seeking asylum from religious and political persecution, and that it grants to the secretary of Homeland Security unprecedented powers to circumvent the judicial branch in matters pertaining to border security. They fear that rather than closing the door to those who would exploit our asylum to do us harm, the law more likely will close the door on real refugees fleeing persecution precisely when we need allies in the fight against international terrorism. The act, they claim, makes the United States less popular and sympathetic in the world, something that we can ill afford at this time. It was also opposed by the National Governors Association and the National Conference of State Legislatures because of its top-down approach and unfunded mandate. The act has measures that enlist military and local law enforcement to help stop illegal entrants and requires employers to verify the legal status of their workers. It approved constructing a 700-mile-long fence along the border in Texas (centered around Laredo). Its provisions turn an estimated 11 million into felons. Foreign students studying here on a visa and suddenly having to drop classes become felons. So too do foreign workers here on H visas who were suddenly laid off. Section 202 of the act, "Alien Smuggling and Related Offenses," turns into felons anyone—employers, aid workers, Catholic nuns—who willingly helped an undocumented person.

The impact of illegal immigrants on the economy is hotly debated, but undoubtedly significant. Economic analysts estimate the shadow economy at over $970 billion, or nearly 9 percent of the goods and services produced by the legal economy. Their filling of jobs, according to economist Vernon Briggs, undermines all of our labor, rips the social fabric, and drives the labor market into a downward spiral. Illegal immigrants hold an estimated 10 to 15 million jobs, about 8 percent of the workforce, and many such jobs are "off the books," meaning that the government does not receive an estimated $35 billion a year in income tax collections. Illegal immigrants earn far less than the rest of the population, with an average income, at $27,400, that is 40 percent below the legal immigrant or native family income of about $47,700, according to a study by the Pew Hispanic Center ("Jobs, Impact Ample in Shadow Economy," 2005). Among illegal alien workers, Mexicans are estimated at 6.3 million, of whom about 3.5 million hold jobs, constituting about 20 percent of the nation's Hispanic workforce. They were drawn here by higher wages. Their average earnings of $300 to $700 per week, while less than half that of legal U.S. workers, are nonetheless nearly three to seven times the average weekly salaries they earned in Mexico. Illegal immigrants are not just randomly relocating. They are following jobs into the suburbs and into states previously seeing fewer unauthorized immigrants, and into job markets that are growing: in areas where the population is growing and where there are more restaurants and grocery stores, more construction work and retail outlets. According to a Pew Hispanic Center study, in the early 1990s, legal immigrants outnumbered illegal immigrants by 675,000 to 394,000; by 2004 the opposite was the case, with an estimated 455,000 legal to 562,000 illegal immigrants entering. From 2003 to 2004, an estimated 1.2 million people arrived, more than half of illegal status.

Building fences in California induces undocumented immigrants to cross elsewhere—through Arizona, Texas, and New Mexico, where the climate and terrain are more dangerous, leading to a number of deaths. A recent notorious incident highlights that fact. A smuggler bringing in seventy-four people across Texas in an eighteen-wheeler, having charged them $7,000 each, lost refrigeration in his truck. Temperatures reached an estimated 173 degrees in the back of the truck, resulting in nineteen deaths, including that of a five-year-old boy, becoming one of the deadliest human smuggling attempts in U.S. history. A record number of more than 415 people died crossing the border illegally in 2004, compared with the previous record of 383 deaths in 2000 ("Smuggling Deaths Net Conviction," 2005). In Arizona alone, in 2005, 279 people died in the effort to cross illegally. A volunteer group, No More Deaths, set up camps along popular smuggling routes in which students conduct daily patrols, transporting immigrants in need to local hospitals or to a Tucson church where they are met by a doctor. Several of their volunteers were arrested and charged with felony aiding and abetting. Another group, Humane Borders, calls the Border Patrol when their volunteers encounter illegal immigrants in dire medical need, and usually secure approval in advance to transport them to the local hospital ("Border: Felony Case Questions Migrant Aid," 2006).

Estimates place annual illegal immigration at roughly 500,000 per year, having peaked in FY1999–2000 (see Figure 6.7). A study by the Pew Hispanic Center documents a downward trend among legal resident aliens, as well as the fact that unauthorized immigrants now annually exceed those who enter legally (see Figure 6.8). The Department of Human Services (DHS), the Department of Labor, and several think tanks estimate that 60 percent of unauthorized immigrants come across the borders, mostly with Mexico, without proper papers, and that about 40 percent enter legally but overstay their visas. Trends in immigration, both legal and illegal, closely follow trends in U.S. employment rates (see Figure 6.9 in Chapter Six). California is home to an estimated 35 percent of illegal aliens (Zuniga and Hernandez-Leon, 14). The two strongest "magnets" drawing illegal aliens to the United States are jobs and family reunion.

The typical Mexican worker earns about a tenth of what his North American counterpart earns, and many U.S. businesses welcome and even rely on such workers, who are seen as cheap and compliant labor. Community networks among recently arrived legal immigrants help establish systems used by illegal aliens and draw more here by helping to provide jobs, housing, and entry to the United States for their illegal relatives and countrymen (Camarota, 2005). A study among day laborers found that 75 percent were here illegally, 49 percent of whom were employed by homeowners and 43 percent of whom worked for construction contractors, most frequently as laborers, landscapers, painters, roofers, and drywall installers. The survey found that 59 percent of day laborers were from Mexico, 28 percent from Central America, and only 7 percent were born in the United States. Among those surveyed, 73 percent said that they were placed in hazardous working conditions ("Study on Day Laborers Tallies Woes of 117,600," 2006).

Throughout the 1990s, more than a million immigrants, both legal and illegal, entered the United States annually. The Census Bureau projects that immigration will help swell total population from its present 270 million to in excess of 400 million. Their numbers are offset by deaths, outmigration, and legalization, leaving an estimated net growth of 275,000 to 300,000 per year. The immigrant population, however, is growing six and a half times faster than the native-born population. The more than 10 million immigrants who arrived between 1990 and 2000 represent 42 percent of the increase in total U.S. population.

After enactment of IRCA, in 1986, there was a slight dip in apprehensions at the borders, but those numbers have climbed again since 1988. Among those caught and deported, Mexicans constituted 97 percent, 99 percent of whom were EWIs (entries without inspection). While it had responsibility for the Border Patrol apprehension function (until 2002), the INS estimated that for every illegal alien apprehended at the borders two to three evaded capture and made it through. One must remember, however, that the INS counted apprehensions, not individuals, and that many persons apprehended and repatriated to Mexico return to the border to cross again, sometimes that same day.

In 1996, the Border Patrol apprehended about 1.6 million persons nationwide, of whom 1.5 million were Mexicans crossing along the 1,952-mile southwestern border. An estimated 93 percent of Mexicans who entered without documentation had a job waiting or came to work. The Border Patrol caught 122,233 aliens who were smuggled into the country and seized about $1.2 billion worth of narcotics (INS Statistical Yearbook, 1997). The increased crackdown, dubbed Operation Gatekeeper, leads to riskier crossings and fuels the growing use of smugglers. An estimated 800 have perished between 2000 and 2002 (*Washington Post Weekly Edition*, August 19–25, 2002: 17).

The flood of illegal immigrants inspired some citizens to act as do-it-yourself immigration law enforcers. A number of vigilante groups have become activists, patrolling the border for migrants. Groups like the American Border Patrol, Ranch Rescue, the Minuteman Project, and the Colorado Minutemen patrol the deserts of Texas, New Mexico, and Arizona. Members claim that they seek only to report migrants to the U.S. Border Patrol. But the groups use such high-tech equipment as homemade drones, sophisticated listening devices, and at least sixteen light aircraft. A proimmigrant group, Border Action Network, argues that this is an inherently dangerous mix of people motivated by racism and xenophobia clashing with undocumented immigrants. The Arizona desert has become the main entry crossing point, accounting for more than half of the 1.1 million border crossers apprehended in 2004. For these vigilante groups, the 350-mile Arizona/Mexico border has become the very symbol of the government's lack of enforcement of the country's borders and illegal immigration laws. One vigilante group member estimated that he spent $1,500 during his time in the desert, including the price of night-vision equipment, a directional microphone, and body armor capable of withstanding a round fired from an AK-47 assault rifle. The Minuteman Project has been supported by the Aryan Nation and the National Alliance, neo-Nazi organizations ("Smuggling Deaths Net Conviction," 2005).

The situation has become so dire that Arizona lawmakers are considering creating a state border patrol. The state already assigns twenty-seven state patrol officers near the border to assist federal authorities in looking for illegal entrants. A bill to create a 100-member squad funded at $20 million would empower the Arizona Department of Public Safety to operate surveillance equipment, construct border barriers, target immigrant and drug smugglers, and patrol the border. Texas Republican governor Rick Perry has ordered the Texas National Guard to deploy along the border when emergencies arise, setting up a fifty-member team of state troopers and guardsmen. He advocates construction of "border jails" as a stopgap measure, since the ICE (Immigration and Customs Enforcement) Border Patrol lacks sufficient detention space to hold apprehended illegal immigrants.

The situation in Arizona and New Mexico became critical enough that their governors declared a state of emergency. Governor Bill Richardson (D-NM) declared that four of the state's counties were crippled by the effects of burgeoning illegal immigration, and he called for national reform. His executive order declares that the four counties "are devastated by the ravages and terror of human smuggling, drug smuggling, kidnapping, murder, property destruction and death of livestock." The order freed up $750,000 in state emergency funding, and the governor pledged an extra $1 million in aid. He cited the total inaction and lack of resources from the federal government and the Congress. Part of the money will be used to build and staff a field office for the New Mexico Office of Homeland Security. By linking illegal immigration to homeland security, the governor is attempting at least partially to reframe the debate over U.S. borders. Near the city of Columbus, New Mexico, 300,000 undocumented immigrants were apprehended in 2004. In July 2005, someone shot at the city's chief of police, and area ranchers witnessed the attempted kidnapping of three female undocumented immigrants by three masked and armed men on a New Mexico ranch. Governor Jane Napolitano (D-AZ) declared a state of emergency in Arizona's border counties, pledging $1.5 million in aid for extra sheriff's deputies and other officers, overtime costs, and upgraded equipment.

Governor Richardson's voice added weight to the issue. As a Hispanic, a Democrat, and a possible vice presidential or even presidential candidate in 2008, his is an important addition to the calls for illegal immigration reform. Rep. Tom Tancredo (R-CO), an ultraconservative Republican and a leading voice for restriction and illegal immigration reform who is also testing the waters for a possible presidential run in 2008, praised the governors' declaration and chided President Bush to get serious about border security.

The Americans for Immigration Control, Inc. (AIC) launched a state-by-state campaign seeking to enact legislation that would reverse the trend to ever-increasing illegal immigration. Their focus is to build public awareness in every state and to restore, in their words, traditional limits on U.S. immigration policy. In July 2006, a special session of the legislature in Colorado passed a measure that imposes fines on the employers of unauthorized workers and requires them to check the legal status of all prospective employees, verifying their social security number, their citizenship, or their legal right to work. The AIC uses surveys, talk radio, newspaper columns and ads, and television stations across the country to gain support for an "immigration moratorium" that would cease all immigration for a three-to-five-year period. They argue that it is a necessity to give the present immigration population time to assimilate and for the Border Patrol (ICE) to regain control of the borders. In any event, they advocate cutting legal immigration to no more than 300,000 per year.

Rep. Tom Tancredo, chairman of the congressional Immigration Reform Caucus, bewailed the porous nature of the borders, which allow terrorists, drug smugglers, and criminals, in his words, to cross into the United States completely undetected and undeterred. He noted also that an estimated 300,000 people who have been ordered to depart remain in the United States because their deportation orders are not being enforced, despite the ICE's having spent $31.2 million on a computer tracking system to determine whether visa holders overstay their visas; it is a system, he notes, that simply does not work, and for which the DHS is asking another $57 million to fix. Tancredo calls for eliminating local-level "sanctuary policies," quick processing and deportation of all illegal aliens apprehended, an end to nonemergency public assistance to them, abolishment of in-state tuition for illegal alien children, a ban on driver's licenses to unauthorized residents, construction of a 700-mile fence in stretches along the Mexican border with California, New Mexico, Texas, and Arizona, and a crackdown on employers, forcing them to check for legal status before they hire anyone ("House Approves Crackdown on Illegal Immigration," *Denver Post*, December 18, 2005: A-19).

Since 9/11 the federal government has pressured state and local law enforcement agencies to take a more active role in enforcing illegal immigration laws. While a few departments have obliged, many are reluctant to do so because the costs to local departments can be significant. To avoid civil rights lawsuits, local officers need special training. Being in the United States illegally is a civil, not a criminal, violation and historically the purview of federal immigration officials. Many local departments have policies and procedures on their books prohibiting local officers from checking the immigration status of persons they pull over in traffic violations, for example, and it is a concern of local officers in questioning persons suspected of being here illegally that they may be charged with racial profiling. There is also the question of whether ICE officers will show up if persons are detained and the local police report them. ICE is stretched thin. For example, only 200 agents cover all of Colorado, Idaho, Montana, and Wyoming, and they are responsible for more than immigration control matters: child pornography, money laundering, and narcotics smuggling. With the number of unauthorized immigrants estimated at 11 million and climbing, ICE's failure or inability to respond when local departments call regarding apprehended illegal aliens contributes to the problems that localities face. Local departments typically lack the funds, their officers lack the training, and they lack the detention facilities to keep those held for much longer than overnight. Any longer period of detention becomes onerous. Los Angeles and Orange County, California, have reached agreements with ICE on getting training for their officers and will begin to apprehend illegal immigrants with criminal convictions; they will also begin reviewing the citizenship status of inmates and those being held for criminal investigations for felony crimes. Florida and Alabama have entered into agreements with ICE to train members of their state patrols to identify and detain undocumented drivers. Several bills in Congress that would force local governments to enforce civil immigration laws have not passed, in part because groups like the National League of Cities have lobbied against them as unfunded mandates that would divert much needed local resources to enforce federal obligations (Crummy, 2005: A-12.).

Incorporation of Illegal Immigrants and Their Children

A concern closely related to the issue of amnesty is the incorporation of illegal immigrants and their children. Historically, each wave of immigrants has raised anxiety about their ability to assimilate, and that pattern holds true today. Since 1965, the source of immigration to the United States has shifted from Northwestern European nations to Latin America and Asia. Those changes renewed concerns as to the ability of the newcomers to incorporate into the cultural, economic, political, and social systems. Critics of illegal immigration especially fear the trend toward increased illegal immigration from Mexico, South and Central America, and Asia, which is projected to alter the racial makeup of the U.S. population. These critics fear that it is changing the very face of the United States.

Although immigration trends are undeniably reshaping the racial composition of the United States and indeed changing the very way "Americans" look, are illegal immigrants any less able to incorporate into the United States than the legal immigrants of the past? By most measures available at this time, such fears seem to be more xenophobic than real. In large measure, how quickly any immigrant assimilates into society is influenced by the person's age. The median age of recent immigrants is twenty-eight years. This influx of young people is particularly important because the U.S. population, with its relatively low birthrate among native-born citizens, is aging rapidly; by 2025, when about 20 percent of the population will be over the age of sixty-five, more working people will be needed to support them and maintain the Social Security system through their payroll taxes.

Critics fear that today's flow makes efforts at "Americanization" more difficult. Illegal immigrants are highly concentrated, with the top four immigrant-receiving states accounting for a 20 percent larger share of that population than did the top four states in 1975. They argue that illegal immigrants are less varied than were immigrants in the past. More than 50 percent come from Spanish-speaking countries, representing what they feel is a degree of ethnic concentration unprecedented in U.S. history. They also feel that the massive flow hinders the economic incorporation of immigrants. Illegal immigrant wages are well below those of native workers, causing a steady rise in overall immigrant poverty. Finally, they argue that illegal immigrants are anti-assimilationist. They contend that most illegal immigrants undergo at best a superficial assimilation. For the critics, Americanization is more than just learning English or getting a job. They see the development of a visceral, emotional attachment to the United States and its history as part of a "patriotic assimilation" that they fear is unlikely to occur when the schools and the general culture are skeptical, even hostile, to patriotism, and when communication technology enables illegal immigrants to maintain strong psychological and even physical ties to their countries of origin. Some carefully constructed social science studies clearly question the idea that today's immigrants and their children (whether legal or not) are any less able to incorporate, or will be significantly slower to do so, than were the immigrants of earlier eras. The findings of several studies show that their respondents turn conventional expectations on their head, a result that potentially has long-term political consequences. These studies offer a different theoretical view or model of the assimilation process than that traditionally held. In place of viewing assimilation as a homogeneous, linear process, these scholars argue that it is better seen as a highly segmented, non-linear process that does not always lead to "amalgamation." Biculturalism and pluralism are as evident as is traditional assimilation (see, for example, Portes and Rumbaut, 2001).

Of concern to most such scholars is the language ability and adaptation of immigrants. A study among immigrants arriving between 1987 and 1989, and who therefore had little time to learn English in the United States, found that about half of the recently arrived immigrants spoke English well or very well (Jasso et al., 2000). There is considerable variation within immigrant groups depending on the language of the nation of origin and on the educational backgrounds and occupational categories of the immigrants. Post-1965 immigrants are less likely than immigrants during the middle 1900s to have entered the United States with high levels of proficiency in English (Stevens, 2001: 186–187). Census 2000 data, however, show that the children of immigrant families quickly become the family's English translators, and that function helps their own assimilation and their self-image (see Obsatz, 2002a).

Since there is no national policy on the incorporation of immigrants to encourage their learning of English, such efforts are highly variable across local and state areas and over time. While twenty-five states have "Official English" laws, twenty-five do not. California's Proposition 227, passed in 1998, undermined bilingual education programs, and several other states have or are considering enactment of similar laws. This patchwork of public and political responses to the varying language skills of these newest immigrants reflects the difficulties, and benefits, of welcoming newcomers to a nation that prides itself as being a nation of immigrants, although not recognized in national policy as an English-speaking nation (Stevens, 2001: 188–189).

And what of the incorporation of their children? Immigrant children, and the U.S.-born children of immigrants, are the fastest growing segment of the U.S. child-age population. They make up more than 20 percent of all U.S. children. That proportion will increase as a result of continued immigration, both legal and illegal, and the higher birthrate among immigrant parents. "Immigrant stock," first-generation, foreign-born persons and second-generation, U.S.-born persons with at least one foreign-born parent, now exceed 60 million in number. The Children of Immigrants Longitudinal Study (CILS) is a multifaceted examination of the educational performance and the social, cultural, and psychological adaptation of children of immigrants. It is the largest study of its kind in the United States (Rumbaut, 2000; Portes and Rumbaut, 2001).

It found that while more than 90 percent of the children of immigrants lived in homes in which a language other than English was spoken, 73 percent preferred to speak English rather than the parents' native tongue. By three years later, those who preferred English rose to 88 percent. Even among the most mother-tongue retentive group, Mexican youth living in San Diego, with its large Spanish-speaking population and many Spanish-language radio and television stations, the 32 percent originally preferring English rose to 61 percent after three years. Among Cuban-origin youth in Miami, the shift was even more dramatic. There, 95 percent preferred English by three years later (Rumbaut, 2000: 237). The study found a somewhat lower but similar shift in identity in the second generation as well, where the U.S.-born children of foreign-born parents were four times less likely to identify themselves by their parents' national origins than were the foreign-born children. The CILS found an overall picture of resilient ambition and noteworthy achievement (ibid.: 242–257).

Another source of pressure for illegal immigration is the desire for family reunification, coupled with huge backlogs in the processing of applications for legal immigration. Visa application processing delays routinely run from two to eight months for "immediate relatives" and to more than two years in other cases. A Mexican adult son or daughter of a legal permanent resident faces a wait of eight and a half years, as do nationals from other high-source countries like India or the Philippines. Such backlogs fuel pressures for illegal entry. Children in backlog often face the problem of "aging out" of their preference category if the delays result in their passage from under the age of eighteen (minor children) to over eighteen years of age (putting them into the category of "adult children"). In 1997, the Department of State estimated the number of visa-backlogged persons at over 3.5 million (ibid.: 112).

Another processing and due process issue involves "expedited removal." Originally called "expedited expulsion," the process was a reaction to persons claiming asylum upon arrival at a port of entry. Proponents, such as Rep. Bill McCollum (R-FL), led a thirteen-year effort to pass "summary exclusion." Their first success at enactment of the concept was in the Anti-terrorism and Effective Death Penalty Act of 1996. Its provisions were superseded by the Illegal Immigration Reform and Immigration Responsibility Act of 1996 (IIRIRA). It contained provisions now better known as expedited removal (ER). It emphasized asylum reform—preventing, defeating, or deterring the cynical use of asylum by claimants who had destroyed or hidden their identity in order to get past border screening and who then disappear into the country. It has proven to be an overall border control and antifraud tool. Most arrivals subjected to it never assert a plea of "fear of return or of persecution." ER subjects clearly fraudulent violators to a more efficient removal order than before, and it lays the legal groundwork for more severe sanctions should such persons attempt illegal entry at a later date.

The federal government uses ER powers to remove illegal aliens convicted of a crime. During FY2004, ICE deported a record 157,281 persons, more than half of whom had criminal records. ICE agents have swept up a record number of unauthorized immigrants whose sole crime involves violation of visa limits or related immigration laws. This campaign boosted the total number of deportations by more than 45 percent from 2001 to 2004. Nearly 70 percent of those deported returned to Mexico, while most of the remainder went back to Central or South America and the Dominican Republic. In 2004, ICE used four jets that it owns and operates to make 317 flights to return more than 18,500 persons to their native countries. These deportations are but a small faction of the 10 to 11 million estimated unauthorized residents in this country. Most, of course, are unknown to ICE officials, and only those who are caught or otherwise reveal themselves—for example, by committing crimes, applying for asylum, or seeking government benefits—become targets of the ICE for deportation. Despite the record number of deportations, the DHS struggles to reduce the number of illegal aliens who have disobeyed orders to leave the country or who have failed to appear at deportation hearings. That number remains at about 400,000, because new unauthorized immigrants continue to flow into the United States, particularly along the southwestern border, and continue to defy orders to appear at deportation hearings. Agents also track noncitizens who are serving time for serious crimes and bring their cases to an immigration judge. If the judge orders them deported, they can be sent home upon release from prison ("Illegals Going Back by the Planeload," 2005).

Among the 400,000 persons ordered out of the country who continue to defy those orders, some are from countries known to harbor terrorists. Conservative Republicans are skeptical about creating any guest-worker program or the granting of amnesty until substantial progress is made to boost enforcement. From the homeland security-perspective, however, the threat of those ordered deported may be small. A 2003 staff report of the 9/11 Commission noted that only 5,000 of the 400,000 were from countries with ties to al-Qaeda. And of the 1,100 persons from that group captured during the program's first year, none were charged with any terrorism-related offenses ("Feds Face Daunting Task in Push to Deport Illegals," 2005).

Critics of the ER process, such as human rights advocates, legal organizations, and refugee service organizations, fear that admissible individuals are being denied entry and that refugees fleeing persecution may not make it through the inspection process to a "credible fear" interview. They maintain that the secrecy surrounding the ER process, anecdotal evidence regarding mistreatment, and the drop in asylum applications by arriving aliens indicate that these processes are being misused behind closed doors. They argue for independent researchers to monitor and report on the process. Given the concerns raised over the ER process, the Bush administration's strenuous advocacy of "Patriots Act II," and its efforts to increase ER provisions, expedited removal and the debate around it will likely remain a contested issue for the foreseeable future.

Border Control
and Management Issues

The perennial proposals for illegal immigration reform speak to another ongoing concern. Does the United States have adequate control over its borders? The political battles over control of illegal immigration, now more than three decades long, reflect the view of many that the nation has lost control of its borders. The 1986, 1990, and 1996 laws all involved some provisions to "beef up" or to "reform" the Border Patrol. These concerns were exacerbated by the September 11, 2001, attacks, resulting in two laws that address the issue (the USA Patriot Act of 2001 and the Homeland Security Act of 2002). There are extensive, ongoing proposals to further revise and strengthen "homeland security." This is a huge undertaking. The United States shares 5,525 miles of border with Canada and 1,989 miles with Mexico. Ocean borders include 95,000 miles of shoreline and a 3.4-million-square-mile exclusivity zone. Annually, more than 500 million persons cross the borders, among which some 350 million are noncitizens. They enter through no fewer than 350 official ports of entry. Managing the borders, securing transportation systems by sea and air, and control of international airports and seaports are inseparable tasks.

The USA Patriot Act, passed nearly unanimously by Congress with great emotion but little debate, grants the attorney general and the Department of Justice sweeping new powers for domestic surveillance, largely unchecked by judicial review. Then, on May 8, 2002, the House of Representatives overwhelmingly approved establishment of the new Department of Homeland Security (DHS). The vote in the House was 411 in favor, none opposed, with only two House members voting present but neither in favor nor opposed. On April 18, 2002, the bill passed in the Senate by 97 to 0. The final version of the law (H.R. 5005) was passed on November 19, 2002. The DHS has four divisions: Border and Transportation Security; Emergency Preparedness and Response; Chemical, Biological, Radiological, and Nuclear Countermeasures; and Information Analysis and Infrastructure Protection.

The DHS restructures the INS by moving the Border Patrol from the Department of Justice to the Department of Homeland Security. These actions reflect a consensus that the United States faces a severe problem of control of its borders: that the system is obviously broken and needs a major overhaul, not some minor tinkering. The debate over how best to "control" or manage the borders has traditionally hinged on arguments posited as zero-sum, no-win trade-offs, as "rights vs. rights." Strong enforcement is pitted against service. Greater control is opposed to civil liberties. Group interest, identity, and diversity are balanced against shared national goals. Trying to balance such polarized arguments reflects inevitable trade-offs deeply ingrained in fundamental constitutional principles and hence seems to result in a never-ending quest (Bach, 2000: 239–240).

The new DHS, using its bureau of Immigration and Customs Enforcement (ICE), encounters, processes, and daily makes decisions about more than 1 million border crossers. With globalization, the world's economies—and that of the United States—depend increasingly on such border crossings for increased trade, business, mobility, and tourism. The ICE remains the primary agency responsible for the control of the U.S. borders and for catching undocumented immigrants and visa overstayers. Its biggest problems occur along the U.S./Mexican border, although others enter as stowaways on ships or enter through airports.

Past attempts to beef up the border at problematic areas simply resulted in a temporary increase in apprehensions, followed by a shift in the flow of illegal traffic. In 1994, for example, the Border Patrol allocated additional persons to San Diego, California, and El Paso, Texas. In 1993 those two areas accounted for 68 percent of all southwestern border apprehensions. During 1997 apprehensions there were half the rate of 1993 (33 percent). Illegal alien traffic moved to other sectors. New agents were allocated to Tucson, Arizona, and to Del Rio, Laredo, and McAllen, Texas. In 1996, Congress approved adding 1,000 agents a year for the next five years. While 1,148 agents were hired in 1998, fewer than 400 were hired in FY2000 (Information Plus, 2006: 96).

The IIRIRA of 1996 required the attorney general to install additional physical barriers to prevent illegal crossings in high-illegal-entry sectors. In San Diego, bollard-type fencing (reinforced steel) was constructed, adding thirty-two miles to the prior fourteen. Nineteen miles of the new fencing are in the San Diego sector. The fencing, however, has failed to slow down undocumented crossings. It has been tunneled under (ICE has found twenty-one such tunnels since 2001) and bypassed, with the flow moving through Arizona and New Mexico.

In 1995 an international advocacy group for human rights, Human Rights Watch, issued a highly critical report alleging abuses committed by the Border Patrol, including the use of excessive force. The INS commissioner at the time, Doris Meissner, signed a nondeadly force policy, but Human Rights Watch insisted that it was too broad and permitted the use of force in too many circumstances. The Border Patrol countered that they often come into contact with human and narcotics smugglers prepared to use all means, including violence, to enter the United States. Smugglers are dangerous, and Border Patrol agents are not as well armed. Pressure to increase Border Patrol capabilities rose dramatically after the terrorist attacks of 9/11. Individual citizens, mostly ranchers whose land abuts the Mexican border, have formed vigilante groups, some armed with lethal weapons. They patrol border area lands looking for human smugglers and bands of illegal crossers.

Airline companies are responsible for screening passengers and preventing those without proper documentation from boarding. They are required to provide the ICE with a list of all departing and arriving passengers. Airlines are held responsible if they bring in passengers without documents, whether or not such documents were verified before departure. Airlines are fined $3,000 per illegal passenger and bear the cost for alien detentions—costs as high as an estimated $9 million a year. Delta Airlines maintains a motel exclusively for detainees near JFK Airport in New York City. At some high-risk airports, carriers duplicate visas and passports prior to departure, collect and hold documents, or take other precautions to screen out document-flushers and to establish that the passenger is not a stowaway.

Border management is complicated by high volume. Increased security results in cross-border exchanges that are slow and rely on rather primitive technology. In border management, the risk to public safety and the potential risk of law enforcement violation is high. Ports of entry often pose no credible law enforcement risks, and the ability of smugglers and traffickers to adapt their techniques and tactics at border crossings increases the law enforcement problem.

Better border patrol and management service requires improved enforcement. That slows traffic. How do policy-makers accomplish the seemingly contradictory aims of increased security yet speeding up the flow for economic reasons? Future innovations and processes must alter the past zero-sum, either-or approaches (Bach, 2000: 242–250). Since establishment of the DHS, border management relies on new technology and better use of information:

1. At airports, advanced passenger information systems relay biographical data collected from airline passengers to inspectors at the port of entry. ICE officers then analyze these data while the passengers are in flight and can then spend less time with passengers at inspection booths on the ground.

2. Dedicated commuter lanes work well at both the Canadian and Mexican borders. These rely on improved service and facilities that enhance law enforcement control of the traffic at the ports of entry. Participants using such lanes are preregistered and prescreened.

3. The ICE has begun testing an information system that matches information on passengers as they arrive and depart. Non-U.S. citizens now use the system on U.S. Airways flights between Frankfurt, Munich, Philadelphia, and Pittsburgh. Travelers are automatically provided an electronic I-94 form with their boarding passes. Upon arrival, their biographical data is already in the DHS computers, having been transmitted electronically from the air. When the person departs the form is collected and read electronically, better enabling the ICE to track how many travelers overstay their visa conditions, making possible improved enforcement and security.

4. The IIRIRA of 1996 requires implementation of an enforcement system at land borders that is simply not feasible with current technology or without the investment dollars necessary to build the new infrastructure at ports of entry. Whether post-9/11 security concerns will increase the priority sufficiently to develop that technology and to justify those expenditures remains an open question.

5. Current reform discussions emphasize four perspectives with very different assessments of the problems:

(a) The first seeks to "harden the borders." One terrorist who crosses the border undetected is one too many. As long as drugs, guns, and even persons are smuggled across the border, no law enforcement person, no community, can feel comfortable to accept that level of scrutiny. Enforcement strategies responding to this perspective involve tightening inspections of each person and vehicle. This involves stopping traffic long enough to open every trunk and interview every passenger. This approach trades much decreased efficiency for increased security.

(b) A second perspective stresses technology and the capacity to automate inspection activities. It attempts to develop high-volume processing of documents. Such processing emphasizes service in which a certain degree of error and risk is expected and considered "normal." Law enforcement, of course, is then less emphasized. Hope for the future in the technology approach relies on the use of biometrics to ensure that a person's identity and documents match. Technology using the traveler's fingerprints is becoming the common solution. Visual eye-scanning and photographic profiling and scanning are under experimental development.

(c) A third approach focuses on creating exceptions to rules for particular groups of passengers in order to speed their processing at ports-of-entry. Proposals include exempting first-class passengers from long inspection lines, visa waivers for preferred nationalities, special procedures for certain occupations, and even facilitated entry for vacationers who own property. These come at a cost to the general public and an increased security risk.

(d) A fourth approach seeks comprehensive transformation of the principles of border management. Figure 6.12 in Chapter Six presents a map of the new DHS border patrol sectors. The goal of the new approach is to reduce some of the pressures at the border because ports of entry are the weakest locations to achieve either efficient facilitation or effective enforcement. This approach hinges on regional cooperation with the governments of Mexico and Canada. It emphasizes overseas interdiction, including document control and training. Preinspection and preclearance arrangements hold potential for transferring the locus of enforcement overseas, where it can often do the most good and the least harm. Such overseas inspection occurs when the inspectors have greater time, where security is greater, and under circumstances in which the government has the upper hand. A regional framework means a shared set of rules for cross-border activity (ibid.: 244–248).

Domestically, the approach involves cooperation among various agencies of the federal government. Within the DHS, an Information Analysis and Infrastructure Protection Directorate was established to attempt to coordinate information about terrorist threats. It combines six separate programs from agencies that include the FBI and the Department of Energy, as well as the DHS. It is responsible for the much derided color-coded scheme for warnings about terrorist threats. It produces the daily homeland security briefings for the president by analyzing information from the nominally independent Terrorist Threat Integration Center (TTIC) created in January 2003. The center, a joint venture of the FBI, CIA, and DHS, is housed in the CIA headquarters and is staffed largely by the CIA. DHS's top officials are not always privy to the sources and methods used by the center to develop its reports (Lehrer, 2004: 72; Kemp, 2003: 52).

The merger of so many and such varied agencies into the huge Department of Homeland Security makes it more difficult for the agency to fulfill goals of being more responsive, effective, and efficient (Crotty, 2003; General Accounting Office, 2004; Haynes, 2004; Hyong, 2003; O'Beirne, 2002; Stana, 2003). One critic of the merger noted the management case against just such a type of reorganization that adds additional obstacles to achieving the very values it was aimed to promote. These obstacles include the following:

1. **Mission Complexity.** The DHS must monitor 5.7 million cargo containers and 600 million passengers on U.S. aircraft annually, in addition to patrolling 95,000 miles of coastline and 430 major airports. It is charged to prepare for and prevent terrorist attacks, coordinate first responders at state and local levels for emergencies, and monitor intelligence to protect against threats to the homeland. The department's abysmal performance after Hurricane Katrina illustrates how unprepared it was to respond to a natural disaster that it had days of warning about. One can only imagine DHS's response to a large-scale terrorist attack for which it had no advance warning as to time, place, and nature of the damage.

2. **Cultural Incompatability**. Trying to combine disparate organizational cultures, competing technologies used in day-to-day operations such as integrating e-mail databases, networking, and security protocols while maintaining

good communications (internal, between federal agencies, vertically with state and local first responders, governors and their staffs, and with the press and general public) inevitably leads to major problems. Creating a huge bureaucracy results in an organization bogged down with red tape, waste, and fraud. It is likely to delay rather than make more efficient any efforts to tackle the complex illegal immigration problem.

3. **Task Obfuscation.** Reducing the threat to terrorist attack is no easy task. The challenge of merging so many agencies, bureaus, and directorates makes it even harder to tackle. During its first half-decade of operation, the DHS appears to have been more concerned with making Americans feel safe than with the task of improving homeland security from the international terrorist threat posed by sleeper cells entering the nation illegally. Although the DHS has received substantial budget increases every year since its inception, agencies such as FEMA, the Coast Guard, the Border Safety Patrol, and the Secret Service have added responsibilities as well, with smaller levels of additional funding. The very behemoth nature of the structure results in greater overhead and administrative costs.

4. **Symbolic versus Real Performance.** The creation of DHS generates a false sense of safety. The public perceives that something is being done to make the United States more secure when, in fact, much of what is being done is public relations spin rather than anything substantive that truly increases homeland safety from attack or from infiltration by terrorists. Certainly, no statistical evidence is available to indicate that the DHS has had a significant influence on stemming the flow of illegal immigration to the United States (Krauss, 2003; Birkland, 2004; Broder, 2002; Halperin, 2003; Jacobson, 2003; Light, 2002). The reality is that for quite some years to come the upper management level in DHS will be more engaged in coordinating the merged agencies than in gauging their actual performance to ensure that the United States is safer.

In addition to creating the DHS, the administration and Congress set several other policies aimed at the illegal immigration problem. To exemplify one such policy: the president authorized the creation of the U.S. Northern Command to provide integrated homeland defense and coordinated Pentagon support to federal, state, and local governments. The president made countering and investigating terrorist activity the number one priority of his administration and of federal law enforcement and intelligence agencies. Again, however, the Katrina debacle illustrates how much work needs to be done, although certainly the response to that disaster improved after the Coast Guard admiral assumed overall command on the ground and the U.S. military, mostly in the form of National Guard troops, arrived on the scene—albeit not until five days after the storm had struck.

Another policy of import to illegal immigration was enactment of the Intelligence Reform and Terrorism Prevention Act (P.L. 108-458). As with establishing the DHS, at first President Bush resisted the idea of creating an "intelligence czar" and of substantially restructuring intelligence operations. Pressure from the 9/11 Commission and from the general public, however, aroused by the joint hearings held by the House and Senate intelligence committees on the intelligence failures that had contributed to the 9/11 attacks, moved the president to accept the reform legislation. The new law enacted H.R. 5150 and S. 2845, introduced in September 2004 and passed in early October 2004. The bill was signed into law by President Bush on December 17, 2004. The act creates a director of national intelligence (DNI) to oversee the fifteen government agencies involved in intelligence and a National Counterterrorism Center (NCTC), among other sections. The new law gives the DNI authority to be certain that there is adequate exchange of information, a condition so obviously lacking prior to the 9/11 attacks. President Bush quickly appointed John Negroponte, the U.S. ambassador to Iraq, to serve as the first DNI. The law also authorized an additional 2,000 border security agents each year for five years, imposed new standards on the information that must be contained to issue driver's licenses, and made it easier to track suspected terrorists not tied to known terrorist groups.

Critics of the new law are skeptical of the "czar" approach (O'Hanlon, 2005). They question whether the new DNI structure will have much impact on the way in which minority views on analysis of information is handled, voiced, and heard. Before 9/11, the CIA basically ignored the State Department's analyses on WMD, for instance. Whether a strong DNI at the top will make it more likely that minority views are being heard is open to question.

At the very heart of the issue of homeland security is the concept of national sovereignty. A unilateral perception of national security arises from the traditional sense and definition of sovereignty, which sees a nation-state as having the power and rightful authority to govern its territory and secure its borders. In a democratic nation-state, that requires a delicate balancing act between the needs of security and the traditions of civil liberty. When confronted by an international terrorist movement such as al-Qaeda, whose announced strategy is to infiltrate our society and avoid attention until they strike, it makes finding that delicate balance all the more difficult. The use of sleeper cells among immigrants, a number of whom were found to be here illegally, and suicide bombers in Western Europe (England, Spain, and France, most notably) as well as in the United States suggests that a more multinational approach to security is needed.

A particularly feared form of international terrorism concerns the issue of bioterrorist attack. While the likelihood of a bioterrorist attack remains low, the potential for large numbers of fatalities remains high, with one estimate up to 1 million (O'Hanlon, 2005: 6). The public is especially fearful of an efficient biological attack employing a contagious agent such as cholera, ebola, smallpox, or anthrax. In part, the extra edge to this fear results from the realization that suicide terrorists could infect themselves with one of these dreaded pathogens whose incubation period is several days or longer, then simply fly to the United States on a tourist visa. Because travel time by air is so short, the symptoms would not be visible upon arrival. If such an individual, while in the contagious stage, then traveled extensively, purposively passing through airport, bus, or train terminals, the potential spread could be significant and extremely difficult to protect against. Indeed, such pathogens could even be introduced without the perpetrators even entering the country—by infecting cargo, feed grain, and agricultural imports. Consider the economic devastation to the beef industry in Great Britain from a relatively few cases of mad-cow disease. Infecting U.S. cattle, pigs, sheep, or other animals with infectious diseases would have similarly drastic effects on the U.S. economy. Any policy to effectively cope with these types of international terrorist attacks requires multinational cooperation and coordination and therefore a more collective sense of national security.

A more difficult set of trade-offs involves enforcement of immigration laws within the United States. The failures of IRCA's employer-sanctions approach led to calls for new strategies bringing people together rather than pitting them against one another. Former INS commissioner Bach suggests four such strategies:

1. Target criminals who should be imprisoned and removed.
2. Target smuggling operations and rally all interest groups against trafficking.
3. Target worksite enforcement by increasing enforcement on the labor market and on individual firms and their unauthorized workers by tactics that dismantle the labor market mechanisms—such as recruitment schemes between employers and labor contractors—that encourage smuggling. Such improvement would involve increasing the ability of the Department of Labor, the Equal Employment Opportunity Commission, and state labor law agencies to enforce laws against those employers.
4. A fourth priority involves visa and document abuse. In FY2000 the INS completed 4.7 million adjudications and issued almost 16 million documents. Controlling fraud is essential to providing better services (Bach, 2000: 248-250).

The Cost of Illegal Immigration

Controversy over immigration centers on whether immigration is of overall benefit to the nation or is a huge drain on resources. Sentiment against illegal immigration registered in public opinion polls emphasizes use of public education, health, and welfare services or added costs to the criminal justice system by illegal immigrants. These costs are viewed as a drain on the citizen taxpayer and a strain on state and local governments. Critics maintain that illegal immigrants take away jobs from native-born citizens. State governments, especially those with high immigration-receiving rates, are concerned that federal laws impose huge financial burdens. Others, however, dispute the "burden" argument. Proimmigration advocates contend that the United States, in the long run, benefits economically, culturally, and socially from immigration, whether legal or illegal. Immigration brings workers, and workers create wealth. These advocates point out that the United States benefits greatly from the "brain drain," wherein highly talented persons come from developing nations to the United States, bringing their talents with them. Immigrants add workers to the labor force, and with their higher birthrates, continue to add to the employee base upon which an increasingly aged native-born population depends for the continued solvency of Social Security and Medicare. This controversy is unlikely to be resolved soon, as the two perspectives use different measures in their assumptions to assess both costs and benefits of immigration.

The "cost debate" over immigration first came to national attention in 1993, when economist Donald Huddle completed a report for the Carrying Capacity Network, an environmental group concerned over rapid population growth. Huddle calculated that for every one hundred unskilled immigrants who were working, twenty-five unskilled U.S.-born were displaced from jobs. In 1992, Huddle placed the net costs of immigration at $42.5 billion. In 1997, he estimated that net costs had risen to $68 billion.

An Urban Institute study by Jeffrey Passel disputed Huddle's findings. Passel maintained that Huddle neglected to account for the positive economic impact of immigrant business and consumer spending. Passel claimed that Huddle overstated costs and displacement effects. He calculated that immigrants pay more than $70 billion in taxes, $50 billion above Huddle's estimate.

Because the different approaches to measuring the cost/benefit ratio of immigration use different assumptions in their calculations, it is difficult to assess which is more accurate. Their estimates of economic gains and losses differ substantially. The General Accounting Office (GAO), in a 1995 report, examined three national studies of costs and benefits associated with illegal aliens. All three concluded that illegal aliens cost more than they generated in revenues to federal, state, and local government. They found that the estimates of that cost ranged from $2 billion (the Urban Institute study) to about $19 billion (Huddle's updated estimates in 1993; General Accounting Office, 1995). Estimates of the primary fiscal benefits of immigrants focus on their positive impact on the Medicare and Social Security systems. A study by Stephen Moore noted that while they pay into the Medicare and Social Security systems, their own parents are not collecting benefits. This creates a one-generation windfall to the Social Security system that will help ease the financial hardship projected to the system by the so-called Baby Boom generation (about 40 million people), who will begin collecting retirement benefits in 2011. A 1998 *Social Security Board of Trustees Report* projects that, if net immigration remains at 800,000 over the next twenty-five, fifty, and seventy-five years, working immigrants would contribute an average of $19.3 billion, $22.3 billion, and $25.8 billion, respectively, to the Social Security Trust Fund benefit (*Board of Trustees Report,* 1998). Moore estimates that, in 1997, the total immigrant income was $390 billion, generating $133 billion in taxes (*Fiscal Impact of the Newest Americans,* 1998). A 1996 Census Bureau study found that families with a naturalized citizen member pay an average of $6,580 in federal taxes, while those with U.S. citizen members pay an average of $5,070.

By contrast, George Borjas, a Cuban immigrant and professor of public policy at the John F. Kennedy School of Government at Harvard University, believes that immigration is harming the country, claiming that the lower educational levels of recently arrived immigrants mean that they remain at an economic disadvantage and in the long run will result in greater use of welfare.

The National Research Council, in a 1997 report, concluded that immigration had little negative effect on the wages and job opportunities of most native-born Americans, and that the estimates of immigrants' costs to state and local taxpayers may be inflated (*The New Americans,* 1997). In 2005, it estimated that immigrants, on average (not distinguishing between legal and illegal status), pay $1,800 in taxes to local, state, and federal government above what they "cost" in services or benefits received, but NRC notes that costs to state and local government are higher (Ewing, 2005: 5).

Guest-Worker Issues

The policy of allowing for guest workers has been a recurring issue since the end of the Bracero Program in 1964. Guest workers are temporary immigrants who are legally admitted to the United States for a given period of time (for example, nine months of a fiscal year). Historically, most have been associated with agricultural work. U.S. growers import such workers through the H-2A program. Congressmen associated with the growers have consistently sought to expand H-2A. Since 1990, the computer, electronic, and similar high-tech industries have successfully lobbied for increased numbers in the annual allotment of H-1B visas for high- or special-skilled workers.

In 1980–1981, there were approximately 44,000 guest-workers admitted into the United States. That number had increased to 139,000 by 1990 and to 227,000 by 1996 (Center for Immigration Studies, 2006). While growers argue that their sector of the economy could not survive without either illegal aliens or guest-workers, critics contend that the inflation of the low-skilled agricultural labor market simply encourages farmers to use more labor-intensive harvesting processes, which retards the progress of U.S. agriculture.

The H-1B visa program was established with the IMMACT (the Immigration Act of November 29, 1990) in reaction to a labor shortage that was projected but never occurred. This program allows for 65,000 temporary visas, good for up to six years, for people in specialty occupations and tied to a specific employer. The drawing card of the H-1B visa is that the employer sponsors the "green card." Government audits, however, have identified it as rife with abuse. The current system allows unscrupulous employers to exploit workers and retaliate against them if they try to assert labor workplace rights (Nevins, 2002). In the 1990s, the guest-worker programs were aimed at filling a narrower range of vacancies in the labor market, such as foreign nurses in areas with few medical personnel. The 1990 act was a response to an anticipated need for more scientists and engineers. It was established just as the Cold War was ending, leading to a layoff of many such professionals. The number was capped at 65,000 a year, with a maximum of 300,000 such H-1B workers being employed at any given time. In 1997 employers lobbied for more than the 65,000 cap, led by the computer industry, which convinced the Congress that more foreign professionals were needed. The program has been controversial. During the Clinton administration, Labor Secretary Robert Reich testified against the H-1B visa program, stating that industry was using it to replace skilled U.S. workers with cheaper foreign workers.

The American Competitiveness and Workforce Improvement Act of 1998 increased the number of H-1B visas available by 142,500 over the course of three years. It imposed two employer requirements, however, for those seeking H-1B workers: that the employer must pay a $500 fee per applicant, the funds from which were to support scholarships for Americans studying computer and related fields; and that employers with 15 percent or more such workers in their labor force had to certify that U.S. workers were not laid off to make room for the H-1Bs ninety days before or after the H-1B workers arrive at the workplace. The Department of Labor estimated that about 50,000 employers filed 250,000 applications in 1999. Some 44 percent of H-1B workers admitted are from India, and most are computer programmers (Martin, 2001: 49). In 2001 another bipartisan Senate bill was introduced to increase further the H-1 cap. The American Competitiveness in the Twenty-First Century Act (ACTFCA) would raise the visa cap for H-1B to 195,000 for three years (S. 2045). A similar House bill sets the total at 200,000.

H-2As are certified foreign guest-workers—meaning that the employer seeking the workers must certify the need through the DOL. Growers have been trying to obtain guest-workers without going through a certification process. A bill to do just that passed the House in 1984, and the Senate approved a measure authored by Sen. Pete Wilson in 1985. Congress approved a Replenishment Worker program in 1986, and the Senate approved a revision of the H-2A program, called Agjobs, in 1988 (ibid.: 50). The Agjobs program was part of a proposed pilot project and introduced the concept of farmworker registries, lists of farmworkers whom local ES offices have screened and determined to be legally authorized to work in the United States. Growers liked that feature, since if farmers request 5,000 workers and only 1,000 were listed in the local registry, they would get virtually automatic approval to have 4,000 more admitted. Critics contended that Agjobs would make it too easy for farmers to reject qualified U.S. workers; would in effect eliminate the Adverse Effect Wage Rate, a government-set minimum wage designed to offset the wage-depressing effects of foreign workers; and would eliminate the requirement for employers to provide housing to the workers. It has not yet been enacted, and growers continue to press for an Agjobs guest-worker program.

There are pros and cons to the guest-worker approach. Foreign-born farmworkers earning low wages by U.S. standards are better off than they would be at home. However, they and U.S.-born farmworkers then find it difficult to get work above the poverty-level farm earnings. U.S. farmers are better off, enjoying higher profits. U.S. consumers pay less for fresh produce and other commodities. The critical policy choice is this: Which is more valuable to U.S. society, cheaper food or higher farm wages? Another choice involves the time frame used to assess the impact of a guest-worker program: today or over some period of time into the future? (ibid.: 53–54). Advocates argue that the United States needs such programs to find the skilled labor by which to stay competitive with its trading partners who do have such programs: Australia, Canada, and the United Kingdom, especially. They argue that these workers fill a vital niche in the global economy and global workforce (Shotwell, 2001: 56).

Restructuring the INS

Many of the issues discussed above involved criticism of the INS. Calls for its restructuring go back to legislative proposals that predate the enactment of the IRCA. During the Iran embassy hostage crisis, when the INS could not establish even how many Iranian students were in the United States, some in Congress called for its restructuring. More considered proposals emerged after 1990. The 1990 IMMACT established a Commission on Immigration Reform (CIR). The commission issued a report in 1997 calling for a restructuring of the INS (Meissner, 2000: 3; Gardner, 2000: 7–8).

The Jordan Commission, as it came to be known, held hearings, consultations, and roundtable discussions. It defined four core functions of government in implementing immigration policy. It held that there were two major systemic flaws in carrying out those functions—(1) mission overload, and (2) fragmentation and diffusion of responsibility. Among its several recommendations was a call for a newly created Independent Agency for Immigration Review (Gardner, 2000: 17–21).

After the Jordan Commission report, several representatives introduced, in 1998, variations to restructure the INS, but those measures were put on hold when the House Judiciary Committee undertook its impeachment referral. In 1999 a new bill was introduced by Reps. Rogers, Reyes, and House Subcommittee on Immigration and Claims chairman Lamar Smith. This bill called for creating two bureaus, a Bureau of Immigration Services and a Bureau of Immigration Enforcement. Had it passed, the bill would have transferred to the director of the Bureau of Immigration Enforcement all functions, personnel, infrastructure, and funding in support of the following programs: the Border Patrol, the Detention and Deportation program, the

Intelligence program, the Investigations program, and the Inspections program. It would also have established a chief financial officer within the bureau (Ries, 2001: 101). Another proposal to restructure the INS came from the International Migration Policy Program of the Carnegie Endowment for International Peace (Papademetriou et al., 1999). There were several areas of consensus among these proposals. All agreed that a dramatic structural change of the INS was needed. All agreed that a separation of enforcement and service functions and chain of command was needed. All agreed on the need for drastic improvement in management. Finally, all agreed that the detention function, like asylum, needed to be separated (Aleinkoff, 2001: 22–27).

The terrorists attacks of September 11, 2001 made the proposals moot, although many of their ideas were incorporated into DHS law. The failure of the INS to prevent the terrorists from entering the country, combined with the announced approval, some six months after the attack, of visa applications for several of the highjackers to come to the United States to attend flight training schools, raised the level of rhetoric and the political support for—indeed, the demand for—something to be done. The Bush administration developed and announced a plan to establish a new cabinet-level Department of Homeland Security. Its creation involves the most extensive reorganization of the executive branch in decades. On November 19, 2002, President Bush signed the law establishing the new DHS. It moved twenty-two agencies and 190,000 employees into the new department, the most massive reorganization since the Department of Defense was established after World War II. The Congressional Budget Office placed the number of affected workers at 225,000, of the federal civilian workforce of 1.7 million, and pegged the cost of creating the department at $3 billion. That was the cost of the reorganization, not the increased cost of additional security technology and the like. Scholars at the Brookings Institution warned that with such a massive reorganization, the new department's top management will for some time be concerned with the integration of the agencies into a new management and budget system. The twenty-two agencies being moved have varied financial management systems and one hundred personnel systems, and the new department managers have to negotiate contracts with eighteen labor unions. Some of the agencies moved to the

DHS were widely viewed as "worst-run agencies" (the Customs Service, the INS, and the Border Patrol, in particular). INS investigators and Border Patrol agents were notoriously undertrained, overworked, and overstressed. Its information management system was abysmal (Light, 2002b).

Congressional debate on the measure generally followed party lines, with a majority of House Democrats voicing concerns that the bill would gut civil service protection for employees, seriously limit civil liberties, and give companies involved in homeland security excessive protection from legal liability. They also wanted airport security guards to be federal employees rather than private sector employees under contract with airport authorities or airline companies.

Among the twenty-two agencies transferred to the new department are the Coast Guard, the Customs Service, the Border Patrol, the Secret Service, the Transportation Security Administration, and the Federal Emergency Management Agency. Figure 6.13 presents a diagram of the new department. The department separates the visa processing, immigration services, and Border Patrol (now called Border Security) functions.

Current Proposals

The issues and concerns noted above are addressed by the dozens of bills before the Congress or introduced into various state legislatures. Collectively they confront major challenges: how to reduce unauthorized migration, how to reform legal migration, how to integrate newcomers, and how to address unfunded mandates and costs associated with illegal immigration. Several of the major proposals are discussed here. They focus on guest-worker programs, identification programs, border security enhancement, the USA Patriot II Act, a congressional reapportionment amendment, and a proposal to encourage state and local enforcement agencies to become more involved in illegal immigration enforcement. These proposals take different approaches to problems associated with illegal-immigration reform, a ticklish and difficult task facing Congress, with social and economic ramifications along with diplomatic and domestic security impacts. Finally, some sample state legislative proposals are discussed.

To get illegal immigration reform through Congress, a comprehensive bill needs three essential components: a guest-worker program pairing willing employers with willing employees; a new and more punitive round of criminal penalties for employers who knowingly hire illegal aliens; and a tamperproof identification card and increased border control.

A number of bills concern a guest-worker program. The Comprehensive Enforcement and Immigration Reform Act of 2005 (S. 1438) is one such, proposed by Sen. Jon Kyl (R-AZ) and Sen. John Cornyn (R-TX). Their bill would establish a new visa category for foreign workers to enter and work up to two years. Workers could reapply to participate for a total of six years. It would add 10,000 new detention center beds and increase penalties for smuggling and document fraud, drug-trafficking, and gang violence. It reaffirms state and local law enforcement authority to enforce federal immigration law and requires their communication with DHS about unauthorized immigrants. It would add 1,250 Customs and Border Enforcement agents and 10,000 Border Patrol agents over five years (National Conference of State Legislatures, 2006, and "Temporary Worker Bill Proposal," 2005).

Another bill, one likely to have greater consideration, is the Secure America and Orderly Immigration Act of 2005 (S. 1033 and H.R. 2330). Sponsored by Sen. John McCain (R-AZ) and Sen. Ted Kennedy (D-MA) with several bipartisan cosponsors in the Senate, and by Rep. Kolbe (R-AZ) in the House, with eighteen cosponsors from both parties, it represents the attempt to forge a broad consensus and includes several ideas floated by President Bush. These increase its likelihood for passage. It would legalize the status of illegal workers currently in the United States with an H-5B visa, require them to pay a $2,000 fine and back taxes, pass a criminal background check and medical exams, demonstrate knowledge of English and civics, and register for military service. These unauthorized immigrants could then apply for three-year guest-worker visas (without having to return to their nation of origin), renewable once. After six years they could apply for permanent resident status for themselves and their families, and, after an additional five years, apply for U.S. citizenship. It allows U.S. employers to hire up to 400,000 workers the first year (but only after showing that no residents are willing to take the jobs) and authorizes $750 million for FY2006, $850 million for FY2007, and $950 million for FY2008 for the State Criminal Alien Assistance Program (SCAAP) to reimburse states for indirect costs such as court costs, detention costs, and so on for unauthorized immigrants charged with crimes (special consideration is given to border states and states with large numbers of unauthorized aliens). It extends federal reimbursement to hospitals that provide emergency health care to unauthorized immigrants and adds new H-5A and H-5B temporary guest-workers as eligible patients. Despite its bipartisan support, it faces an uphill battle on both sides of the aisle. Republicans tend to oppose its amnesty provisions while favoring its guest-worker provisions. Democrats favor the legalization but fear that it will result in cheap labor, depressing domestic wages.

The Bush administration's proposal for temporary workers allows foreign citizens to apply for work permits good for one year, renewable for up to six years. After three years the person would have to return to the country of origin, but could then apply for a visa under improved status. More recently, the White House has let Congress know that President Bush would accept a revision not requiring the return to the country of origin.

Rep. Tom Tancredo (R-CO) is sponsoring legislation that would allow guest-workers for a short period to fill jobs for which there are no American workers. It would reduce legal immigration to 300,000. It calls for a secure border utilizing the U.S. military until the Border Patrol is up to full strength. It stiffens penalties for employers of the illegal. His bill died in the 2003–2004 session, but Tancredo began a national campaign using Team America, a political action group he founded, and was considering a run for the presidency in 2008 based on an anti–illegal immigration theme. Although Tancredo was elected to the Congress only in 1998 and has a maverick reputation in Congress, his growing national reputation and visibility on the illegal immigration issue and possible presidential bid have the potential to give him added clout in the new Congress. His stand on the threat of the Balkanization of the United States and the "dire threat of multiculturalism" give him wide public appeal.

Gov. Bill Owens (R-CO) and former House majority leader Dick Armey (R-TX) endorsed another guest-worker program, one developed by Helen Krieble, president of the Vernon K. Krieble Foundation and coauthored by Greg Walcher, who served in Gov. Owens's cabinet. Under this proposal, unauthorized immigrants would have to return to their country of origin, pass a background check proving that they have work waiting for them in the United States, and obtain a visa from a private, commercial agency before they could legally return to the United States. Gov. Owens emphasized the proposal's unique focus on partnership between government and business, in which private employment agencies would handle applications and the task of matching workers with jobs. This partnership had the potential to garner greater Republican support and was endorsed by Armey's group, FreedomWorks. Its critics said it favored big business and was biased toward wealthier undocumented immigrants who can afford to return to their country of origin and go through the legalization process ("Owens Calls for Visas," 2005).

All such proposals face the hurdle of being likened to the Bracero Program of the 1950s, which was notorious for its human-rights abuses and exploitation of workers but an enormous incentive for illegal immigration when the program ended. Critics maintain that there is no such thing as "temporary workers." They hold that these programs would expand permanent legal immigration by the hundreds of thousands, since guest-workers, when here legally and having children, would add to the number of citizens who are native-born; also, the guest-workers, on becoming resident aliens and then naturalized citizens, would draw additionally higher numbers of family members who would qualify for legal immigration under family reunification preferences.

Other Proposals

House Judiciary chairman Rep. James Sensenbrenner, Jr. (R-WI), is the sponsor of the Border Protection, Anti-terrorism and Illegal Immigration Control Act of 2005 (H.R. 4437). Cosponsored by Homeland Security chairman Peter King (R-NY), it passed the House by a vote of 239 to 182 in December 2005. Referred to as the Real ID Act, it addresses illegal immigration by strengthening interior enforcement of immigration laws and adding border security measures. It excludes any guest-worker program. If passed again and approved in the Senate, it would set new standards for driver's licenses. If states opted not to adopt the federal standards, their licenses could not be used for federal identification purposes, such as boarding an airplane. The measure requires applicants for licenses to prove their citizenship or legal resident status and requires licenses for foreign residents to expire on the same day that their visa expires, with such date displayed on the card. It would ease the government's denial of entry to foreigners and deportation of those in the country by broadening the definition of "terrorist activity." Giving any sort of support to a terrorist organization would constitute a terrorist activity and could be applied retroactively to anyone who gave support to an organization deemed in the future a terrorist group by the Department of State. The bill allows the secretary of Homeland Security to waive any local laws deemed to impede the building of physical barriers (fences) along U.S. borders. It authorizes SCAAP funding at $1 billion each fiscal year. It provides for a variety of new technology to assist DHS in monitoring ports of entry and land borders and establishes a Border Security Advisory Committee that includes representatives of state and local government; it approves about 700 miles of new fencing along the southern border and authorizes a study to examine the construction of a fence along the northern, Canadian border. Finally, it tightens asylum by requiring applicants to prove through a police report or other similar means that they are victims of persecution.

Sen. Larry Craig (R-ID) with forty-seven cosponsors and Rep. Chris Cannon (R-UT) with thirty-four cosponsors introduced the Agricultural Jobs Opportunities, Benefits, and Security (AgJOBS) Act of 2005 (S. 359, H.R. 884). This bill adjusts the status of unauthorized agricultural workers and revises and expands the H-2A agricultural guest-worker visa program. Similarly, the Defense Security Enforcement Act of 2005 (H.R. 3162), commonly called the USA Patriot Act II, renews the sunset provisions of the 2001 act and expands on its powers. Like the Sensenbrenner bill, it expands the definition of terrorism and terrorist organizations. The House of Representatives passed its version of the bill on March 18, 2006.

As Congress moved to renew the Patriot Act by passing the Domestic Security Enforcement Act, battle lines were drawn over its counterterrorism powers by an unlikely coalition of liberal civil-rights groups and conservative libertarians, gun-rights supporters, and medical privacy advocates. Led by former Republican congressman Bob Barr, who voted for the USA Patriot Act but later became a sharp critic of it, the new coalition, called Patriots to Restore Checks and Balances, joined conservative groups such as the American Conservative Union, the Center for Privacy and Technology Policy, and Free Congress, as well as more liberal groups such as the American Civil Liberties Union and the American Librarians Association. The nationwide grass-roots coalition claimed that 383 communities and seven states passed anti–Patriot Act laws, called "civil liberties safe zones" ("House Passes Patriot Act," 2006 and Lindorff, 2005).

Advocates for Patriot Act II argue that separation of powers is impeding the ability of the government to capture terrorists, and the law is needed to renew and expand Patriot Act I. They point to the breakup of an alleged cell in Portland, Oregon, which the attorney general at the time, John Ashcroft, claimed was only possible because the act allowed dots to be connected and criminal charges to be fully developed against the so-called Portland Six. That case was launched when a local deputy sheriff in rural Washington State spotted a group of Middle Eastern men with a cache of automatic weapons target-shooting at a gravel pit and called in the FBI ("Powers of the Patriot Act in Eye of the Beholder," 2003).

Critics of renewal counter by pointing to an October 2004 raid by the FBI on the offices of a small charity called the Islamic-American Relief Agency (IARA). Its attorney stated that the charity was effectively shut down under a little-known provision of the Patriot Act that expanded the International Emergency Economic Powers Act to allow the government to seize the assets of organizations while it investigates for links to terrorism. The government presented no credible evidence that IARA was funding terrorism, but by taking their funds and interviewing their donors, they effectively destroyed the charity and created a chilling effect in the Muslim community. Their lawyer stated that the FBI confused IARA—founded two decades ago as the Islamic African Relief Agency and which changed its name during the Bosnia conflict when demand for aid shifted and expanded beyond the Africa focus—with a Sudan-based charity called the Islamic African Relief Agency, which the U.S. government claims has links to terrorists. Critics charge that often ICE and FBI targeting is more like racial profiling of some minorities who become "suspects" merely because of their looks or names. Civil libertarians note the slaying by police in London of a Latin American who was mistakenly shot in the head and killed after the London bombings, apparently because he simply looked Middle Eastern and did not stop when challenged. They also look skeptically at programs like the Total Information Awareness Project of the Department of Defense, which focuses on people who speak certain languages—Afghan, Arabic, Farsi,

Korean, and Mandarin (Torr, 2004: 61). The government's reluctance to provide any information about the implementation of the USA Patriot Act, as well as stealthy actions to expand its powers and avoid judicial checks and balances, has further raised civil liberty concerns. In December 2005 the House voted to extend the USA Patriot Act into March 2006, by which time its proponents hope to secure sufficient compromises to enact Patriot Act II. At issue are sixteen provisions that Congress wanted reviewed and renewed by the end of 2005. Despite such reservations, the Defense Security Enforcement Act passed in the Senate on March 3, 2006, by a vote of 89-10. It passed in the House on March 8, 2006, by a vote of 280-138, just two more votes than needed to enact. Its passage in the Senate was accomplished when Senator John Sununu (R-NH) sponsored some compromise new civil liberties protections and then worked the House floor to get the needed Republican member votes to pass the bill.

Rep. Candice Miller (R-MI) has a bill for a constitutional amendment that would require congressional districts to be apportioned on the basis of resident *citizens* only. Currently, total population is used for the purpose of apportionment. The current system lessens representation in Congress from states with small populations of illegal aliens and increases representation for those states having large illegal populations. Language in the Constitution specifies apportionment on the basis of "persons." Rep. Miller's proposed amendment would replace "person" with "citizen."

Rep. Charles Norwood (R-GA) is sponsor of the CLEAR Act (H.R. 3137). It encourages state and local police agencies to become involved in illegal immigration law enforcement. In 2004 his measure was cosponsored by 125 legislators. While promoting local and state cooperation with federal authorities to enforce illegal immigration laws, it would require federal reimbursement to the localities for the costs of their efforts. It also increases the civil penalties against foreigners who reside illegally in the United States.

Rep. Bob Goodlatte (R-VA) introduced H.R. 1219, which ends the "visa lottery." The lottery program is part of the IMMACT of 1990 and admits 55,000 immigrants per year on the basis of a random lottery drawing. The lottery provision requires no skills or abilities, and allows illegal immigrants residing in the United States to participate. The inspector general of the State Department reported that the "visa lottery poses significant threats to national security" from entry of hostile intelligence officers, criminals, and terrorists, although to date no one apprehended as such has entered using the visa lottery.

State-Initiated Proposals

Chapter One identified the top ten immigration-receiving states (gateway states with traditionally high rates of immigration). Other states have more recently seen explosive growth rates in their immigrant populations, among which more than half are unauthorized. Between 1990 and 2000, the states that experienced the greatest increases were North Carolina (174 percent), Georgia (233 percent), Nevada (202 percent), and Arkansas (196 percent). Between 1996 and 2000 more than 90 percent of new job growth was the result of immigration in the following states: Connecticut, Iowa, Kansas, Maine, Massachusetts, Minnesota, Missouri, Nebraska, New Hampshire, New Jersey, New York, North Dakota, Pennsylvania, Rhode Island, South Dakota, and Vermont (National Conference of State Legislatures, 2006). Not surprisingly, then, in the first six months of 2005, state legislatures considered 300 bills on immigration policy issues and passed 47. Governors signed 36 bills and vetoed 7. Areas with the most legislative activity included benefits, education, employment, human trafficking, identification/driver's licenses, and law enforcement. The illegal immigration flow presents a number of serious challenges for state governments: new settlement areas, aspects related to the No Child Left Behind Act, temporary workers as potential future citizens, their incorporation into the economic and social fabric of the community, community tensions and the legitimate concerns of those already here, federal-state relations and issues of unfunded mandates, and, of course, security issues. Proposed actions by state legislatures are highlighted here.

Several states have expanded benefits to legal immigrants: Colorado, Florida, Maine, and Washington. Washington reinstated eligibility to immigrant children (whether the parents were here legally or not) after a five-year federal ban. Fifteen states, however, considered bills to restrict benefits: Alabama, Arizona, Arkansas, Colorado, Florida, Georgia, Idaho, Maryland, Mississippi, New Hampshire, New York, North Carolina, South Carolina, Tennessee, and Virginia. Only Virginia's bill was signed into law, in 2005. It prohibits unauthorized immigrants from receiving state or local public benefits. In a special session of the legislature held in July 2006, Colorado passed a bill that restricts assistance to illegal residents.

In education, nine states had bills granting in-state tuition to unauthorized immigrant students (Arkansas, Connecticut, Massachusetts, Mississippi, Nebraska, New Jersey, New Mexico, Oregon, and Rhode Island). Only New Mexico passed and signed into law such a provision, joining nine other states that extend in-state tuition benefits. By contrast, seven states (Arizona, California, Florida, Kentucky, North Carolina, Tennessee, and Wyoming) saw bills prohibiting in-state tuition for unauthorized immigrants. Arizona passed its bill, but it was vetoed by its governor. Georgia, New York, and Virginia also considered but have not yet passed bills that bar unauthorized immigrants from enrolling in state postsecondary institutions.

Employment issues were covered in several bills before state legislatures. Florida, Kansas, Maine, Mississippi, Missouri, and Tennessee considered but did not pass bills that prohibited the awarding of government contracts to firms that employ unauthorized workers. Arizona, Connecticut, Georgia, New York, and South Carolina had bills introduced—though none passed—that would variously punish employers of unauthorized workers by imposing fines and revoking the licenses of such businesses. South Carolina and Virginia sought to deny workers' compensation benefits to unauthorized workers. Arizona passed a measure that prevents cities from constructing day labor centers if such centers assist unauthorized workers.

Twelve states considered human-trafficking issues, and bills were enacted in nine of them: Arizona, Colorado, Idaho, Illinois, Kansas, Louisiana, Missouri, New Jersey, and Washington. All involved increased fines, penalties, and the creation of standards. Identification was at issue in twenty-seven states considering bills on identification documents and variously requiring proof of citizenship or permanent legal residency in order to engage in activities such as voting, receiving governmental services, obtaining a driver's license, and owning a handgun. Nine of the twenty-seven state measures were passed, in Arkansas, Illinois, Kentucky, Montana, Tennessee, Texas, Utah, Virginia, and Washington. Washington's bill was a ballot initiative that requires proof of citizenship to register to vote and is similar to Arizona's Proposition 200, which passed in 2004. Law enforcement bills emerged in Arizona, California, Colorado, Georgia, Maryland, New York, and South Carolina. Three of them were enacted into law, in Arizona, Arkansas, and Colorado. In 2006, Arizona has a ballot initiative denying bail to unauthorized immigrants (National Conference of State Legislatures, 2005).

Conclusion

The restructuring of immigration policy-making by the merger of the multiplicity of agencies into the DHS is an elephantine problem. Illegal immigration control is likely to be more difficult to describe and assess in the near future as the management of the DHS struggles to coordinate and manage so many and so disparate an array of agencies, bureaus, directorates, divisions, and programs. Instead of a new and relatively simple independent agency devoted exclusively to immigration and citizenship services, as recommended by many reformers prior to 9/11, the dissolving of the INS and merger of its functions into the DHS suggest continued problems for decision-making. It is a merger fraught with management problems and a likely source of many unanticipated consequences that will keep the illegal immigration issue on the front burner of the congressional agenda for years. Despite the crackdown and increased restrictions, illegal immigration pressures remain high. Policy-making to cope with it is likely to continue to be complex and less predictable. The total Hispanic population in the United States has surged, as has illegal immigration, because federal sanctions against employers who hire illegal immigrants (whether undocumented or visa overstayers) are at best poorly enforced. IRCA's provisions and the continued discussion of possible amnesty or a guest-worker program raise expectations and likely fuel the movement for more illegal immigration. Every year hundreds of thousands of Mexicans arrive illegally. Tighter controls since 9/11 seem to have done little to stanch the flow. Those controls have more often resulted in shifting the traffic to more dangerous routes.

What is the likely immediate future for illegal immigration policy-making? The era of fortress America will likely prevail for another decade or two. We can expect more of the same—increased restriction—for the foreseeable future. Congressional mandates on how states issue driver's licenses, increased expedited removal, and so on are probable for the remainder of this decade. Increased funding for the DHS is likely as well. A portion of that will go to increase the implementation ability of the Bureau of Citizenship and Immigration Services (BCIS). Technology making possible better tracking and control of nonimmigrants is on the near horizon. Although likely to require another half-decade or more to implement, improvements in the management of the DHS and particularly its BCIS are likely. In the post–Hurricane Katrina catastrophe, Congress will likely consider removing FEMA from the DHS and reestablishing it as an independent agency.

References

Aleinkoff, T. Alexander. 2000. "Reorganizing the U.S. Immigration Function." In Lydio Tomasi, ed., *In Defense of the Alien, XXII.* New York: Center for Migration Studies, 22–32.

_____. 2001. "Policing Boundaries: Migration, Citizenship, and the State." In *E Pluribus Unum? Contemporary and Historical Perspectives on Immigrant Political Incorporation*, ed. Gary Gerstle and John H. Mollinkopf. New York: Russell Sage.

"Arizonans Weigh State Border Patrol." *Colorado Springs Gazette*, February 5, 2006: Metro-2.

"Assaults against Border Patrol Double." *Colorado Springs Gazette*, November 10, 2005: A-13.

Associated Press. 2002a. "House Panel Approves Homeland Security Agency." Washington, DC: July 20.

Associated Press. 2002b. "INS Is Years Behind in Processing Records." Washington, DC: August 5.

Bach, Robert L. 2000. "Looking Forward: New Approaches to Immigration Law Enforcement." In Lydio Tomasi, ed., *In Defense of the Alien, XXII.* New York: Center for Migration Studies, 239–251.

Bean, Frank D., and Gillian Stevens. 2003. *America's Newcomers: Immigrant Incorporation and the Dynamics of Diversity.* New York: Russell Sage.

"Bipartisan Backing for Immigration Bill." *Denver Post*, December 17, 2005: 6-A, 11-A.

Birkland, Thomas A. 2004. "The World Changed Today: Agenda-Setting and Policy Change in the Wake of 9/11 Terrorist Attacks." *Review of Policy Research* 21, no. 2 (March): 179–201.

Board of Trustees Report. Washington, DC: U.S. Government Printing Office, 1998.

"Border Bill Not Enough, Some Say." *Denver Post,* December 19, 2005: A-14.

"Border: Felony Case Questions Migrant Aid." *Denver Post,* January 2, 2006: A-7.

"Border Shooting Raises Tensions in Mexico over U.S. Policy." *Denver Post,* January 6, 2006: A-15.

Borjas, George J. 1994. "The Economics of Immigration." *Journal of Economic Literature* 32: 1667–1717

Broder, David. 2002. "Security in the Homeland." *Washington Post Weekly Edition,* September 2–8: 4.

"Bush Signs Homeland Measure." *Press-Enterprise,* Riverside, CA, November 26, 2002: A-1, A-5.

"Bush Taps Intelligence Chief." *Denver Post,* February 18, 2005: A-2.

"Bush Touts Border Plan." *Denver Post,* November 29, 2005: A-1, 16.

Calavita, Kitty. 1992. *Inside the State: The Bracero Program, Immigration and the INS.* New York: Routledge.

Camarota, Steve A. 1999. *Immigrants in the United States—1998: A Snapshot of America's Foreign-Born Population.* Washington, DC: Center for Immigration Studies.

_____. 2005. "Economy Slowed, but Immigration Didn't: The Foreign-Born Population, 2000-2004." Washington, DC: Center for Immigration Studies.

Center for Immigration Studies. "Guestworkers." www.cis.org/topics/guestworkers.html. Accessed July 20, 2006.

Cohen, Steve, Beth Humphries, and Ed Mynott, eds. 2001. *From Immigration Controls to Welfare Controls.* New York: Routledge.

Cranston, Alan. 2004. *The Sovereignty Revolution.* Stanford: Stanford University Press.

Crotty, William. 2003. "Presidential Policymaking in Crisis Situations: 9/11 and Its Aftermath." *Policy Studies Journal* 31, no. 3 (August): 451–465.

Crummy, Karen E. 2005. "The Reluctant Enforcer." *Denver Post,* May 31: A-12.

Ewing, Walter A. 2005. "The Economics of Necessity." *Immigration Policy in Focus, Report of the American Immigration Law Foundation* 4, no. 3 (May).

"Feds Face Daunting Task in Push to Deport Illegals." *Denver Post,* January 16, 2005: A-15.

"Firebrand Tancredo Puts Policy over Party Line." *Denver Post,* November 27, 2005: A-1, 10-11.

Francis, Samuel T. 2001. *America Extinguished: Mass Immigration and the Disintegration of American Culture.* Monterey, VA: Americans for Immigration Control.

Freeman, Gary P. 2000. "Democratic Politics and Multilateral Immigration Policy." In Lydio Tomasi, ed., *In Defense of the Alien, XXII.* New York: Center for Migration Studies, 223–235.

"Fresh Ideas on Immigration." *Denver Post,* December 28, 2005: B-6.

Gardner, Robert. 2000. "Restructuring the INS: Draft Design Proposal." In Lydio Tomasi, ed., *In Defense of the Alien, XXII.* New York: Center for Migration Studies, 6–10.

General Accounting Office. 1995. *Illegal Aliens: National Net Cost Estimates Vary Widely.* Washington, DC: U.S. Government Printing Office.

———. 1997. *Illegal Aliens: Extent of Welfare Benefits Received on Behalf of U.S. Citizen Children.* Washington, DC: U.S. Government Printing Office.

———. 1998. *Illegal Aliens: Significant Obstacles to Reducing Unauthorized Alien Employment Exist.* Washington, DC: U.S. Government Printing Office.

———. 1999. *Illegal Immigration: Status of Southwest Border Strategy Implementation.* Washington, DC: U.S. Government Printing Office.

———. 2000a. *H1-B Foreign Workers: Better Controls Needed to Help Employers and Protect Workers.* Washington, DC: U.S. Government Printing Office.

———. 2000b. *Illegal Aliens: Opportunities Exist to Improve Expedited Removal Process.* Washington, DC: U.S. Government Printing Office.

_____. 2002. *Alien Smuggling: Management and Operational Improvement Needed to Address Growing Problem.* Washington, DC: U.S. Government Printing Office.

_____. 2004. *Overstay Tracking: A Key Component of Homeland Security and a Layered Defense.* GAO-04-82. Washington, DC: U.S. Government Printing Office.

Gerstle, Gary, and John Mollenkopf, eds. 2001. *E Pluribus Unum? Contemporary and Historical Perspectives on Immigrant Political Incorporation.* New York: Russell Sage.

Gorman, Siobhan. 2004. "The Endless Flood." *National Journal* 6 (February 7): 378–384.

Gotcham, Benjamin, and Rutilio Martinez. 2005. "Mexicans in the U.S. Send Billions Home—And It All Comes Back." *Denver Post,* February 19: C-13.

Halperin, Morton H. 2003. "Safe at Home." *American Prospect* 14, no. 10 (November): 36–40.

Haynes, Wendy. 2004. "Seeing around Corners: Crafting the New Department of Homeland Security." *Review of Policy Research* 21, no. 3 (May): 369–396.

"Homeland Security Gets OK." *Press-Enterprise,* November 20, 2002: A-1, A-5.

"House Approves Crackdown on Illegal Immigration." *Denver Post,* December 18, 2005: A-19.

"House Approves License Ban for Illegal Immigrants." *Denver Post,* February 11, 2005: A-2.

"House Bill Addresses Casino Debt, Illegal Aliens, Movers, ID Theft." *Colorado Springs Gazette,* February 5, 2006: B-1.

"House of Cards? Point-Counterpoint Commentary." *Denver Post,* February 19, 2005: C-12.

"House Passes Patriot Act," *San Bernardino Sun,* March 8, 2006: A-3.

Huddle, Donald. 1993. *The Costs of Immigration.* Washington, DC: Carrying Capacity Network.

Hyong, Y. 2003. "Building a Department of Homeland Security: The Management Theory." *Public Manager* 32, no. 11 (Spring): 55–57.

"Illegals Going Back by the Planeload." http://www.aolsvc.news .aol.com/news/article.adp?ids=205. Accessed February 17, 2005.

"Immigration Debate Illuminates Rift in GOP." *Denver Post,* December 16, 2005: 6-A.

"Immigration Lays open Fault Lines in GOP." *Denver Post,* October 23, 2005: E-1, 4.

Immigration and Naturalization Service. 1997. *Statistical Yearbook, 1996.* Washington, DC: U.S. Government Printing Office.

"Immigration Reform Plan Must Embrace Three Key Ideas." *San Diego Union-Tribune,* June 1, 2005: editorial page.

Information Plus. 2006. *Immigration and Illegal Aliens: Burden or Blessing?* Farmington Hills, MI: Thomson/Gale.

"INS Should Put Its House in Order." *Atlanta Journal-Constitution,* August 9, 2002: A-1.

"Intelligence: First Director Will Help Define the Institution." *Colorado Springs Gazette,* February 18, 2005: 8-A.

Interpreter Releases. 2002. "INS Proposes Requiring Aliens to Acknowledge Advance Notice of Change of Address Requirements: 200,000 Cards Remain Unfiled." August 5. Department of Justice. Washington, DC: U.S. Government Printing Office.

Jacobson, Gary C. 2003. "Terror, Terrain and Turnout: Exploring the 2002 Midterm Elections." *Political Science Quarterly* 118, no. 1 (Spring): 1–23.

Jasso, G., et al. 2000. "The New Immigrant Pilot Survey (NIS-P): Overview and New Findings about U.S. Legal Immigrants at Admission." *Demography* 37: 127–138.

"Jobs, Impact Ample in Shadow Economy." *Denver Post,* December 4, 2005: A-12.

Kamau, Pius. 2005. "Illegal Immigrants Jam Our Emergency Rooms." *Denver Post,* December 22, 2005: B-7.

Kemp, Roger L. 2003. "Homeland Security: Trends in America." *National Civic Review* 92, no. 4 (winter): 45–53.

Kerwin, Donald. 2001. "Family Reunification and the Living Law: Processing, Delays, Backlogs, and Legal Barriers." In Lydio Tomasi, ed., *In Defense of the Alien, XXIII.* New York: Center for Migration Studies, 107–116.

Kondrake, Morton. 2004. "Guest-Worker Program Could Add to Our Safety." *Colorado Springs Gazette.* December 18: M-5.

Krauss, Elishia. 2003. "Building a Bigger Bureaucracy: What the Department of Homeland Security Won't Do." *Public Manager* 32, no. 1 (Spring): 57–59.

Krauss, Erich, and Alex Pacheco. 2004. *On the Line: Inside the U.S. Border Patrol.* New York: Citadel, Kensington.

Kraut, Alan. 1994. *Silent Travelers: Germs, Genes, and the "Immigrant Menace."* Baltimore: Johns Hopkins University Press.

Lamm, R. D., and G. Imhoff. 1985. *The Immigration Time Bomb.* New York: Truman Tally.

Lehrer, Eli. 2004. "The Homeland Security Bureaucracy." *Public Interest* 1156 (Summer): 71–86.

LeMay, Michael. 1994. *Anatomy of a Public Policy: The Reform of Contemporary American Immigration Law.* Westport, CT: Praeger.

_____. 2001. "Assessing Assimilation: Cultural and Political Integration of Immigrants and Their Descendants." In Lydio Tomasi, ed., *In Defense of the Alien, XXIII.* New York: Center for Migration Studies, 163–176.

Light, Paul C. 2002a. *Homeland Security Will Be Hard to Manage.* Washington, DC: Brookings Institution Center for Public Service.

———. 2002b. "Homeland Security Debate on Hold." Washington, DC: Brookings Institution Center for Public Service, Interpreter Releases, August 25.

Lindorff, Dave. 2005. "Patriot Act II? Alternet." http://www.alternet .org/rights/22134. Accessed August 23, 2005.

Lopez-Garza, Marta, and David R. Diaz, eds. 2001. *Asian and Latino Immigrants in a Restructuring Economy: The Metamorphosis of Southern California*. Stanford, CA: Stanford University Press.

Martin, David. 2000. "Expedited Removal, Detention, and Due Process." In Lydio Tomasi, ed., *In Defense of the Alien, XXII*. New York: Center for Migration Studies, 161–180.

———. 2005. "With a Whisper, Not a Bang: Bush Signs Parts of Patriot Act II into Law—Stealthily." *San Antonio Current*. http://www.sacurent.com/site/news/cfm? Accessed August 23, 2005.

Martin, Philip. 2001. "Temporary Workers at the Top and Bottom of the Labor Market." In Lydio Tomasi, ed., *In Defense of the Alien, XXIII*. New York: Center for Migration Studies, 44–55.

McCarthy, Kevin F., and Georges Vernez. 1997. *Immigration in a Changing Economy: California's Experience*. Santa Monica, CA: Rand.

Meissner, Doris. 2000. "Management Challenge and Program Risks." In Lydio Tomasi, ed., *In Defense of the Alien, XXII*. New York: Center for Migration Studies, 1-5.

"Migrant-Aid Case Puts Border Policy under Microscope." *Denver Post*, January 2, 2006: A-1, 7.

Mintz, John, and Christopher Lee. 2003. "The Homeland Security Wish List." *Washington Post National Weekly Edition*, February 3–9: 31.

"Minutemen Propel Border Concerns to Political Forefront." *Denver Post*, December 20, 2005: A-9.

Moore, Stephen. 1998. *A Fiscal Portrait of the Newest Americans*. Washington, DC: National Immigration Forum and the Cato Institute.

Mosisa, Abraham T. 2002. "The Role of Foreign-Born Workers in the U.S. Economy." *Monthly Labor Review* [U.S. Department of Labor] 125, no. 5: (May).

National Conference of State Legislatures. 2005. "Immigrant Policy: News from the States, 2005." http://www.ncsl.org/programs/immig/immigstatelegis080105.htm. Accessed July 20, 2006.

National Conference of State Legislatures. 2006. "Immigrant Policy." http://www.ncsl.org/programs/immig/. Accessed July 20, 2006.

National Immigration Forum. *Fiscal Impact of the Newest Americans*. Washington, DC: National Immigration Forum and the CATO Institute, 1998.

Nevins, Joseph. 2001. *Operation Gatekeeper: The Rise of the "Illegal Alien" and the Making of the U.S.-Mexico Boundary*. New York: Routledge.

O'Beirne, Kate. 2002. "Bureaucratic Nightmare on the Way?" *National Review*, public opinion page, *Press Enterprise*, Riverside, CA, August 25: D-1.

Obsatz, Sharyn. 2002a. "Between Two Worlds." *Press Enterprise,* Riverside, CA, August 27, 2002: B-5.

———. 2002b. "Vandals Turn Desert Deadly." *Press Enterprise,* Riverside, CA, September 14: A-1, 10.

"Odd Cast Boosts Immigration Reform." *Denver Post,* June 12, 2005: E-4.

O'Hanlon, Michael E. 2005. *Defense Strategy for the Post-Saddam Era.* Washington, DC: Brookings Institution.

O'Harrow, Robert, Jr. "Who's Minding the Passengers?" *Washington Post National Weekly Edition,* Washington, DC, September 16–22, 2002: 29.

"1,000 Activists to Patrol Arizona Border for Migrants." *Denver Post,* March 31, 2005: A-6.

Owens, Bill [Governor]. 2005. "A Plan for Workers." *Denver Post,* December 24, 2005: C-8.

"Owens Calls for Visas." *Denver Post,* December 15, 2005: A-1, 8.

Papademetriou, Demetrios, Alexander Aleinkoff, and D. W. Meyers. 1999. *Reorganizing the U.S. Immigration Function: Toward a New Framework for Accountability.* Washington, DC: Carnegie Endowment for International Peace.

Passel, Jeffrey. 1994. *Immigration and Taxes: A Reappraisal of Huddle's "The Cost of Immigration."* Washington, DC: Urban Institute.

Passel, Jeffrey S., and Rebecca L. Clark. 1994. *How Much Do Immigrants Really Cost?* Washington, DC: Urban Institute.

"Patriot Act Hits Wall." *Denver Post,* December 17, 2005: A-30, 32.

Podesta, John, and Peter Swire. 2002. "Speaking Out about Wiretaps." *Washington Post National Weekly Edition,* September 9–15: 27.

Portes, Alejandro, and Ruben G. Rumbaut, eds. 2001. *Ethnicities: Children of Immigrants in America.* New York: Russell Sage .

"Powers of the Patriot Act in Eye of the Beholder." *Los Angeles Times,* September 2, 2003: A-15.

"A Question of Numbers: Lack of Data on Illegal Population Clouds Immigration Debate." *Colorado Springs Gazette,* February 12, 2006: Metro-1.

Ries, Lora. 2001. "An Update from Capitol Hill." In Lydio Tomasi, ed., *In Defense of the Alien, XXIII.* New York: Center for Migration Studies, 99–103.

"Rising Immigrant Tide Reaches Deeper in U.S." *Denver Post,* December 6, 2005: C-1, 10.

Roberts, Marta. 2005. "20/20 Spy Sight." *Security Management* 59, no. 2 (February): 76–80.

Rumbaut, Ruben G. 2000. "Transformation: The Post-Immigrant Generation in an Age of Diversity." In Lydio Tomasi, ed., *In Defense of the Alien, XXIII*. New York: Center for Migration Studies.

Russell, James C. 2004. *Breach of Faith: American Churches and the Immigration Crisis*. Lexington, VA: Representative Government Press.

Sanchez, Rene. "Deadly Smuggling at the Border." *Washington Post Weekly Edition*, August 19–25, 2002: 17.

"Senate Passes S. 2845, the National Intelligence Reform Act of 2004." http://www.ssa.gov/legislation/legis.bulletin 102704.html. Accessed August 18, 2005.

Shotwell, Lynn Frendt. 2001. "Comparison of the H-1B Bills." In Lydio Tomasi, ed., *In Defense of the Alien, XXIII*. New York: Center for Migration Studies, 87–95.

Simcox, David. 1997. *Measuring the Fallout: The Cost of the IRCA Amnesty after 10 Years*. Washington, DC: Center for Immigration Studies.

"Six Killed in Suspected Human Smuggling." *Denver Post*, January 27, 2006: A-4.

Smith, James P., and Barry Edmonston, eds. 1998. *The New Americans: Studies of the Economic, Demographic, and Fiscal Effects of Immigration*. Washington, DC: National Research Council, National Academy of Sciences Press.

"Smuggling Deaths Net Conviction." *Denver Post*, March 25, 2005: A-1, 16.

Social Security Trust Fund. 1998. *Board of Trustees Report*. Washington, DC: SSTF, U.S. Government Printing Office.

Spencer, Jim. 2005. "Immigration Economics vs. Emotion." *Denver Post*, December 14, 2005: B-1.

Stana, Richard M. 2003. *Homeland Security: Challenges to Implementing the Immigration Interior Enforcement Strategy*. GAO-03-660T. Washington, DC: U.S. Government Printing Office.

"States Fear Nationwide Driver's License Law Is a Lemon." *Denver Post*, January 13, 2006: A-12.

Stevens, Gillian. 2001. "U.S. Immigration Policy and the Language Characteristics of Immigrants." In Lydio Tomasi, ed., *In Defense of the Alien, XXIII*. New York: Center for Migration Studies, 177–191.

"Study on Day Laborers Tallies Woes of 117,600." *Denver Post*, January 22, 2006: A-3.

"Tancredo Takes Immigration Fight on the Road." *Denver Post*, January 19, 2006: A-14.

"Tancredo Working to Turn the Tide." *Denver Post*, June 5, 2005: A-1, 8.

"Temporary Worker Bill Proposal." *Denver Post,* August 9, 2005: B-7.

Torr, James D. 2004. *Homeland Security.* San Diego: Greenhaven Press.

"Two Tons of Pot Found in Border Tunnel." *Denver Post,* January 29, 2005: A-12.

"Unusual Coalition Pans Patriot Act." *Denver Post,* March 23, 2005: A-5.

U.S. Department of Justice. "Undocumented Aliens in U.S." http://www.usdoj.gov/graphics/aboutins/Statistics/illegalalien/index.htm. Accessed November 14, 2001.

Wolbrecht, Christina, and Rodney E. Hero. 2005. *The Politics of Democratic Inclusion.* Philadelphia: Temple University Press.

Wolchok, Carole Leslie. 2000. "Where Do We Go from Here? The Future of the Expedited Removal Process." In Lydio Tomasi, ed., *In Defense of the Alien, XXII.* New York: Center for Migration Studies, 181–192.

Zuniga, Victor, and Ruben Hernandez-Leon, eds. 2005. *New Destinations: Mexican Immigration to the United States.* New York: Russell Sage.

3

Worldwide Perspective

Introduction

Given that illegal immigration policy-making is "intermestic" in nature—that is, it inherently involves both international and domestic policy—it is not surprising that many of the issues and concerns discussed in Chapter 2 as facing domestic policy-makers are similar to those concerns faced by other illegal immigration–receiving nation-states and by the organizations of the international community. International migration is estimated at 200 million worldwide and growing rapidly. As is the case for flows coming to the United States, worldwide migration is driven by various disparities. The strongest push-pull factors arise out of economic disparities between Third World and First World economies. Failed economies with severe unemployment and underemployment in many Third World nations push citizens to emigrate. The population explosion and the demographic disparities between the rich and the poor nations likewise fuel the international migration. In many nations civil rights disparities between ethnic, racial, and religious minorities and their majority societies compel mass migrations and refugee crises. The international migration of hundreds of millions is sustained by *chain migration*—by networks based on family and sending communities and assisted by labor recruiters, smugglers, and human traffickers.

Since mass migration is global in scale, and since illegal immigrants flow into and through many nations around the world, the policy issues involved in controlling illegal immigration are likewise global in nature. And just as the development of international terrorism and international terrorist organizations affected U.S. domestic policy with respect to illegal immigration, so too do they influence policy-making in a worldwide perspective. The fear of and experience with international terrorist attacks being associated with immigration and illegal immigration flows has affected Western Europe, particularly the nations of England, France, Germany, Spain, and, more recently, the European Union as a whole. So, too, has the danger that episodic epidemic diseases may spread with massive migration flows and become true pandemic disease outbreaks, like the flu pandemic of 1918–1919, which various estimates conclude may have killed between 50 and 80 million people worldwide. Just as the present era of U.S. policy directed at illegal immigration may be referred to justifiably as a "storm-door era" designed to erect a "Fortress America," European policy-making on the issue led to a "Fortress Europe" mentality.

This chapter will cover several topics from the worldwide perspective. It focuses on amnesty and legalization issues, on the control of illegal immigration, on global refugee issues and how they are caused or affected by illegal immigration flows, on border management issues, on the spread of plagues in the context of illegal immigration flows and how best the international community might control pandemics, on how issues of economic development are affected by illegal immigration, on the economics of illegal immigration, and on regional or multinational approaches to the problem of illegal immigration.

Amnesty or "Regularisation" Issues

Nearly every major immigration-receiving nation has experienced some degree of illegal immigration. Like the United States, several have enacted or are considering some sort of amnesty program to legalize undocumented or otherwise illegal resident aliens. Australia, Canada, France, Italy, the Netherlands, Spain, Portugal, the United Kingdom, and the United States have all enacted some sort of legalization programs, which in Europe is more usually referred to as "regularisation." Greece is considering a bill to legalize thousands of undocumented immigrants, and labor shortages in Malaysia have forced that country to reverse its immigration policy regarding the crackdown on and expulsion of former illegal migrants.

France has had several regularisation programs, instituted by successive governments, between 1972 and 1998. The French experience with the issue and the most recent large-scale immigrant legalization program of more than 3 million immigrants by the United States as a result of IRCA provide examples of elements that are common to all such amnesty efforts.

Generally, immigration-receiving nations consider legalization after some period of time during which they tolerated illegal immigration, unauthorized employment, or some temporary guest-worker program that became an entrenched part of their labor markets. Their economies became "addicted" to the supply of cheap labor. Several countries have had a period of negative or near-zero population growth that created a situation in which domestic labor could no longer supply the economy's needs, and foreign labor—in the guise of a temporary or guest-worker program—filled the gap in the economy's labor supply. Temporary workers soon became permanent, if not legally recognized, residents within their populations. Most countries that tried guest-worker programs lacked any type of organized policy or programs to ensure the incorporation of the migrants into their societies, since they were legally only "temporary" resident aliens.

Legalization programs are generally promoted by a particular political party, such as the Democratic Party in the United States and the Socialist Party in France and other European states. Most of these programs have involved some degree of the carrot-and-stick approach, wherein amnesty is balanced with increased enforcement in the labor market against employers who encourage or who exploit illegal alien employment. Legalization programs have been successful only when backed by a coalition of interests: trade unions, the Catholic Church or other religious organizations, a plethora of immigrant assistance, mutual aid, and welfare groups, and so on. In the French regularisations, which occurred between 1981 and 1983, protests were brought to bear on the government. The National Assembly and the Senate never debated these programs; they were authorized by the government after protest campaigns succeeded in mounting sufficient pressure. In the experience of the United States, both with the Immigration Reform and Control Act (IRCA) and with current calls for a legalization program, public protests demanding amnesty have not occurred. Rather, change in the United States has mostly been the result of behind-the-scenes lobbying. If anything, public sentiment is consistently registered as opposed to legalization or amnesty as a reward for unlawfulness. Where amnesty is viewed as encouraging illegal immigration, it is generally opposed by a majority of citizens in public opinion polls.

Legalization programs have generally sparked anti-immigration reflexes, as evident both in France and the United States. All such programs have experienced a degree of fraudulent applications. They are costly and difficult to administer and implement. They have not "resolved" the illegal immigration influx problem at which they were, in large measure, aimed. Critics marshal evidence to show that such programs induce further illegal immigration rather than inhibit or rescind it. Whatever their shortcomings, such programs have allowed significant numbers of illegal residents to achieve legal status. In doing so, they diminish to some degree the sociopolitical concerns arising from the illegal status of many long-term resident aliens. Observers contend that illegally resident and employed populations have grown after such programs—in the United States, as we have seen, to an estimated 5 million or more. In France, the 1981–1983 programs were followed by several additional "specialized" legalizations directed at applicants for asylum, at those who had been turned down in the 1981 and 1983 programs, and at those who had been "wrongfully denied" legal status by conservative governments. The most recent regularisation in France ended on December 31, 1998. It legalized some 80,000 applicants, most of whom had family members in France, out of some 130,000 applicants in all. That represents a higher success ratio than those during the 1981–1983 procedure (Miller, 2000: 259–269).

Both France and the United States have experienced anti-immigrant backlashes to their respective amnesty programs, but one cannot rule out future recourse to the process, even in a political period of more restrictive immigration control. Amnesty programs provide a symbolic counter to stricter immigration control by expressing solidarity with a vulnerable and often exploited foreign population who provide what many see as much needed labor market services in relatively affluent democracies. Amnesty programs offer humane and practical solutions to what are enormously complex problems that resist easy solution. They endow rights and privileges that facilitate the social and political incorporation of those foreign-born populations.

Amnesty programs also provide the formerly illegal aliens with the legal status to organize into ethnic, political, or racially based political pressure groups that can then advocate in favor of those ethnic and racial minorities gaining more rights or redressing discriminatory patterns and practices in the majority society. In some cases, they provide a mechanism for the formerly illegal alien to seek naturalization or citizenship.

There are, however, several drawbacks to such programs. They undercut legal immigration and processes, they seem to reward lawbreakers, they violate equity by rewarding a group or class of aliens for special consideration, and they fuel anti-immigrant backlash. As various nation-states struggle with amnesty proposals, it is clear that whether or not such legalizations will be enacted or otherwise authorized depends on a complex calculus of interest group interaction and bargaining, electoral considerations that often affect political party coalitions for decades, and how the programs impact foreign policy concerns, just as was evident in Chapter Two with respect to U.S. domestic illegal immigration policy.

Control of Illegal Immigration

Amnesty programs are closely tied to another perplexing global concern—how to control illegal immigration. Table 6.3 in Chapter Six lists more than fifty countries whose illegal alien problems were discussed in an article on the CIS News site in just a few days in mid-July 2002. Recent developments following a series of terrorist attacks in England, Spain, and France, moreover, have certainly cooled public opinion for support of any type of legalization in Europe. Indeed, a number of countries experienced a political backlash and have passed or are considering legislation that cracks down on illegal immigration. New Zealand is reviewing its immigration laws aimed at halting bogus refugee appeals, and in 2005 it made restrictive changes to its residency and temporary entry immigration policy. In the Netherlands, the Dutch immigration minister insisted on stricter compliance with anti–illegal immigration measures. Russia announced new requirements and fees for Lithuanian visitors and in 2005 adopted a new microchip passport procedure. The European Union ministers, in December 2005, approved the use of a new biometric card, and they are discussing plans for anti–illegal migration and

EU border-protection policies. In November 2005, Hong Kong began temperature screening of all inbound travelers. In October of that year, the High Court in the United Kingdom approved rules easing deportation, and in August 2005 the government introduced new and stricter requirements for asylum and for naturalization. Japanese government officials revived fingerprint requirements for all foreign nationals. In 2005, France initiated numerous procedures to tighten immigration regulations and crack down on illegal immigration, and expelled hundreds of unauthorized immigrants and adopted a process for using biometric visas. In 2005, Russia multiplied fines imposed for hiring illegal workers. Spain tightened controls of illegal immigration in May 2005 (Littler Mendelson, P.C., 2006).

Problems associated with illegal alien streams in these countries echo those facing the United States—undocumented persons entering for jobs, human trafficking or smuggling, visa overstayers, their impact on the economy, their incorporation into society, and security concerns regarding bioterrorism and epidemic disease outbreaks, rioting, and terrorist cells.

A number of countries experience problems associated with illegal aliens who are passing through on their way to more preferred nations for more permanent residency. In short, they are stepping-stone counties in the illegal alien flow: for example, the Dominican Republic, Georgia, Hong Kong, Ireland, Mexico, Poland, and Turkey. The European Union approved a plan to help fund Poland's efforts to tighten controls on its eastern border. The EU governments were concerned that Poland could become a gateway for human trafficking, drugs, arms, and prostitution. Under the agreement, Poland would hire 5,300 extra border guards by 2006, a 50 percent increase in staff, and build more border stations as well as buy new equipment, such as helicopters and infrared detection devices. In December 2005, Poland began requiring larger financial guarantees for visa applicants. These measures are needed to crack down on the trafficking of women for prostitution and to curb the flow of illegal immigrants from East Asia and poor Eastern European countries (mostly from new republics that were formerly a part of the Soviet Union) who seek better lives in Western Europe. Bulgaria and Romania are closing in on preparations to join the EU in 2007, and they are considering illegal immigration measures necessary to be in compliance with EU policy on the matter. Bosnia and Herzegovina are much further away from joining EU status, but they have begun negotiations on doing so. This step will likewise require those countries to revise policy to comply with that of the EU (Littler Mendelson, P.C., 2006).

The German Migration Council, a nongovernmental body, projects the movement of 5 million immigrants from Eastern to Western Europe by 2020. As the former Eastern European bloc nations improve economically, there will be more opportunity at home and less pressure to emigrate. The Czech Republic, Slovenia, and Hungary—the three richest of the Central European republics—have few emigrants, and many former migrants have returned home. But the current trend is to the Central and Western nations: Ukrainians are often seen in the Czech Republic and Poland; Romanians serve as farm labor on Hungarian farms. In Hungary, the fourth largest foreign community comprises more than 10,000 Chinese. EU immigration rules are getting tougher as border areas in Germany and Austria attract increased unskilled labor and increased cross-border commuting.

Every year thousands of Africans try to enter Spain seeking work and to escape war and grinding poverty at home. Many of these sail west from Morocco to the Canary Islands, while others cross the Strait of Gibraltar and seek to enter Spain at its southern tip. Muslim immigrants, many of whom entered as unauthorized migrants, are particularly evident in Spain, France, and England, and came from former "colonies" in Africa of those European nations. Because of former colonial ties, the governments often were hesitant or reluctant to crack down on the illegal flow, but all three have begun to do so after the attacks on trains and buses in London and Madrid and the rioting in Paris and other parts of France.

Italy, Spain, and Portugal are among the European countries experiencing new immigration, and they share three principles in their respective immigration policies in a multinational agreement referred to as the Barcelona process: an openness to working immigrants on a (temporary) visa basis, massive regularization based on economic criteria, and increasing restrictions cracking down on illegal immigration. The Barcelona process aims at creating partnerships to establish an area of prosperity and security in the Mediterranean region. The Barcelona process links security, promotion of economic exchanges, and control of people movement. These countries, which serve as entrant countries to others in the EU as well, envision that increased economic stability and prosperity in the region will provide an alternative to migration flows. While that eventually may be the case, in the short run free trade agreements seem to spur migration to and through countries in the EU rather than inhibit such migration.

News reports exemplify this illegal alien influx. In 2002, for example, Turkish police detained two vans jammed with seventy-one illegal immigrants who had each paid $800 to be smuggled across Turkey and over the border into Greece. Turkey is under considerable pressure from EU nations, such as Greece, to clamp down on the thousands of illegal aliens who use Turkey's borders and coasts every year for illegal entry to EU countries.

In France, 400 illegal aliens occupied a famous basilica in a northern Paris suburb where they had sought refuge for ten days; they were demanding legal papers to live and work in France. In 2005, Paris experienced weeks of violent rioting by Turkish and other Muslim immigrants protesting, by burning automobiles, the discrimination they felt aimed at them in jobs, housing, and social relations. An anti-immigrant group calling itself the "Committee of St. Louis" is believed to be behind a false bomb threat that forced the immigrants to evacuate the basilica.

Malaysian authorities have been enforcing new immigration restriction laws that allow whipping, imprisonment, and large fines for illegal workers found there. Immigration officials estimate that as many as 600,000 illegal workers are in the country, as that wealthy nation has become a magnet to migrants from nearby poorer Southeast Asian neighbors. Dozens of illegal immigrants have been sentenced to prison terms and beaten with rattan canes. An estimated 300,000 illegal immigrants fled Malaysia during a prosecution amnesty before its 2002 deadline. The Philippines foreign minister protested the crackdown and treatment of its citizens, who make up much of the illegal alien population in Malaysia, calling the conditions in detention centers unduly harsh and the congestion appalling. In Indonesia, another major source of the pass-through illegal alien population, demonstrators burned a Malaysian flag in protest against the crackdown. Some 60,000 Filipinos returned home from Malaysia in 2002, and 4,000 more were deported. An estimated 180,000 Filipinos are estimated to be staying illegally in Malaysia's state of Sabah. In 2005 the Philippines sent its largest-ever number of skilled workers abroad, but it also saw many of those who had been working in Iraq to restore its ravaged oil industry return home in response to attacks on foreigners there. In June 2005, Malaysia reversed its crackdown on illegal immigrants in response to its booming economy and continued labor shortages. The Malaysian case illustrates a major concern about the mass movement of illegal aliens and refugees—protection of their basic human rights. As one scholar puts it:

> The number of international migrants moving around the world estimated by the UN Population Agency of approximately 120 million is bound to increase. [By the end of 2005 the estimates had risen to 200 million.] This trend and the problem of their vulnerability as subjects of human rights . . . imply a spectrum of instability and conflict as one of the most serious problems of the twenty-first century, negatively affecting peaceful relations in the community of nations. (Bustamante, 2002: 354)

Widespread anxieties have arisen throughout Europe as a result of rapid social and economic changes. These conditions provide fertile ground for political entrepreneurs all over Europe who promote anti-immigration and especially anti–illegal immigration sentiment. While rarely referring openly to racist ideology, the more extreme-right groups and parties have popularized views on national homogeneity in which the majority culture is more clearly defined in ethnic terms, assumes uniformity, and is seen as a quality to be preserved rather than loosened up.

> Demographers in several countries are now applying similar perspectives. Increasingly, declining birth rates and longer life expectancy in Europe are viewed as a ticking time bomb. The European Commission has proposed that member states reintroduce the practice of recruiting specific types of labour, partly for competitive reasons and partly to combat illegal immigration. Germany and Britain have introduced so-called green-card measures. But politically, a U-turn able to redefine the issue of immigration in all its complexity does not appear very feasible. All over Europe, parties hostile to immigration have altered the political frame of reference. No one in the European political establishment

has dared to speak the truth—that more immigrants are an inevitable and essential part of a future Europe. (Ruth, 2006)

In Great Britain's general election in 2005, an anti-immigration political party called the Get Britain Back Party ran on the premise that "Great Britain is full, we are closed for business." It promoted four main cornerstone policies: (1) zero immigration; (2) withdrawal from the EU; (3) keeping the pound, defined as currency sovereignty; and (4) referendums—using them to enable popular sentiment to decide important public policy issues (Hylton-Potts, 2005).

Global Refugee Issues and Illegal Immigration

Often pressures for illegal migration result from mass migration movements of refugees, some of whom attempt illegal entry into other countries. Refugee movements are generated by civil war or strife, ethnic conflicts, war, political persecution or repressions that often follow regime changes, and natural disasters such as famine, floods, earthquakes, hurricanes, or outbreaks of epidemic disease. Mass refugee movements happen when thousands of persons conclude that it is a matter of life or death that they depart their home or native country.

In the international context, the term "refugee" is defined in the UN Convention relating to the Status of Refugees of July 1951, which established the Office of the High Commissioner for Refugees (UNHCR) based on the statute adopted by the UN General Assembly on December 14, 1950, and refined by a January 31, 1967, protocol that took effect October 4, 1967. To date, 130 nations have signed the convention or protocol. The UN convention defines "refugee" to mean "any person who is outside any country of such person's nationality, or, in the case of a person having no nationality, is outside any country in which such person habitually resided, and who is unable or unwilling to return to, and is unable or unwilling to avail himself or herself of the protection of that country because of persecution or a well-founded fear of persecution on account of race, religion, nationality, membership in a particular social group, or political opinion." This convention and related protocols are occasionally up-dated by the office of the UNHCR, such as the Guidelines on Applicable Criteria and Standards relating to the Detention of Asylum Seekers, agreed upon in Geneva in February 1999.

Estimates of the number of worldwide refugees place the figure at 19.5 million. The United Nations estimates that there were 4 million Afghan refugees abroad; 0.2 million returned to Afghanistan from Pakistan alone in 2002. The flood of refugees returning to Afghanistan overwhelmed the UN budget for refugees. By regional area the United Nations estimated that the number of persons of concern (asylees/refugees) who fall under the mandates of the UNHCR as of January 1, 2002, were as follows: Asia, 8,820,700; Europe, 4,855,400; Africa, 4,173,500; North America, 1,086,800; Latin America and the Caribbean, 765,400; and Oceania, 81,300; for a total of 19,783,100. The United Nations, however, registered a sharp decline from 2002 to 2005 in the number of asylum seekers arriving in industrialized countries. The Office of the UN High Commissioner for Refugees was established on December 14, 1950, to lead and coordinate international action to protect refugees and resolve refugee problems worldwide. Its primary purpose is to safeguard the rights and well-being of refugees, to ensure that everyone can exercise the right to seek asylum and find safe refuge in another country, with the option to return to their nation of origin voluntarily if conditions allow, and to integrate locally or to resettle in a third country. The United Nations estimates that, since the Geneva Convention for Refugees was established in 1951, it has aided 50 million people to restart their lives in new countries. Its current staff exceeds 6,500 people in 116 countries, while it continues to help 19.2 million persons (UN High Commission for Refugees, 2006). Figure 6.14 presents graphically the number of asylum seekers of concern to the UNHCR, their region of location, and their category of status.

Internationally, five organizations provide the primary programs for refugee assistance: the UN High Commissioner for Refugees (UNHCR), the International Committee of the Red Cross (ICRC), the United Nations Relief and Works Agency for Palestinian Refugees in the Near East, the International Organization for Migration (IOC), and the World Food Program (WFP).

In 2004, the United States accepted more refugees than ten other countries involved in resettlement. It accepted 54 percent of the world's refugees resettled in FY2004. The other countries with substantial resettlement programs were Australia, Canada, Denmark, Finland, Ireland, the Netherlands, New Zealand, Norway, Sweden, and the United Kingdom. The State Department's Bureau of Population, Refugees, and Migration (PRM) reported that the U.S. cost of resettlement for FY2004 was about $3,500 per refugee admitted, an almost 60 percent increase from 2001. It anticipated that this cost would become a "funding impediment" that would curtail the resettlement effort in 2005. The United States contributed $125 million to the UNHCR's refugee-assistance efforts for FY2005, allocated at $50 million for Africa, $2.9 million for the Near East, $14.1 million for Europe, $20.3 million for South Asia, $5.2 million for East Asia, $4.6 million for the Western Hemisphere, and $27.9 million for global operations and reserves. The PRM report also noted that in FY2005 the United States committed an additional $13.9 million to four specific nongovernmental organizations (NGOs) with refugee-related programs: the International Catholic Migration Commission for programs in Turkey; the Shelter for Life program in Iraq; the United Israel Appeal to facilitate resettlement and integration of humanitarian migrants to Israel; and the World Food Program, to support returnee food rations in Burundi (PRM Report, Funding Actions, February 2005).

The Organization for Economic Cooperation and Development of the European Union estimates that there are 3 million Eastern European refugees in the EU, among which 2 million refugees are from the former Yugoslavia. Others are Poles, Romanians, and Albanians.

Asylees and refugees under the mandate of the UNHCR are hosted in 150 nations around the world. While space does not permit listing all of those countries and their numbers of refugees, Table 6.4 names those countries in which 100,000 or more reside in the host nation. Four countries currently host more than 1 million refugees: Pakistan at over 2,199,000; Iran with over 1,868,000; Afghanistan at over 1,200,000; and Russia with over 1,100,000. Table 6.4 lists the host countries, the number of refugees/asylees, or those internally displaced. Table 6.5A presents the number of applications for asylum in the twenty-eight most industrialized nations submitted during January 2001 to June 2002, according to the UNHCR, and Table 6.5B presents the nation of origin from the top twenty source nations. The top five such countries are, in order of the size of their refugees applying for asylum, Iraq, Afghanistan, Turkey, the former Federal Republic of Yugoslavia, and China.

The desperation driving mass refugee movements often results in their use of exceedingly dangerous means of travel. New Zealand, for instance, recently agreed to take in 136 refugees rescued from a sinking boat. They were to be transferred from Auckland to the Managere Refugee Resettlement Centre. They were to be part of an annual quota of 750 refugees that New Zealand has accepted under convention by the UN High Commissioner for Refugees. They came from Tampa, Manus, an island of Papua New Guinea, and from Nauru. Previously from Afghanistan, Iraq, and other countries, they were boat people who had been sent to Pacific islands to have their refugee claims processed. These 136 refugees represent the first time that New Zealand has accepted refugees whose claims had been determined by Australia, but a spokesperson for the Immigration Ministry noted: "The quality of their [Australia's] determination is equal to our own and the UNHCR. I am satisfied that they are genuine refugees." More than a thousand asylum seekers remain in Australia's Pacific detention centers, where their applications for refugee status were being processed ("More Refugees to Arrive from Pacific Island Camps," 2002).

Border-Management Issues

The massive, worldwide migration of refugees and illegal immigrants has strained the resources of all of the major receiving countries. They all struggle with border management issues. Among the favored receiving nations of this flow are Australia, Canada, France, Germany, the Netherlands, New Zealand, and the United Kingdom. Each has its own general pattern in terms of the source of the flow and each its own particular management issues. Each has a comparatively strong economy that borders developing areas with weak economies, and the migration to find labor is enhanced and often difficult to manage. Australia, New Zealand, and the United Kingdom share a common heritage, flows predominated by persons from the former British Commonwealth of nations, and an island geography that enables them to better control their borders. Their management issues concern primarily visa overstays and those smuggled into the country. France, Germany, and the Netherlands, having land borders with sending sources, have additional border management concerns. They also struggle with illegal immigrants who came initially as guest-workers and then stayed beyond their time or smuggled in family members. These countries have one distinct advantage over the United States with respect to their border management concerns: the much smaller flow of migration makes it easier to finance the effort. Most charge special "exit" stamps or fees to visitors, and the funding from that source supports border management efforts. They are better computerized and seem more able to keep track of the flow and manage the information and record keeping far better than does the ICE in the United States.

Mexico issues ID cards for Mexicans and now for other nationals who travel through Mexico and into the United States. Guatemala has begun issuing such cards, and El Salvador and Honduras are following Mexico's example. The cards are considered helpful in fraud prevention. Mexican ID cards are accepted by banks and nearly 1,000 police departments in the United States. They resemble a California driver's license. They are used to cash checks and are accepted by police departments to establish identity and Mexican citizenship. Anti-immigrant groups contend that the acceptance of the ID cards provides a quasi-legal status to such unauthorized resident individuals and are virtually a "mini-amnesty." Mexico issued 500,000 such cards in its first year of using them (Associated Press, 2002b).

As discussed in Chapter Two, strict border enforcement measures involving increased numbers of agents, fences, and the like seem unable to stem the flow of unauthorized immigrants crossing land borders. Demetrious Papademetriou of the Migration Policy Institute, notes: "There is a certain emperor-has-no-clothes aspect to these enforcement only bills. The only way they can work would be if you totally militarize the border. And even then, people would find some other way to come in" ("Border Bill Not Enough, Some Say," 2005). Indeed, ironically, building border fences may have a counterproductive effect. The United States built more such fences in the early 1990s, under President Clinton, and the flow of unauthorized immigrants has increased dramatically since then. Those immigrants changed to include more women, children, and skilled workers. The number of undocumented children returned to Mexico from the United States rose 63 percent from 2003 to 2004. The border fences signaled to the unauthorized that traveling back and forth would be more difficult, and led many of them to stay in the United States and to bring their families in to join them, rather than traveling back or sending remittances to wives and children remaining at home. The more recent unauthorized immigrants are no longer simply farm laborers seeking work. They increasingly work in construction, commerce, and manufacturing and are more educated than those coming prior to 2001. Despite fences, border patrol increases, and other border management efforts, illegal immigration will continue, driven by cultural connections, family reunification necessities, and simple economic forces. The European Union tends more than the United States to try to engage in economic assistance to poorer sending countries, assuming that economic development at home will better stem the tide. If the United States invested what it spends to "militarize" or "harden" the border on investment in economic development of Mexico, it would more likely reduce illegal immigration in a decade.

Plagues and Illegal Immigration

It is a simple but often deadly fact that microbes migrate along with people. And especially when people move in mass migrations, disease spreads with them. Epidemic outbreaks of diseases in one place or nation have on numerous occasions spread throughout the world—becoming pandemics. It is also a simple fact that epidemic disease outbreaks occur more often in Third World, or lesser developed, nations. Migration, and particularly illegal immigration, from the Third World to the more developed nations of the world is therefore a source of rather considerable and consistent threat. Epidemics and the fear of a pandemic drive a good deal of the increased fear of and concern over illegal immigration worldwide. In an age of the "global village," a new potential threat to a very ancient peril arises from world travel. Diseases that once took months to cross the Atlantic can now circumnavigate the globe in a single day. Today, one after another, plagues previously dismissed as having been "conquered" return to haunt us. New plagues, every bit as deadly as anything seen in history, threaten the world community (Ryan, 1998: 9). In many respects, the "frontline" in the battle to cope with the threat of pandemics is international organizations such as the World Health Organization (WHO), the International Red Cross (IRC), the Centers for Disease Control (CDC), and the International Immigrants Foundation (IIF).

The CDC is part of the WHO's global surveillance system, which connects 110 laboratories in more than 80 countries where scientists study new outbreaks of epidemic disease. Should a new pandemic arise, the various CDC labs would lead an all-out effort to develop a vaccine and would contract with vaccine manufacturers to rush vaccines to inoculate people. Having learned from past pandemics, the CDC would vaccinate entire populations, beginning first with priority groups like firemen, policemen, and health care workers needed to care for the sick. Next would come high-risk groups: the elderly, those with heart ailments or respiratory illnesses, diabetes, and so on. But poorer countries would be in severe danger, since there the vast majority of their populations lack the resources of Europe, the United States, Australia, and Canada to cope with epidemic outbreaks and to pay for massive vaccination campaigns (Getz, 2000: 75–76).

The World Health Organization was launched in June 1948, with fifty-five national signatories. It had as its declared goal to establish "a state of complete physical, mental and social well-being and not merely the absence of disease or infirmity." Today it is governed by 192 member states through the World Health Assembly, composed of representatives from the WHO's member states. The WHO has regional offices in Africa, the Americas, Southeast Asia, Europe, the Eastern Mediterranean, and the Western Pacific (World Health Organization, 2006). It funded campaigns for immunization of the world's children against six dreaded diseases that had for ages plagued mankind: diphtheria, tetanus, whooping cough, measles, poliomyelitis, and tuberculosis. The WHO monitors international disease developments by collecting statistics, improving cooperation, intervening in health crises, and developing plans for Third World health improvements. WHO works closely with the UN's International Children's Emergency Fund (UNICEF) and the UN Educational, Scientific and Cultural Organization (UNESCO), and it cooperates closely with international agencies such as the International Red Cross to spearhead famine relief and epidemic interventions (Porter, 1997: 485–486).

The WHO scored its most notable success by eradicating smallpox, which as recently as 1966 killed 2 million people among the 10 to 15 million persons who suffered from the disease in thirty-three countries. In 1976, the WHO eliminated smallpox from the face of the earth (McNeill, 1976: 9). Other successes, although falling short of eradication, were against infectious diseases such as malaria, tuberculosis, measles, whooping cough, diphtheria, and polio. Collectively, these endemic diseases still kill millions worldwide every year. One difficulty in coping with them is that diseases can develop resistance to modern medical treatments. Between 1985 and 1991, for example, after having been beaten back to where some scientists felt that eradication was imminent, tuberculosis increased by 12 percent in the United States, 30 percent in Europe, and 300 percent in parts of Africa where TB and HIV frequently go together. Today, an estimated 10 million people have active tuberculosis. It kills 3 million annually, 95 percent of whom reside in Third World nations.

In the 1980s, the transmission route of the AIDS virus was thought to have been identified: from Africa to Haiti to the United States. But the distinguished medical historian Mirko Grmek proposed in 1989 that AIDS was really a long-standing human infection widely dispersed around the earth but hidden from medical attention. Changes in medical science and in human behavior may have provoked the AIDS epidemic (ibid., 11).

Modern medicine essentially began the battle against plagues when medical scientists discovered germs and viruses as the causes of many diseases and began to unravel how they were contracted and how they spread. In 1882, Robert Koch won instant fame when he announced discovery of the TB bacillus. He was also the first to identify, in 1884, the cholera bacillus (ibid., 286–287). International medical organization of a formal and official kind dates back to 1909, when the International Office of Public Hygiene was set up in Paris to monitor outbreaks of plague, cholera, smallpox, typhus, and yellow fever. The League of Nations set up special commissions to deal with incidences of such diseases as malaria, smallpox, leprosy, and syphilis (ibid., 291). The administration of antimalarial campaigns passed from private hands (the Rockefeller Foundation) to the WHO when it was established in 1948 (ibid., 286).

Cholera is another disease thought to have been near eradication that has returned. In 1961 the seventh pandemic of cholera erupted, initially in Indonesia, then quickly spreading through Asia and Africa, attacking twenty-nine countries in two years. It reached Peru in 1991, then raced through Chile, Colombia, Ecuador, Bolivia, Brazil, Argentina, and Guatemala. By 1992 it had affected 400,000 Latin Americans, killing 4,000 (Porter, 1997: 491).

The AIDS pandemic continues to spread. It is so difficult to cure or to develop a vaccine against because it mutates so rapidly. By 1996, it had killed an estimated 1,390,000 people. Ironically, AIDS appeared in Africa at the same time that WHO was eradicating smallpox. It may be more than coincidental, in that during the 1970s, WHO teams were reusing needles fifty to sixty times. Live vaccines (such as smallpox) directly provoke the immune system and can awaken sleeping giants such as viruses (ibid., 492).

Poor immigrants, and especially unauthorized immigrants, are particularly at risk in spreading natural outbreaks of infectious diseases when they migrate internationally. They are more likely to speak the language of their host country. Hospitals rarely have or use interpreters. Nationalization movements, like the Americanization movement of the 1920s and the English-Only movement today, discourage perpetuating foreign languages even in a hospital setting, and few foreign workers take nurses' training. Lower-class legal immigrants and illegal immigrants are isolated from the mainstream hospital system by barriers of language, class, income, and the culture of aloofness and impersonality that prevails within the routines of mainstream hospitals; they more often use health clinics set up to assist them in their neighborhoods. Most modern hospitals—staffed by sophisticated, busy, efficient-minded doctors, nurses, and employees buzzing about rapidly from one duty or patient to another—seem to have little time for the poor immigrant. For the unauthorized immigrant, an experience with a major hospital is frightening. The large city hospitals that typically serve the poor handle large numbers of cases, dealing with tuberculosis, venereal diseases, and contagious diseases. They become imbued with an "almshouse" tradition of providing primary care for the poor, with second-class social status and a certain moral stigma. Such hospitals continue to attract a large portion of the poorest residents, with large portions of racial and ethnic minorities. These hospitals are typically "teaching hospitals" at which medical schools develop a pattern of viewing patients more as "teaching material." The largest portions of welfare patients are treated in academic medical centers (Stevens, 1989: 10).

Outbreaks of epidemic disease in poor countries could develop into pandemics as their citizens immigrate illegally. Poorer countries do not have adequate health care programs and can ill afford to produce and distribute many of the medicines needed to protect their citizens against such outbreaks. Dr. Nancy Cox, of the Atlanta CDC, is responsible for keeping an eye on flu outbreaks around the world. She identifies certain conditions under which a flu pandemic could arise. First, the RNA of the flu virus must mutate and change so much that people around the world have little immunity to the new strain. Second, a pandemic strain must be sturdy and contagious, capable of traveling easily from person to person. Third, the new strain must reproduce well in epithelial cells. If a new flu virus arises that meets those conditions, a pandemic is possible. The flu pandemic of 1918–1919, often called the Spanish influenza, killed an estimated 50 to 80 million persons worldwide.

Influenza develops from birds and some then transfer to humans. The current avian bird flu has spread from Asia to Western Europe, in Italy and Greece. The twenty-five-nation EU announced in February 2006 that they had detected the deadly H5N1 strain of the virus in dead swans. This strain, which has infected 166 people and killed 88, mostly in Asia, has also been detected in Bulgaria. This latest outbreak raised concern that the spread of the disease, which ravaged poultry stocks across Asia since 2003, would increase chances of its mutating into a form easily transmissible among humans, who generally catch it from domestic poultry. The human deaths from the disease have been linked to contact with infected birds. The infected birds in Italy and Greece likely arrived from the Balkans, having been pushed south by cold weather. The disease has also been suspected in Africa, having spread to humans, after several people were reported ill of it in Nigeria. China suffered 8 deaths from the disease and Indonesia reported 18. The scientific study of past pandemics, moreover, has failed to discover how viral mutation occurs ("Bird Flu Discovered," 2006; "Scientists Must Wing It on Future of Avian Flu," 2005).

Even diseases once thought conquered or controlled are potential epidemic and even pandemic threats. The WHO estimates that in the 1980s and 1990s some 2.5 million children died annually from measles because of the failure to vaccinate. After decades of trying to eliminate the disease, global eradication is now projected by 2020, but with rapid travel to all parts of the world, those coming from areas where the measles virus still circulates pose a very real hazard to susceptible people in distant countries. WHO studies indicate that measles still infects 40 million children and kills about 1 million per year (Oldstone, 1998: 88–89). The WHO launched its second worldwide crusade (against measles) in the 1960s (Etheridge, 1992: 164–165).

Likewise, poliomyelitis has nearly been wiped out, but it, too, occurs in epidemic episodes in some areas. In 1995, the WHO immunized 300 million people, yet in 1996 it still reported 2,200 cases worldwide. WHO committed to its eradication by the end of 2005, but it did not achieve eradication by that target date.

Mutations of previously pandemic diseases break out episodically. In the 1970s a new strain of cholera, called the El Tor strain, broke out and spread rapidly. In the 1980s it arrived in Latin America (Colombia and Chile experienced notable outbreaks), probably in the ballast tanks of a ship from China that discharged its pestilential cargo in Peruvian coastal waters. The discharge infected shellfish, crabs, lobsters, fish, and then people. The CDC estimates that by the mid-1980s more than 1 million persons were infected, and 10,000 deaths occurred throughout Latin America. It kills quickly, from massive dehydration due to fulminant diarrhea. In 1994, India had an outbreak of bubonic plague. In 1995, most of the world was hit by the "superbug" MRSA (Ryan, 1998: 115–133).

The Vietnam war, with its massive troop movements, spread outbreaks of malaria in the late 1960s. India experienced another smallpox epidemic during the same period. In 1980 the Marburg virus broke out in Africa, near Nairobi. It is one of the new "hot viruses" that has no known cure and is deadly, with a 90 percent mortality rate. Ebola is another such hot virus that seems to have spread from monkeys to man (Preston, 1994).

The world's deadliest pandemic, known as the Spanish influenza of 1918–1919, resulted from a particular mutated influenza virus. It killed at least 50 million worldwide and over 500,000 in the United States. Long a mystery as to why it was so virulent, its genetic code was finally deciphered by Dr. Jeffery Taubenberger of the Armed Forces Institute of Pathology (Sternberg, 2005; Barry, 2005). Medical scientists have feared the return of some similarly lethal influenza virus. The first major change in the flu virus that caused an influenza pandemic, though one less lethal than that of 1918–1919, occurred in 1957–1958. Another was the Hong Kong flu of 1968.

Epidemiologists warn of the inevitability of another pandemic on the scale of the influenza pandemic of 1918–1919. "Warning" episodes include the current HIV/AIDS pandemic. In late 2002, SARS, a previously unknown virus, struck, first breaking out in Hong Kong. The Ebola hemorrhagic fever outbreak and a new strain of Lyme disease portend similar warnings of a disaster to come (Walters, 2003: 148–151).

Of particular concern with the unauthorized immigration flow is its potential to be used by international terrorist organizations to spread infectious diseases intentionally, as agents of bioterrorism. Richard Preston's chilling account of such an attack, in *The Cobra Event*, while fictional, is based on real science. Indeed, the CDC has identified a number of diseases as potential bioterrorism threats: anthrax, botulism, *Chlamydia psittaci*, cholera, Ebola virus hemorrhagic fever, E. coli 0157H7, food safety threats (for example, various salmonella species), lassa fever, Marburg virus hemorrhagic fever, plague (*Yersenia pestis*), Q fever, Ricin toxin, smallpox (*viriola major*), and typhoid fever (Centers for Disease Control and Prevention, 2006).

Dr. D. A. Henderson, who founded the Center for Civilian Biodefense Strategies, became, in 2001, the director of the Office of Public Health Preparedness (OPHP) in the U.S. Department of Health and Human Services. It was established to defend against bioterrorism. He had helped in the eradication of smallpox and sees it potentially as one of the deadliest of bioterrorism agents (Drexler, 2002: 238). The OPHP was established after the anthrax cases struck via the U.S. Postal Service in the autumn of 2001. Anthrax spores are deadly and capable of jumping continents with ease. The danger of bioterrorism was very real to the government. Its potential had long been recognized. During World War II the U.S. Army experimented with bioweapons and concocted a botulinum toxin so potent that one pound of it, if expertly dispersed, could kill 1 billion people (ibid., 232).

The list above suggests that many diseases are potential bioterrorism agents whose spread might well be enhanced by developing new strains resistant to known treatments. These are dubbed "superbugs." Each year, the WHO estimates, drug resistance contributes to more than 14,000 U.S. hospital deaths (ibid., 129). In the late 1990s a staph infection developed that was resistant to penicillin and even methicillin, which accounted for its name of MRSA (methicillin-resistant *staphylococcus aureus*).

Illegal Immigration and Economic Development Issues

The push and pull of international migration is another important global issue. Many countries in the developing world are sending nations. The emigration they experience often results in a "brain drain" problem. A significant portion of their talented population emigrates to immigration-receiving countries. Sometimes, even more developed countries experiencing economic difficulties struggle with this issue. South Africa, for example, is currently experiencing emigration outflow and brain drain difficulties. The causes of the exodus include such factors as the uncertainties of majority rule, fears about rising crime, the AIDS pandemic, massive unemployment, the government's policy of affirmative action favoring black South Africans, corruption, and declining standards of health care and education. Violent crime is cited by an estimated 60 percent of emigrants leaving the country as a major reason for their decision. Others leave for better opportunities available since South Africa's reintegration into international business after the long period of isolation associated with the apartheid policy.

Salaries paid in the rand (South Africa's currency) make South African labor cheap to hire, and the falling value of the currency has increased white middle-class anxiety about their future spending power in relation to the European and U.S. middle classes. Favored destinations for South Africans are Australia, New Zealand, Canada, the United States, and the United Kingdom. As many as 800,000 South Africans hold British passports and are thereby able to enter the UK and to work. Others can extend their stay in the United Kingdom on the strength of British ancestry. They are able to gain permanent residency status after four years, and in six years may claim a British passport. South Africa is shedding skilled labor at a worrying rate in comparison with its global economic competitors. Similarly, there are more than 1 million Moroccan nationals who are officially resident in the European Union, according to a Push and Pull Migration Study research project of the Netherlands Interdisciplinary Demographic Institute and the statistical office of the European Commission.

Thailand struggles with controlling the pull of its economy from nearby nations such as Myanmar (formerly known as

Burma). Its comparatively booming economy acts like a magnet for foreign workers, and a significant illegal flow is a migration both dangerous and highly exploited. Hundreds of thousands of Myanmar migrants have fled to Thailand to escape their impoverished and military-ruled homeland. Laotians and Cambodians annually join them. The Thai government has registered 400,000, allowing them to work, but tensions along its 1,300-mile border remain high. Thai officials estimate that there are more than 250,000 illegal Myanmar workers in the country. Migrants pay smugglers $100 to $250 to get them into the country, where they work in factories, farms, fishing boats, the construction industries, or as domestic workers. Some work as prostitutes by choice or by coercion. Amnesty International reports indicate that most were paid less than Thailand's legal minimum wage of $3.30 to $4.20 per day, depending on the region. Typically, farm workers were paid as little as $1.25 per day. In construction, they perform the dirtiest, most dangerous, and most difficult jobs.

Thailand has no systematic protection against the abuse and prejudice that migrants encounter. In March 2002, the bodies of thirteen immigrants, including women and children, were discovered in a waste dump where a smuggling gang admitted to having dumped the corpses; the migrants had suffocated while packed under vegetables in a truck being used to smuggle them into the country. In February 2002, twenty ethnic Myanmars were found along a trail used for smuggling. In July, an eighteen-year-old girl died shortly after being found north of Bangkok. Before her death, she told Thai police that she had been working as a maid at the house of a factory owner who kept her a virtual prisoner. He accused her of stealing a gold necklace. She denied the charge but was beaten up, taken away, doused with gasoline, and set afire (Associated Press, 2002a).

Emigration has emerged as among the greatest of challenges to postapartheid South Africa. The country's skilled workers are easily snapped up abroad. The emigration flow is seriously undermining the country's efforts to rise above a 3 percent economic growth rate. An estimated 39,000 South Africans left in 1999, joining some 1.6 million South Africans living abroad. One study found that 70 percent of skilled South Africans are considering emigrating, and an estimated 20 percent have already left. The brain drain costs South Africa about 2.5 billion rand ($250 million) annually. Each skilled professional leaving the country costs it as many as ten unskilled jobs, according to a University of South Africa study (Lamont, 2002).

Southeast Asia loses many skilled workers to Malaysia, Europe, Australia, Canada, and the United States. In Australia's current immigration flow, two-thirds are from Africa, the Middle East, and Southeast Asia. The Australian immigration minister said that the country's migrant intake for FY2001–2002 was the largest in a decade and the most skilled ever, numbering over 93,000. Per capita, Australia had a greater net overseas migration than any other comparable country. Its immigration minister noted: "What you've got is 53,520 highly skilled and educated young people and their families bringing their energy, their skills and knowledge, and their experience to Australia and helping our economy to grow" (Ruddock, 2002).

Canada also benefits from the brain drain flow. Its immigration minister, Denis Coderre, released a major proposal to encourage new immigrants to come to Canada and to settle in the country's smaller urban centers. The plan intends to put a million newcomers into the nation's less populated regions by 2011, and if accomplished would constitute the most dramatic effort to channel immigrants since the settlement of western Canada during the early decades of the twentieth century. Under the plan, only skilled workers, who make up about 60 percent of the inflow, are eligible to sign a social contract under which they would agree to reside in the Atlantic provinces, the Prairie provinces, or rural areas of Ontario, Quebec, and British Columbia provinces for three to five years. In advocating the program, Mr. Coderre noted:

> It's not complicated. You know why? It's everybody's business and everybody participates in the process. Because immigration is not just a port of entry. By bringing them to a specific place, first of all its economic, it's a matter of quality of life because it provides services to the citizens living there, and thirdly, it sends a clear sensitivity to a regional approach that Canada is the country to come to and that it is serious about plans to encourage settlement in all of its regions and that people from Flin Flon or North Bay or Kelowna have a right to have the same services. There's no such thing as a second-class citizen. (Curry, 2002)

Canada has good reason to welcome Italian tradesmen, medical doctors from India, and similarly skilled workers from around the globe who fill jobs and pay taxes. They ease Canada's significant demographic crunch. Canada is experiencing a tumbling birth rate among its native population precisely as its baby boomer generation retires. By 2020 an estimated million jobs will go unfilled, a projection of huge implications for government revenues, for businesses seeking employees, and even for retirees relying on government health care and pensions.

Ireland is also experiencing a long economic boom and its first-ever wave of immigration. Long considered one of the major sending nations, particularly to Australia, Canada, New Zealand, and the United States, Ireland is now attracting immigrants to its growing economy. Current census figures show a population surge that is at the highest level in modern history. The Republic of Ireland (which excludes British North Ireland) has seen an 8.2 percent increase in its population since 1996, reaching nearly 4 million. It, too, benefits from the brain drain flow (Associated Press, 2002c).

The Economics of Illegal Immigration

When developing countries are close to countries with relatively healthy to booming economies, the migration flow is virtually unstoppable. Sending countries rely on emigration to relieve economic, social, and political pressures. Receiving countries enjoy a source of cheap and easily exploitable labor. Migrants, both legal and illegal, send support to their families at home, significantly enhancing the economies of the sending countries. The Banco de Mexico, for example, reported that during the first half of 2002, Mexicans living and working in the United States sent a record $4,753 billion dollars in remittances, an 11 percent increase over the previous year. Competition among banks and wire-money transfer services over the lucrative business increased when the banks agreed to accept the *matricula consular* documents issued to Mexicans to establish Mexican citizenship.

With the ID cards, Mexicans can open bank accounts from which ATMs in Mexico with corresponding banks can be used to withdraw funds for family members at lower costs and with immediate access, thus making it easier to "send" money home.

The Mexican economy is highly susceptible to economic trends in the United States. An old Mexican refrain states, "When the U.S. economy sneezes, the Mexican economy catches a cold." The U.S. recession in 2001–2002 gave Mexico a case of economic pneumonia. Unemployment and underemployment have reached epidemic proportions, necessitating more Mexicans to seek employment in the United States to send money home—vastly increasing the flow of remittances to help out and vastly increasing the unauthorized immigration discussed in Chapter Two. A 2004 study by Banco de Mexico found that most of the remittances sent to Mexico came from illegal immigrants, most of whom were working in the United States. Between January and October 2004 those came to more than $13.8 billion, an increase of 23 percent over the previous year. In 2005 they were estimated to reach $17 billion and have become the top driving force of the Mexican economy.

While migrants have traveled to other Latin American countries, Europe, and Japan, the overwhelming migration has been to the United States. An Inter-American Development Bank report found that in 2003 remittances exceeded all combined foreign direct investment and official development assistance to the region, accounting for some 10 percent of the gross domestic product in Haiti, Nicaragua, El Salvador, Jamaica, the Dominican Republic, and Guyana. Remittances to Mexico exceeded total tourism revenues, and equaled more than two-thirds of the value of petroleum exports and about 180 percent of total agricultural exports ("Remittances—the Flow of Money Out of the United States to Latin America," 2006: 100–101).

Regional Approaches to Illegal Migration Issues

The worldwide refugee crisis is but one issue illustrating an increasingly important trend in global migration movements: the effort to cope with problems generated by such mass migrations with an approach that emphasizes the use of regional governmental or even nongovernmental organizations. Regional or multilateral agreements have been forged as a better way to cope with several illegal immigration issues: antitrafficking strategies to deal with human smuggling across national borders; the effects of illegal immigration on economic development in both sending and receiving countries; the human rights afforded or guaranteed to migrants, especially unauthorized migrants, desperate refugees, and asylees; the illegal immigrants' right of return; how nation-state policy interacts with cooperative or multilateral links; and technical cooperation. As one scholar notes:

> The global and regional contexts within which immigration and refugee policies are made are changing in ways that produce pressures for states to forego their traditional practices of devising and executing autonomous immigration policy and increasingly to participate in more coordinated, jointly-produced, multilateral policies fashioned in participation with their neighbors and the governments of the countries from which immigrants come. (Freedman, 2000: 223)

One such international migration issue, for example, that is benefited by use of the multilateral approach concerns trafficking. Trafficking in human beings is defined as a process involving the recruitment, transportation, harboring, sale, or receipt of persons through the use of deceit, fraud, coercion, force, or abduction, for the purpose of placing such persons in situations of slavery-like conditions, including forced prostitution, bonded sweatshop labor, domestic servitude, or other debt-bondage (Helton and Jacobs, 2001: 120–121).

Trafficking in men, women, or children poses relatively few risks and promises significant financial rewards to the traffickers. The United Nations estimates that 4 million persons are trafficked around the world each year, with an estimated profit to criminal syndicates perpetrating the traffic at more than $7 billion dollars annually. In 2000, an estimated 50,000 women and children were smuggled into the United States for bonded sweatshop and domestic servitude. Men are also brought in to forced labor. This problem prompted Rep. Christopher Smith (R-NJ) to sponsor, in November 1999, the Trafficking Victims Protection Act, which provides up to 5,000 T-visas, for humanitarian relief of those so abused, to enter the United States annually (ibid., 122; Centre for International Crime Prevention, 2006).

The United Nations has touched on the issue in several ways: agreements and protocols based on the Universal Declaration of Human Rights, passed by the UN General Assembly in

1948, and on the International Covenant on Civil and Political Rights, passed by the United Nations in December 1966. The UNHCR issued suggested guidelines for dealing with aspects of the issue—for example, "Guidelines on Policies and Procedures in Dealing with Unaccompanied Children Seeking Asylum" (Geneva, 1997); "Guidelines on Applicable Criterion and Standards Relating to the Detention of Asylum Seekers" (Geneva, 1999); most important, the UN Protocol on Human Trafficking and Immigrant Smuggling (Palermo, Italy, 2002). This latter protocol has been signed by 141 countries. The issue is clearly illustrated by a story reported by the Associated Press on July 24, 2002, which related the story of a Greek court that convicted a British yacht captain of smuggling seventy-two Iraqi and Syrian illegals, including nine children, from Turkey to Greece. Each illegal alien paid $2,000 to be smuggled into Greece. The captain was sentenced to ten years for smuggling.

While the United Nations is undoubtedly the largest and most important international organization when it comes to international policy to deal with worldwide migration, it is not alone. Several regional approaches are highlighted here. The Central American region has developed multilateral approaches, mostly in response to the massive emigration of refugees from El Salvador, Guatemala, and Nicaragua in response to their civil wars of national liberation. Ten countries of the region formed what has become known as the Puebla Group, after a 1996 conference in Puebla, Mexico: Belize, Canada, Costa Rica, El Salvador, Guatemala, Honduras, Mexico, Nicaragua, Panama, and the United States. The Regional Conference on Migration has developed into an ongoing cooperative mechanism, with vice ministers meeting annually to discuss common problems and trying to develop mutual approaches and solutions. They deal specifically with irregular (illegal) immigration, migrant trafficking, cross-border labor issues, and human rights issues.

The Regional Conference on Migration seeks migration management strategies across the region. In recent years they have invited participation by nongovernmental organizations involved in refugee assistance. U.S. and Canadian NGOs (most of which are affiliated with a particular religious group) are joined by Mexican and Central American activists in relief efforts on behalf of refugees. In 1989 a coalition of such groups formed the Conference for Central American Refugees (CIREFCA, after its

Spanish-initials), and later the National Coordination of NGOs to Assist Refugees (CONONGAR, for its Spanish initials). Although those largely ended after the civil strife declined in the mid-1990s, they developed into the Asociación Regional para las Migraciones Forzedas (the Regional Association on Forced Migration, ARMIF). This regional network operates currently and cooperates with the RCM. The RCM vice ministers, meeting in Ottawa, Canada, in 1998, formally invited the NGOs to participate in the annual conference. Another related group of NGOs involved in the issue was formed as a communication network in 1995, the Heartland Alliance for Human Needs and Human Rights, which is a Chicago-based NGO for binational and regional coalitions (Gzesh, 2000: 207–222).

ARMIF formed in January 1999, after Hurricane Mitch devastated the Central American region. They attended the Regional Conference on Migration meeting held in San Salvador and helped form the International Organization for Migration, which successfully advocated for the Nicaraguan and Central American Relief Act, in which the U.S. Congress approved a program to give Nicaraguans treatment equal to that afforded Salvadorans and Guatemalans. The Puebla Group also deals with intraregional migration. South-to-south migration affecting the area is exemplified by large-scale and mostly illegal immigration from Colombia to Panama and from Nicaragua to Costa Rica.

The European Union

Regional cooperation in Europe that addresses the immigration flow, both legal and increasingly illegal flows, is exemplified by the EU Dublin Convention on Refugees and Asylees and by the United Kingdom's Empire Settlement Scheme. Several of the EU member states have ratified the UN's Palermo, Italy, convention outlawing the trafficking in women and children for forced labor sweatshops or "sex slavery." Organized crime involvement in human trafficking is one of the most serious transnational threats that EU nations face.

Illegal immigration for purposes of employment is a larger and more contentious issue over which the EU is still developing a consensus approach. Moreover, since the mid-1990s migration between East and West Europe has become much more fluid, with movements into the EU often being nearly offset by movements back to the former communist states. The Organization for Economic Cooperation and Development is an EU-based organization established, in part, to deal with the issue.

Conclusion

The world is increasingly becoming "a global village." As the worldwide economy becomes more intermingled, the flow of migration becomes ever more massive (200 million plus) and nearly uncontrollable. Illegal immigrants flow from impoverished Third World countries and economies to those of the First World, often transitioning through other "stepping-stone" nations. Nearly every developed nation grapples with legalization programs and controversies over how best to control illegal immigration. The global refugee issue amounts to an enormous pool of potential illegal migration and taxes the best efforts of receiving states to develop effective and comprehensive border management policy.

The unprecedented worldwide flow of migration portends the danger of epidemic diseases becoming pandemics threatening the lives of millions worldwide. Illegal immigration exacerbates the problem and has become increasingly linked in the developed nations to policies aimed at protection against both natural disease outbreaks and bioterrorism.

The complex economics that drive illegal immigration render single-nation efforts in domestic policy to control the flow ineffectual. The developed nations of the world, as illegal immigration–receiving states, increasingly rely on multinational and regional approaches to cope with the problem.

References

Al-Ali, Nadje, and Khalid Koser, eds. 2001. *New Approaches to Migration: Transnational Communities and the Transformation of Home.* New York: Routledge.

Associated Press. 2002a. "Between Two Worlds." *Press Enterprise,* Riverside, CA, September 1: A-24.

Associated Press. 2002b. "Consulates to Issue ID Cards Following Mexican Success." *Los Angeles Times,* September 7: B-4.

Associated Press. 2002c "Irish Population Soars above 3.9 Million." *Press-Enterprise,* Riverside, CA, July 24: B-1.

Barry, John M. 2005. *The Great Influenza: The Epic Story of the Deadliest Plague in Human History.* New York: Penguin.

Bauer, Thomas, and Klaus F. Zimmerman. 1998. "Looking South and East: Labor Market Implications of Migration in Europe and Developing Countries." In Ed O. Memodovic et al., eds., *Globalization of Labor Markets, Challenges, Adjustment and Policy Response in the European Union and the Less Developed Countries.* Dordrecht: Kluwer Academic, 75–103.

Bauer, Thomas, et al. 2002. "Portuguese Migrants in the German Labor Market: Selection and Performance." *International Migration Review* 36, no. 2 (Summer): 467–491.

"Bird Flu Discovered in Western Europe." *Colorado Springs Gazette,* February 12, 2006: A-6.

"Border Bill Not Enough, Some Say." *Denver Post,* December 19, 2005: A-14.

Brettell, Caroline B., and James F. Hollifield, eds. 2000. *Migration Theory: Talking across Disciplines.* New York: Routledge.

Bureau of Population, Refugee, and Migration, U.S. Department of State. 2002. "Migration and Refugee Assistance: Emergency Refugee and Migration Assistance, FY 2003." http://www.state.gov/g/prin/vls/rpt/2002/1428.htm.

Bustamante, Jorge A. 2002. "Immigrants' Vulnerability as Subjects of Human Rights." *International Migration Review* 36, no. 2 (Summer): 333–354.

Castles, Stephen, and Alastair Davidson, eds. 2000. *Citizenship and Migration: Globalization and the Politics of Belonging.* New York: Routledge.

Centers for Disease Control and Prevention. 2006. "Bioterrorism Agents/Diseases." http://www.bt.cdc.gov/agent/agentlist.asp. Accessed February 16, 2006.

Centre for International Crime Prevention. 2000. United Nations Office of Drug Control and Crime Prevention. "Introduction to the Centre for International Crime Prevention." http://www.uncjin.org/CICP/cicp.html. Accessed June 6, 2000.

Curry, Bill. 2002. "Immigrants Coming to Flin Flon." *National Post,* August 27. http://www.nationalpost.com.

Drexler, Madeline. 2002. *The Menace of Emerging Infections: West Nile Virus, Anthrax, E. Coli.* New York: Penguin.

Etheridge, Elizabeth W. 1992. *Sentinel for Health: A History of the Centers for Disease Control.* Berkeley: University of California Press.

Freedman, Amy L. *Political Participation and Ethnic Minorities: Chinese Overseas in Malaysia, Indonesia, and the United States.* New York: Routledge, 2000.

Gallogher, Stephen. 2002. "Towards a Common European Asylum System: Fortress Europe Redesigns the Ramparts." *International Journal 57,* no. 3 (summer): 375-394.

Getz, David. 2000. *Purple Death: The Mysterious Flu of 1918.* New York: Henry Holt.

Guiraudon and Christian Joppke, eds. 2001. *Controlling a New Migration World.* New York: Routledge.

Gzesh, Susan. 2000. "Advocacy for Human Rights in an Intergovernmental Forum: The Puebla Process from the Perspective of Non-governmental Organizations." In Lydio Tomasi, ed., *In Defense of the Alien, XXII.* New York: Center for Migration Studies, 207–222.

Helton, Arthur, and Eliana Jacobs. 2001. "Combating Human Smuggling by Enlisting the Victims." In Lydio Tomasi, ed., *In Defense of the Alien, XXIII.* New York: Center for Migration Studies, 119–128.

Hughes, Helen. 2002. *Immigrants, Refugees, and Asylum Seekers: A Global View.* New Providence, Australia: Center for Independent Study.

Hylton-Potts, Rodney. 2005. "Get Britain Back: The Party Manifesto for the General Election 2005." www.getbritainback.com/gbbpmanifesto.htm. Accessed February 12, 2006.

Inter-American Development Bank. 2004. "Sending Money Home: Remittance to Latin America and the Caribbean." http://www.iadb.org/mif/v2/files/StudyPE2004eng.pdf. Accessed July 24, 2006.

International Organization for Migration [IOM]. 2002. *Trafficking in Women and Prostitution in the Baltic States: Social and Legal Aspects.* Washington, DC: International Organization for Migration.

Karim, H. Karim, ed. 2002. *Diaspora and Communication: Mapping the Globe.* New York: Routledge.

Karlen, Arno. 1995. *Man and Microbes.* New York: Touchstone.

Kennedy, Paul, and Victor Roudometof, eds. 2002. *Communities across Borders: New Immigrants and Transnational Cultures.* New York: Routledge.

Kofman, Eleonore, et al. 2001. *Gender and International Migration in Europe.* New York: Routledge.

Lamont, James. 2002. "Skilled South Africans Leave to Find Fortune." *Financial Times,* July 23. http://www.cisnews.org. Accessed August 26, 2002.

LeMay, Michael. 1989. *The Gatekeepers: Comparative Immigration Policy.* New York: Praeger.

Littler Mendelson, P.C. 2006. "Global Migration Insights." http://www.littler.com/presspublications/index.cfm?event=detail&childViewID=318. Accessed July 21, 2006.

Lynch, James B., and Rita J. Simon. 2003. *Immigration the World Over: Statutes, Policies, and Practices.* Lanham, MD: Rowman and Littlefield.

McNeill, William H. 1976. *Plagues and Peoples.* New York: Doubleday/Anchor.

Miller, Mark. 1989. "Continuities and Discontinuities in Immigration Reform in Industrial Democracies." *International Review of Comparative Pubic Policy* 1: 131–151.

———. 2000. "Legalization and the Capacity of Democratic States to Prevent Illegal Alien Residency and Employment: French and American Experiences." In Lydio Tomasi, ed., *In Defense of the Alien, XXII.* New York: Center for Migration Studies, 259–272.

"More Refugees to Arrive from Pacific Island Camps." 2002. Associated Press, August 27.

Morris, Lydia. 2003. *Managing Migration: Civic Stratification and Migrants' Rights.* New York: Routledge.

Oldstone, Michael B. A. 1998. *Viruses, Plagues and History.* New York: Oxford University Press.

Pew Hispanic Center. 2003. *Remittance Senders and Receivers: Tracking the Transnational Channels.* Washington, DC: Pew Hispanic Center.

Porter, Roy. 1997. *The Greatest Benefit to Mankind: A Medical History of Humanity.* New York: W. W. Norton.

Preston, Richard. 1994. *The Hot Zone.* New York: Doubleday/Anchor.

———. 1997. *The Cobra Event.* New York: Ballantine.

"Remittances—the Flow of Money Out of the United States to Latin America." *Information Plus.* 2006. Farmington Hills, MI: Thomson/Gale.

Robinson, Eugene. 2005. "Proof that Multi-culturalism Works." *Washington Post* editorial in the *Denver Post,* November 13, 2005: E-5.

Russell, James C. 2004. *Breach of Faith: American Churches and the Immigration Crisis.* Lexington, VA: Representative Government Press.

Ruth, Anne. 2006. "The European Battle between Civil Rights and Nationhood." *Humanity in Action,* http://www.humanityinaction.org. Accessed February 12, 2006.

Ryan, Frank. 1998. *Virus X: Tracking the New Killer Plagues.* Boston: Little, Brown.

"Scientists Must Wing It on Future of Avian Flu." *Denver Post*, November 20, 2005: 16-A.

Sergeant, Harriet. 2001. *Immigration and Asylum in the U.K.* London: Center for Policy Studies, Chameleon Press.

Sharp, Nancy. 2001. "International Assignments and the Immigration Issues Surrounding Spousal Employment." In Lydio Tomasi, ed., *In Defense of the Alien, XXIII*. New York: Center for Migration Studies, 59–63.

Sorenson, Ninna, and Karen Fog Olwig, eds. 2001. *Work and Migration: Life and Livelihoods in a Globalizing World.* New York: Routledge.

Sternberg, Steve. 2005. "Catastrophic Flu Virus of 1918 Is Decoded." *U.S.A. Today,* October 6: 7-D.

Stevens, Rosemary. 1989. *In Sickness and in Wealth: American Hospitals in the Twentieth Century.* Baltimore: Johns Hopkins University Press.

UN High Commission for Refugees. 2006. "The U.N. Refugee Agency," http://www.unhcr.org/cgi-bin/texis/vtx/home. Accessed February 9, 2006.

Walters, Mark Jerome. 2003. *Six Modern Plagues and How We Are Causing Them.* Washington, DC: Island/Shearwater.

World Health Organization. 2006. "About WHO." http://www.who.int/about/en/. Accessed February 16, 2006.

Zimmerman, Klaus F. 1995. "Tackling the European Migration Problem." *Journal of Economic Perspectives* 9: 45–62.

Zolberg, Aristide, Astri Suhrke, and Sergio Aguayo. *Escape from Violence: Conflict and the Refugee Crisis in the Developing World.* New York: Oxford University Press, 1989.

Zucker, Norma, and Naomi Flink Zucker. 1987. *The Guarded Gate: The Reality of American Refugee Policy.* San Diego: Harcourt Brace Jovanovich.

4

Chronology

Precursor Legislation:
Setting the Stage for Things to Come

1790   In one of its first official actions, the U.S. Congress estab-
        lishes a uniform rule of naturalization that imposes a
        two-year residency requirement for aliens who are "free
        white persons of good moral character."

1802   Congress revises the 1790 act to require a five-year resi-
        dency requirement and that naturalizing citizens re-
        nounce allegiance and fidelity to foreign powers.

1819   Congress enacts law requiring shipmasters to deliver a
        manifest enumerating all aliens transported for immi-
        gration and requiring the secretary of state to inform
        Congress annually of the number of immigrants admit-
        ted. This act, for the first time, keeps count of the num-
        ber of immigrants who enter "legally" for the purpose of
        permanent immigration. In short, it is the first official
        "immigration act."

1848   Treaty of Guadalupe Hidalgo guarantees citizenship to
        Mexicans remaining in the territory ceded by Mexico to
        the United States. This action sets the first base for the
        flow of Mexicans to the United States and provides for a

1848, citizen base from Mexico into which future immigrants,
cont.   both legal and undocumented, can assimilate. It forges
        the first link into what develops as "chain migration"
        from Mexico and even Central America to the United
        States.

1855   Castle Garden becomes New York's principal port of en-
       try for legal immigration. Its volume of immigrants sets
       the stage for later development of "visa overstayers"
       who are able to remain because such extensive numbers
       overwhelm the ability of immigration authorities to keep
       accurate track of them.

1862   Congress enacts the Homestead Act, granting acres of
       free land to settlers who develop the land in frontier re-
       gions and remain on it for five years, spurring heavy lev-
       els of immigration.

1868   The Fourteenth Amendment is ratified. It guarantees
       that all persons born or naturalized in the United States
       and subject to its jurisdiction are citizens and states that
       no state may abridge their rights without due process or
       deny them equal protection under the law. The amend-
       ment ensures citizenship rights of the former slaves and
       thereby changes the "free white persons" phrase of citi-
       zenship to include blacks. It further establishes the su-
       premacy of federal law over actions by state govern-
       ments in matters pertaining to citizenship,
       naturalization, and immigration.

1870   Congress enacts a law granting citizenship to persons of
       African descent.

1882   Congress passes the Chinese Exclusion Act, barring the
       immigration of Chinese laborers for ten years and deny-
       ing Chinese eligibility for naturalization. The act is reen-
       acted and extended in 1888, 1892, and 1904. Its harsh
       provisions induce many Chinese immigrants to get
       around the law by using falsified documents—such as
       "paper sons and daughters." This sets a precedent for
       using phony documents by illegal aliens that persists to
       the present day.

1885   Congress passes an act making it unlawful for laborers to immigrate to the United States under contract with a U.S. employer who in any manner prepays passage to bring the laborer to the country. In some ways it serves as the precursor to employers who hire illegal aliens using fake documents: the employer simply does not verify the accuracy of the documents, in some cases knowing or suspecting that they are illegal.

1886   *Yick Wo v. Hopkins* overturns a San Francisco municipal ordinance against Chinese laundry workers as discriminatory and unconstitutional on the grounds that the Fourteenth Amendment prohibits state and local governments from depriving any person (even a noncitizen) of life, liberty, or property without due process.

1888   Congress expands the Chinese Exclusion Act by rescinding reentry permits for Chinese laborers and thus prohibiting their return (also known as the Scott Act).

1889   In the case of *Chae Chan Ping v. United States*, the Supreme Court upholds the right of Congress to repeal the certificate of reentry as contained in the 1888 act, thereby excluding ex post facto certain Chinese immigrants who had previously entered legally.

1891   Congress expands the classes of individuals excluded from admission, forbids the soliciting of immigrants, and creates the position of superintendent of immigration.

1892   Ellis Island is opened as the nation's leading port of entry. It becomes the source of many visa overstayers from European countries.

1894   Congress extends the Chinese Exclusion Act and establishes the Bureau of Immigration within the Treasury Department, the first of several such home departments to immigration services.

1897   A federal district court decides the case *In re Rodriquez*. This west-Texas case affirms the citizenship rights of

1897, Mexicans based on the 1848 Treaty of Guadalupe Hi-
cont. dalgo and notwithstanding that such persons may not
be considered "white."

1898 In the case of *Wong Kim Ark v. United States,* the Supreme
Court rules that a native-born son of Asian descent is indeed a citizen of the United States despite the fact that
his parents may have been resident aliens ineligible for
citizenship.

1903 Congress enacts a law making immigration the responsibility of the Department of Commerce and Labor.

1906 The Basic Naturalization Law codifies a uniform law for
naturalization. With some amendments and supple-
ments, it forms the basic naturalization law thereafter.

1907 Congress adds important regulations about issuing passports and the expatriation and marriage of U.S. women
to foreigners. It continues to stir controversy until Section 3 of the act is repealed in 1922. President Theodore
Roosevelt issues an executive order, known as the Gen-
tleman's Agreement, by which Japan agrees to restrict
emigration of laborers from Japan and Korea (which was
then under Japanese jurisdiction). Picture brides, however, are permitted to emigrate. Congress passes the
White-Slave Traffic Act forbidding importation of any
woman or girl for the purpose of prostitution or similar
immoral purposes.

1911 The Dillingham Commission issues its report, whose
recommendations form the basis for the quota acts of the
1920s.

1915 The Americanization/100 Percentism campaign begins
and is supported by both government and private enterprise. These social movements represent the first attempt
at "forced assimilation" encouraging the adoption of the
English language and social customs. After World War I,
its perceived failure will contribute to the disillusion-
ment that set the stage for the quota acts of the 1920s.

1917   The United States enters World War I in April. Congress enacts an immigration act that includes a literacy test and bars all immigration from a specified area known thereafter as the Asian barred zone. The Departments of State and of Labor issue a joint order requiring passports of all aliens seeking to enter the United States and requiring that the would-be entrants be issued visas by U.S. consular officers in their country of origin rather than seeking permission to enter the United States only when arriving at the port of entry. Puerto Ricans are granted U.S. citizenship.

1918   Congress gives the president sweeping powers to disallow the entrance or the departure of aliens during time of war. Similar presidential declarations are used in virtually all periods of war thereafter.

1919   Congress enacts a law granting honorably discharged Native Americans citizenship for their service during World War I. In the summer, the Red Scare following the Bolshevik revolution in Russia leads to the summary deportation of certain specified "radical" aliens deemed thereby to be a threat to U.S. security. It serves as a precursor to the USA Patriot Act in that respect.

1921   Congress passes the first Quota Act, in which immigration from a particular country is set at 3 percent of the foreign-born population from that country based on the 1910 census.

1922   Congress passes the Cable Act, stating that the right of any woman to become a naturalized citizen shall not be abridged because of her sex or because she is a married woman unless she is wed to an alien ineligible for citizenship. This latter provision is later repealed.

1923   The U.S. Supreme Court rules in *United States v. Bhagat Singh Thind* that "white person" means those persons who appear and would commonly be viewed as white. Thus, East Asian Indians, although Caucasians, are not "white" and are therefore ineligible for citizenship through naturalization.

1924   Congress enacts the Immigration Act, known as the Johnson-Reed Act, setting the national-origin quota for a particular country at 2 percent of the foreign-born population from that country as of the census of 1890. This new system drastically shifts the sources of immigration from South, Central, and Eastern Europe to Northwestern Europe. The act bars the admission of most Asians, who are thereby classified as "aliens ineligible for citizenship." Congress passes an act granting citizenship to those Native Americans who had not previously received it by allotments under the 1887 Dawes Act or by military service during World War I.

1925   Congress establishes the Border Patrol, charged with policing the U.S. borders against illegal or undocumented entrants. It is also charged with finding and deporting illegal aliens from the interior who had managed to elude apprehension at the border.

1929   President Herbert Hoover proclaims new and permanent quotas in which national-origin quotas for European immigrants are based on the proportion of those nationalities in the total population as determined by the 1920 census. The total number of such to be admitted is fixed at just over 150,000.

1929–   U.S. immigration levels slow dramatically in response to
1939   the worldwide Great Depression.

1940   Congress passes the Registration Law, which requires noncitizens to register their addresses every year. The process remains in effect until 1980. Millions of such forms are backlogged and "lost" in INS warehouses. The failure of this program contributes to the calls during the 1980s to crack down on illegal immigration and visa overstayers through enhanced capability of the INS, which is never achieved.

1941   President Franklin D. Roosevelt issues a proclamation to control persons entering or leaving the United States based on the first War Powers Act.

1942   Agreement with Mexico to allow migrant farmworkers to enter as temporary labor to satisfy wartime labor shortages in agriculture.

       President issues Executive Order 9066, leading to the evacuation, relocation, and internment of Japanese and Japanese Americans into relocation camps.

1943   The Supreme Court rules, in *Hirabayashi v. United States,* that the executive orders for curfews and evacuation programs were constitutional based upon "military necessity."

1944   The Supreme Court decides *Korematsu v. United States*, again affirming the constitutionality of the executive orders excluding Japanese Americans from remaining in certain "excluded zones."

       The court also rules, in *Ex Parte Mitsuye Endo,* that the internment program was an unconstitutional violation of the habeas corpus rights of U.S. citizens—namely, the Nisei.

1949   Congress passes the Agricultural Act with provision to recruit temporary farmworkers from Mexico—the Bracero Program.

1956   President Eisenhower establishes a "parole" system for Hungarian freedom fighters. Two years later, Congress endorses the procedures to an act to admit Hungarian refugees.

1959   Congress amends the Immigration and Nationality Act of 1952 to provide for unmarried sons and daughters of U.S. citizens to enter as "nonquota" immigrants.

1960   Congress enacts a program to assist resettlement of refugees from communist countries who have been paroled by the attorney general (mostly Cubans).

       President John F. Kennedy is elected.

1963   President Kennedy is assassinated.

1964   Bracero Program ends.

The Revolving-Door Era, 1965 to 2000

1965   Congress passes the Immigration and Nationality Act. It amends the 1954 act by ending the quota system and establishing a preference system emphasizing family reunification and meeting certain skill goals, standardizing admission procedures, and setting per-country limits of 20,000 for Eastern Hemisphere nations, with a total of 170,000. The first ceiling on Western Hemisphere immigration is set at 120,000.

1966   Congress amends the 1965 act to adjust Cuban Refugee status. This sets up the distinction between refugees based on anticommunist U.S. foreign policy goals and those based on economic refugee status.

1967   UN Convention and Protocol on Refugees; 130 nations sign the protocol accords. Refugees entering under its provisions (such as Cuban refugees) get resettlement assistance, whereas those entering based on economic grounds (Haitian refugees) are excluded.

1968   Bilingual Education Act is passed.

        President Johnson issues a proclamation on the UN Protocols on the Status of Refugees, essentially endorsing the U.S. commitment to the multinational protocols.

1972   The House passes, but the Senate kills, a bill that would have made it illegal to knowingly hire an illegal alien. It becomes the first of many attempts prior to 1986 to impose what becomes known as "employer sanctions" for hiring illegal aliens.

        Haitian boat influx of illegal aliens begins arriving on the East Coast, mostly in Florida. Haitian detention camps are set up in Miami.

France implements its *regularisation* program.

1975   The fall of Saigon, then Vietnam along with Cambodia and Laos, precipitates a massive flight of refugees to the United States from the Indochina region. Vietnamese, Cambodians, and Laotians are classified as refugees from communist countries and are thereby assisted in re-settlement and aided by "assimilation assistance" pro-grams, many conducted by church-based organizations that assist immigrants.

President Carter establishes and Congress funds the Indochinese Refugee Resettlement Program.

Soviet Jews begin fleeing in large numbers. Civil war in El Salvador leads to beginning of their refugee move-ment. Haitians continue arriving in large numbers.

1976   Congress amends the 1965 act by extending the per-country limits of visa applicants on a first-come, first-served basis to Western Hemisphere nations as regu-lated by the preference system.

The U.S. Supreme Court rules, in *Matthews v. Diaz*, that an alien has no right to Social Security or Medicare ben-efits.

The Ford administration establishes a cabinet-level committee to study immigration options.

1978   President Carter and the Congress set up the Select Commission on Immigration and Refugee Policy (SCIRP).

1979   SCRIP begins its work.

Vietnamese and Southeast Asian Boat People influx.

1980   Congress passes the Refugee Act to systematize refugee policy. It incorporates the UN definition of refugee, ac-cepting 50,000 persons annually who have a "well-

1980,
cont.

founded fear" of persecution based on race, religion, nationality, or membership in a social or political movement. Provides for admission of 5,000 "asylum seekers."

1981 Economic recession begins.

March 1: The SCIRP issues its Final Report, recommending many changes in policy that form the basis of IRCA and other subsequent reform acts, several of which underlie proposed reforms even after 2001.

President Reagan creates Task Force on Immigration and Refugee Policy, which reports in July.

France implements its second *regularisation* (amnesty) program.

1982 Federal district judge rules the lockup of Haitians unconstitutional, ordering release of 1,900 detainees.

Major bill to amend the Immigration and Nationality Act is introduced into House.

1983 Immigration reform bill is reintroduced into Congress.

The Supreme Court rules, in *INS v. Chadha* et al., that the use of the legislative veto to overturn certain INS deportation proceedings, rules, and regulations by the House of Representatives was unconstitutional.

France implements its third "legalization" program.

1984 Immigration reform bill passes in different versions in both chambers, dies in conference.

1985 Sen. Alan Simpson (R-WY) reintroduces what becomes known as the Simpson/Mazzoli/Rodino bill.

1986 The Supreme Court rules in *Jean v. Nelson* on INS denial of parole to undocumented aliens. Congress enacts IRCA's employer sanctions/legalization approach granting amnesty to about 1.5 million illegal aliens and more than 1 million special agricultural workers.

1987   In *INS v. Cardoza-Fonseca,* by a vote of 6 to 3, the Supreme Court rules that the government must relax its standards for deciding whether aliens who insist that they would be persecuted if they returned to their homelands are eligible for asylum.

1988   The Senate passes, but the House kills, the Kennedy-Simpson bill in what becomes the 1990 act.

U.S.-Canada Free Trade Implementation Act is signed.

Congress amends the 1965 Immigration Act regarding H-1 category use by nurses.

1989   Conference for Central American Refugee is held.

1990   Congress passes a major reform of the laws concerning legal immigration, setting new ceilings for worldwide immigration, redefining the preference system for family reunification and employment, and setting up a new category of preference called "the diversity immigrants." It enacts special provisions regarding Central American refugees, Filipino veterans, and persons seeking to leave Hong Kong. Significant changes were included with respect to naturalization procedures.

1993   Congress ratifies the North American Free Trade Agreement (NAFTA).

Donald Huddle issues his report, "The Cost of Immigration," setting off the decades-long debate over the relative costs and benefits of immigration and illegal immigration.

1994   California passes Proposition 187, the "Save Our State" initiative.

Congress enacts the Violent Crime Control and Law Enforcement Act, the "Smith Act," giving the attorney general more authority to issue visas, the "S Visas."

1994,   Congress passes the Violence against Women Act with
cont.   provision to grant special status through cancellation of
         removal and self-petitioning provisions.

1995   Federal district court for California rules, in *LULAC et al.
         v. Wilson et al.*, that many of Proposition 187's provisions
         are unconstitutional.

         The General Accounting Office issues its first major and
         comprehensive report on the costs of illegal aliens to
         governments and to the overall economy.

         A Human Rights Watch report is highly critical of the
         INS and alleged abuses.

1996   June: The Board of Immigration Appeals (in re: Fauziya
         Kasinga, A73479695) grants the first woman asylum on the
         basis of gender persecution (female genital mutilation).

         Congress enacts Personal Responsibility and Work Op-
         portunity Act (welfare reform), with numerous immigra-
         tion-related provisions. Congress essentially enacts as-
         pects of Proposition 187 regarding welfare and other
         public benefits that had been overturned.

         Congress passes the Illegal Immigration Reform and Im-
         migrant Responsibility Act (IIRIRA), the sixty-plus im-
         migration-related provisions of the Omnibus Spending
         Bill. It removes other welfare and economic benefits to il-
         legal aliens and to some legal resident aliens.

         The Anti-terrorism and Effective Death Penalty Act of
         1996 is passed. Among its provisions, it gives INS in-
         spectors the power to make "on-the-spot credible fear"
         determinations involving asylum. It takes effect on April
         1, 1997, as part of IIRIRA reforms beginning then.

         The Central American Regional Conference on Migra-
         tion is held in Puebla, Mexico.

         Border Patrol makes a record 1.6 million apprehensions
         at the borders nationwide.

Congress authorizes the addition of 1,000 new Border Patrol agents annually.

1997   The Jordan Commission on Immigration Reform, set up by the 1996 law, recommends restructuring of the INS in its final report.

The "Expedited Enforcement Rules" of the IIRIRA of 1996 take effect at U.S. land borders, international airports, and seaports to issue and enforce expulsion orders. Some 4,500 INS officers are added at 300 ports of entry.

The General Accounting Office issues its Report on the Fiscal Impact of Newest Americans.

1998   President Clinton sends another immigration bill to Congress seeking, in part, a restructuring of the INS. It dies in committee when the Judiciary Committee begins hearings on impeachment.

The Agriculture Job Opportunity Benefits and Security Act establishes a pilot program for 20,000 to 25,000 farm-workers.

The Social Security Board of Trustees Report is issued, documenting positive effects of immigration on the status of the Social Security fund but also on the dire, long-term crisis in the Social Security account as the U.S. population ages and fewer active workers support ever-growing numbers of retirees.

Congress passes the American Competitiveness and Workforce Improvement Act, which expands the H-1B category to the computer industry.

California voters approve its Proposition 227, which ends bilingual education programs in state schools. The Children of Immigrants Longitudinal Study is issued.

France implements its latest *regularisation* program.

1999   The Carnegie Endowment for International Peace presents its International Migration Policy Program.

1999, Twenty-one nongovernmental organizations con-
cont. cerned with immigration call for INS restructuring, separation of enforcement from visa and naturalization functions, and the sending of some functions to the DOL and HHS. INS provides Border Patrol/adjudication.

In *INS v. Aguirre-Augirre* (67 U.S.L.W. 4270), a unanimous Supreme Court rules that aliens who have committed serious nonpolitical crimes in their home countries are ineligible to seek asylum in the United States regardless of the risk of persecution when returned to their countries.

Rep. Christopher Smith (R-NJ) introduces the Trafficking Victims Protection Act of 1999.

With a restored economy, President Clinton's administration restores some of the benefits stripped away from legal aliens by the 1996 acts.

November 22, 1999: Elian Gonzalez is rescued off the Florida coast.

UNHCR issues guidelines related to Detention of Asylum Seekers in Geneva, Italy.

Trafficking Victims Protection Act is passed.

2000 Negotiations regarding the Elian Gonzalez case begin.

April: Attorney General Reno approves a Justice Department "raid" on the Miami home to "return Elian Gonzalez" to his father in Cuba.

May: Sen. Sam Brownback (R-KS) introduces a bill to establish "T-Visa."

June 1: In *Gonzales v. Reno,* the 11th circuit court rules that only the father of Elian Gonzalez can speak for the boy.

The Storm-Door Era: 2001–?

2001   September 11: Terrorists attack the World Trade Center's Towers in New York and the Pentagon in Washington, D.C. Immediate calls for a crackdown on terrorists begin.

October 24, 2001: Congress passes the USA Patriot Act, granting sweeping new powers to the attorney general, the FBI, and the Department of Justice regarding immigrants and the authority to detain "enemy combatants" involved in or suspected of terrorism.

American Competitiveness in 21st Century Act is approved.

2002   The INS issues notice to several of the (now dead) hijackers that they are given permission to enroll in U.S. flight training programs. Immediate calls for restructuring of INS to remove Border Patrol functions result.

November: Congress establishes a cabinet-level Department of Homeland Security. The attorney general is granted sweeping new powers for expedited removal. INS is extensively restructured into the new department. As of March 2003, the INS is abolished; the undersecretary for Border and Transportation Security begins oversight of Immigration Enforcement and Citizenship and Immigration Services.

The United Nations issues its Protocols on Human Trafficking and Immigrant Smuggling in Polermo, Italy. The protocols are signed by 141 countries.

2003   January: The Terrorist Threat Integration Center is created.

2004   The 9/11 Commission issues its report detailing the intelligence failures contributing to the success of the terrorist cells and their attacks.

2004,   Congress passes the Intelligence Reform and Terrorism
cont.   Prevention Act. It establishes the director of National In-
           telligence position. President Bush appoints John Negro-
           ponte, ambassador to Iraq, as the first DNI.

           National Counterterrorism Center is created, largely
           housed and staffed in the CIA.

           Unauthorized immigrants within the United States reach
           an estimated record of 11 million. The ICE reports 1.1
           million apprehensions at the nation's borders.

2005   The House passes the Border Protection, Anti-terrorism
           and Illegal Immigration Control Act, also known as the
           REAL ID Act.

           The State of Virginia passes a law prohibiting unautho-
           rized immigrants from receiving state or local public
           benefits.

           New Mexico passes a law extending state tuition to
           unauthorized immigrants.

           Arizona enacts a measure preventing cities from con-
           structing day labor centers if such centers serve unau-
           thorized immigrants.

           Nine states pass anti–human trafficking laws.

           Nine states pass laws banning the issuing of driver's li-
           censes (identification) to unauthorized immigrants.

           Three states pass laws mandating state and local law en-
           forcement agencies to enforce federal immigration laws
           against unauthorized immigrants.

           The governors of Arizona and New Mexico issue "state
           of emergency" declarations because of the extreme ad-
           verse impacts of illegal immigration on their respective
           states.

The AIC launches a state-by-state campaign aimed at enacting state laws against illegal immigration.

The European Union Ministers approve the use of biometric cards for immigration to EU countries.

The Netherlands enacts stricter anti–illegal immigration measures.

Hong Kong imposes the temperature screening of all incoming travelers.

England's High Court approves several measures announced by the government designed to "crack down" on illegal immigrants and ease procedures to deport them.

Japan begins fingerprinting all incoming immigrants.

France expels thousands of illegal immigrants.

Russia imposes fines for hiring illegal immigrants.

2006   Poland increases its border patrol by 50 percent.

Congress extends the USA Patriot Act. In March it renews the Uniting and Strengthening America by Providing Appropriate Tools Required to Intercept and Obstruct Terrorism Act of 2001 (the USA Patriot Act).

References

"Anti-terror Law Passes Senate, Goes to House." *USA Today,* March 3, 2006: A-1.

Bean, Frank, George Vernez, and Charles B. Keely. 1989. *Opening and Closing the Doors.* Santa Monica, CA: Rand Corporation; Washington, DC: Urban Institute.

Chiswick, Barry R., ed. 1988. *The Gateway: U.S. Immigration Issues and Policies.* Washington, DC: American Enterprise Institute.

Department of Homeland Security. 2002. "HR 5005: To Establish the Department of Homeland Security, and for Other Purposes." http://www.dhs/hr5005.html. Accessed April 20, 2003.

Department of Justice. 2002. "Follow-Up Report on INS Efforts to Improve the Control of Nonimmigrant Overstays." Report No. 1–2002–006. Washington, DC: U.S. Government Printing Office.

Department of Justice. 2001. "Undocumented Aliens in the U.S." Available at http://www.doj.gov/graphics/Aboutins/statistics/illegalalien/index.htm. Accessed November 14, 2001.

Fix, Michael, ed. 1991. *The Paper Curtain: Employer Sanctions' Implementation, Impact, and Reform.* Washington, DC: Urban Institute.

General Accounting Office. 1995. *Illegal Aliens: National Cost Estimates Vary Widely.* Washington, DC: U.S. Government Printing Office.

———. 1998. *Illegal Aliens: Significant Obstacles to Reducing Unauthorized Alien Employment Exist.* Washington, DC: U.S. Government Printing Office.

———. 1999. *Illegal Immigration: Status of Southwest Border Strategy Implementation.* Washington, DC: U.S. Government Printing Office.

———. 2000. *Illegal Aliens: Opportunities Exist to Improve Expedited Removal Process.* Washington, DC: U.S. Government Printing Office.

———. 2002. *Alien Smuggling: Management and Operational Improvement Needed to Address Growing Problem.* Washington, DC: U.S. Government Printing Office.

———. 2004. *Overstay Tracking: A Key Component of Homeland Security and a Layered Defense.* GAO-04–82, May. Washington, DC: U.S. Government Printing Office.

Glazer, Nathan, ed. 1985. *Clamor at the Gates: The New American Immigration.* San Francisco: ICS.

Hirschman, Charles, Philip Kasinitz, and Joshua DeWind, eds. 1999. *The Handbook of International Migration: The American Experience.* New York: Russell Sage.

"House Passes Patriot Act." *San Bernardino Sun,* March 8, 2006: A-3.

Information Plus. 2006. *Immigration and Illegal Aliens: Burden or Blessing?* Farmington Hills, MI: Thomson/Gale.

LeMay, Michael. 1987. *From Open Door to Dutch Door: An Analysis of U.S. Immigration Policy since 1820.* New York: Praeger.

———. 1989. *The Gatekeepers: Comparative Immigration Policies.* New York: Praeger.

———. 2004. *U.S. Immigration: A Reference Handbook.* Santa Barbara, CA: ABC-CLIO.

LeMay, Michael, and Elliott Robert Barkan. 1999. *U.S. Immigration and Naturalization Law and Issues: A Documentary History.* Westport, CT: Greenwood.

Massey, Douglas S., et al. 1987. *Return to Aztlan: The Social Process of International Migration from Western Mexico.* Berkeley: University of California Press.

Massey, Douglas S., Jorge Durand, and Nolan J. Malone. 2002. *Beyond Smoke and Mirrors: Immigration Policy in an Era of Free Trade.* New York: Russell Sage.

Nevins, Joseph. 2002. *Operation Gatekeeper: The Rise of the Illegal Aliens and the Making of the U.S.-Mexico Boundary.* New York: Routledge.

Papdemetriou, Demetrious, and Mark Miller, eds. 1984. *The Unavoidable Issue.* Philadelphia: Institute for the Study of Human Issues.

Select Commission on Immigration and Refugee Policy. 1981. *Final Report.* Washington, DC: U.S. Government Printing Office.

Stana, Richard M. 2003. *Homeland Security: Challenges to Implementing the Immigration Interior Enforcement Strategy.* GAO-03–660T. Washington, DC: U.S. Government Printing Office.

U.S. Congress. Senate. *Uniting and Strengthening America by Providing Appropriate Tools Required to Intercept and Obstruct Terrorism (USA PATRIOT ACT) Act of 2001.* HR 3162. 107th Cong., 1st sess. http://www.epic.org/privacy/terrorism/hr3162.html. Accessed April 20, 2003.

Zuniga, Victor, and Ruben Hernandez-Leon, eds. 2005. *New Destinations: Mexican Immigration to the United States.* New York: Russell Sage.

5

Biographical Sketches

This biographical selection is a partial list of the individuals who are key players in the arena of illegal immigration reform. The chapter covers executive branch officials, including several U.S. presidents; legislative branch officials—key senators and members of the House of Representatives; and nongovernmental actors, including important advocates for and against illegal immigration reform legislation, as well as scholars, or "think tank" actors, who have had a particular impact on the debates over illegal immigration policy reform. They are presented here in alphabetical order by last name.

Angelo Amador
(no birth date available)

The Chamber of Commerce is the largest "umbrella" business federation, representing more than 3 million enterprises of various sizes, regions, and sectors. As director, Amador is responsible for working with members to develop the Chamber's position on comprehensive immigration reform, legalization issues, border security concerns, and the guest-worker program endorsed by the Chamber. He advocates on behalf of the Chamber with Congress and the Department of Homeland Security, the Department of State, and the Department of Labor. Amador also chairs the Americans for Better Borders Coalition, which unites regional business organizations to work to ensure the efficient flow of goods and peoples across the borders. He is a graduate of the University of Maryland and has an M.A. in international transactions from George Madison University and a law degree in international and comparative law from Georgetown University. Before joining the Chamber, he practiced law and clerked with Judge David Stitt, 19th Judicial Circuit of Virginia, with the office of the governor of Puerto Rico and as director/legislative counsel in the Intergovernmental Affairs Division, and as a staff attorney in the Mexican American Legal Defense and Education Fund. He is an adjunct professor of law at the George Mason University School of Law and is on the faculty of the Virginia Beach Law Enforcement Training Academy.

John Ashcroft (b. 1942)

John Ashcroft was appointed attorney general by President George W. Bush in 2000. He was born in Chicago, Illinois. He graduated with honors from Yale University in 1964 and received his J.D. from the University of Chicago in 1967. He began his public sector career as Missouri auditor in 1973, was later elected to two terms as the state's attorney general, and served a term as the chairman of the National Association of Attorneys General. He served as governor of Missouri from 1984 until 1993. In 1991, the National Governors Association elected him chairman. He was elected to the U.S. Senate in 1994 and served there until 2000. In the Senate he cosponsored the reauthorization of the Violence against Women Act and served on the Foreign Relations Committee and on the Senate Judiciary Committee, which held hearings on all immigration bills. In the first administration of President George W. Bush, he was at the forefront of efforts to implement immigration law, especially regarding expedited removal and rapid adjudication of asylum cases. As attorney general he had primary oversight responsibility for the INS. He was a leading proponent for the enactment of the USA Patriot Act and for the creation of the Department of Homeland Security with its dissolution and dramatic restructuring of the INS and immigration policy administration.

Roy Beck (b. 1948)

Beck took his degree in journalism from the University of Missouri. In the late 1970s he wrote on business news at the *Cincin-*

nati Enquirer, then covered religion and politics, including covering Congress as chief Washington correspondent for the Booth chain of daily newspapers. He has written two books on immigration, one on its impact on the environment and the other on the U.S. labor market and on local communities. He has published on the topic in the *Atlantic Monthly, New York Times, National Review, Washington Post,* and *Christian Science Monitor.* He has studied immigration policy as an area of special concern while covering Congress. He is a frequent speaker on immigration matters before a wide variety of groups and organizations. His career in print media coverage of immigration policy-making finally led him to develop the Numbers USA Web site.

Robert Beauprez (b. 1948)

Rep. Beauprez is the grandson of a Belgian immigrant. He received a B.S. degree from the University of Colorado in 1970. He was a dairy farmer from 1970 to 1990 and a banker from 1990 to 1992. He served as chairman of the Colorado Republican Party from 1999 to 2002, at which time he was elected to the House in a newly redistricted Seventh District, and was reelected in 2002 and 2004. He serves on the Small Business Committee, on Transportation and Infrastructure, and on Veterans Affairs. Along with Rep. Tancredo, he has become increasingly outspoken on illegal immigration matters and opposes the guest-worker program proposals' amnesty or legalization provisions.

Robert Bennett (b. 1933)

Sen. Bob Bennett is Utah's junior senator, first elected in 1992, then reelected in 1998 and 2004. He grew up in Salt Lake City. At age seventeen, when his father, Wallace Bennett, was elected to the first of two terms in the U.S. Senate, Bob worked as a congressional staffer serving as aide to both U.S. Rep. Sherm Lloyd and to his father. He served as a Mormon chaplain in the Army National Guard from 1957 to 1960. He was the Department of Transportation's chief lobbyist during the administration of Richard M. Nixon and headed a public relations firm that was a front for the CIA. In 1992, when Sen. Jake Garn retired, Bennett ran for and was elected to the seat held by his father. Bennett has a moderate conservative voting record, and he became the chief deputy whip in 2003. In the debate on homeland security he strongly supported the personnel provisions of the Bush administration. He is the sponsor of an amendment that would exempt church volunteers from provisions regarding the provision of aid to illegal aliens. Sen. Bennett serves on the Governmental Affairs Committee and its subcommittee on Budget and International Security, and he chairs the Small Business and Entrepreneurship Joint Economic Committee.

Sandford D. Bishop (b. 1947)

Sandford D. Bishop graduated with his B.A. from Morehouse College in 1968. He took his J.D. from Emory University in 1971. He served in the U.S. Army from 1971 to 1972. He was a practicing attorney from 1971 to 1992. His political career began with his election to and service in the Georgia House of Representatives, 1976–1990; then the Georgia Senate, 1990–1992. He was elected to the U.S. House of Representatives in 1992. He serves on the Agriculture Committee and on the Permanent Select Committee on Intelligence, on whose subcommittee for Technical and Tactical Intelligence he is the ranking minority member (RMM). His most notable effort on the immigration issue was his sponsoring in the House of the 1998 Guest Worker Program bill.

Patrick Buchanan (b. 1938)

Patrick Buchanan was twice—in 1992 and 1996—a candidate for the Republican Party's presidential nomination. He was the nominee for president of the Reform Party in 2000. Buchanan is the founding editor of *The American Conservative* and is the author of seven books. He served in the White House under the administrations of Richard M. Nixon, Ronald Reagan, and George H. W. Bush. He currently is a political analyst for MSNBC and has been a pundit, the founding panelist of three national television shows, and notably, an alumnus of CNN's *Crossfire*. He has been a vocal critic of the lax immigration policies of the United States and especially the proposed guest-worker programs of senators Ted Kennedy (D–MA), John McCain (R–AZ), and the administration of George W. Bush.

George Walker Bush (b. 1946)

George W. Bush was enrolled at Phillips Academy in Andover, Massachusetts, in 1961. He worked on his father's Senate bid in 1964. He graduated Yale University in 1968, then enlisted in the Texas Air National Guard. In 1973 he entered the Harvard Business school, taking his M.B.A. in 1975. He founded an oil and gas exploration company that year. In 1978 he lost a bid to the U.S. House. In 1978 he worked on his father's campaign for the presidency. He joined a group of investors buying the Texas Rangers baseball team in 1989. He was elected governor of Texas in 1994 and reelected in 1998. In 2000 he won the presidency after losing the popular vote but being certified as winner in Florida: he won the electoral college vote and a U.S. Supreme Court case that prevented recounts of disputed votes in Florida. He was inaugurated in 2001. On September 11, 2001, terrorists struck the Pentagon and the World Trade Twin Towers in New York City. President Bush launched a "war on terrorism," and his administration authored and Congress passed the USA Patriot Act, granting the executive branch sweeping powers to deal with terrorism that have had significant impact on illegal immigration control efforts. Congress also passed the administration-backed law to create a Department of Homeland Security that dissolved the INS and moved its activities to the new department. The administration is noted for its crackdown on illegal immigrants and efforts to enforce expedited removal. He appointed the first director of National Intelligence, a position that has the potential to impact on efforts to control international terrorism (which will in turn affect illegal immigration). He is currently promoting enactment of a guest-worker program that could legalize approximately 6 million unauthorized immigrants.

Jeanne Butterfield (no birth date available)

Butterfield is a graduate of Northeastern University and a member of the Massachusetts bar. Before joining the American Immigration Lawyers Association (AILA) she directed refugee and asylum programs in Boston. She is the author of *Immigration Law and Crimes,* as well as many articles on immigration law and policy, and she has been a featured speaker on the matter at immigration-law seminars across the United States and around the world. She is an ardent proponent of a more liberal legal-immigration policy and advocates an amnesty provision for the nearly 12 million undocumented immigrants now residing in the United States. She served as the executive director of the Palestine Solidarity Committee. She has addressed the U.S. Senate's Subcommittee on Immigration, which cited her proposals in their report "Effective Immigration Controls to Deter Terrorism." In her testimony, she expressed doubt that the 9/11 terrorist attacks could legitimately be attributed to the failure of the nation's immigration laws.

Chris Cannon (b. 1950)

Rep. Chris Cannon was born in Salt Lake City. He took a B.S. degree from Brigham Young University in 1974 and a J.D. from there in 1980. He practiced law from 1980 to 1983, then served as assistant and associate solicitor in the Department of the Interior until 1986. He was co-owner of a business and then the founder of Cannon Industries, Inc., from 1990 to 1996. In 1996 he was elected to the House. A devout Mormon, he sponsored a bill to give religious missionaries an exemption from more stringent immigration policy. He is the great-grandson of Utah's first territorial delegate, who was also a counselor to the Mormon church's second president, Brigham Young.

Cannon has a conservative voting record. He serves on the Government Reform Committee; on the powerful Judiciary Committee and its Immigration, Border Security and Claims Subcommittee; and on the Resources Committee. He served on the Judiciary Committee during the Clinton impeachment proceedings. In 2003 he became chairman of the Western Caucus, a group of more than fifty House members who advocate "rational, balanced and sound resource management." In immigration matters he has been outspoken for providing amnesty to illegal immigrants, and he cosponsored the Central American Security Act, which would legalize the status of more than 250,000 Central American immigrants. He is the House sponsor of the AgJobs bill.

James Earl Carter Jr. (b. 1924)

Jimmy Carter was born in Hope, Georgia. In 1941 he entered the Georgia Institute of Technology. In 1943 he entered the Annapolis Naval Academy, where he graduated in 1946. In 1962 he was elected to the Georgia state senate. In 1970 he was elected governor of Georgia.

Carter was elected president in 1976. In 1978 he deregulated the oil industry, pushed the Panama Canal treaty through the Senate, and signed the Camp David Accords. His most significant contribution to immigration policy was the establishment of the Select Commission on Immigration and Refugee Policy (SCIRP), whose recommendations led to the Immigration Reform and Control Act of 1986 (IRCA). The commission's work has formed the basis for much of the debate over illegal immigration reform since then. In 1980, the hostage crisis in Iran and the failure of the Immigration and Naturalization Service (INS) to track Iranian students in the United States contributed to his failed reelection bid. Carter's humanitarian work has led to involvement in negotiations regarding the Haitian crisis, and he has worked with the United Nations on refugee problems and as an external election observer in several countries around the world. He was awarded the Nobel Peace Prize in 2002.

Saxby Chambliss (b. 1943)

Rep. Saxby Chambliss received a B.A. degree from the University of Georgia in 1966 and his J.D. from the University of Tennessee in 1968. He was a practicing attorney from 1968 to 1994. He was elected to the U.S. House of Representatives in 1994. He serves on the Agriculture Committee, Budget Committee, and Armed Services Committee. To date, his most significant involvement in the immigration issue has been his cosponsorship of the 1998 Guest Worker Program bill.

Linda Chavez (b. 1947)

Linda Chavez is founder and chairperson of the Center for Equal Opportunity, a policy research and advocacy organization headquartered in Virginia. She also writes a weekly syndicated column and is a political analyst for Fox News, hosts a daily radio show in Washington, D.C., and has written three books: *Towards a New Politics of Hispanic Assimilation* (1991); *An Unlikely Conservative* (2002); and *Betrayal* (2004). She served as chairperson of the National Commission on Migrant Education (1988–1992); as White House director of public liaison in 1985; as staff director of the U.S. Commission on Civil Rights (1983–1985); and as a member of the Administrative Conference of the United States (1984–1986). She was a Republican nominee for the U.S. Senate from Maryland in 1986. In 1992 she was elected to the UN Human Rights Commission, where she served a four-year term. She chairs the Latino Alliance of the Republican Party. In 2000, she was honored by the Library of Congress as a "Living Legend" for her contributions to America's cultural and historical legacies. In January 2001, President Bush nominated her to be the secretary of labor, but after considerable controversy she withdrew her name from consideration. She was born in Albuquerque, New Mexico, and received her B.A. from the University of Colorado in 1970. Chavez served as editor of the quarterly journal *American Educator* (1977–1983). She also served the American Federation of Teachers as assistant to its president (1982–1983) and as assistant director of legislation (1975–1977). She is a strong advocate of legal-immigration reform and control of illegal immigration, and she opposes amnesty for illegal immigrants.

Michael Chertoff (b. 1953)

Judge Michael Chertoff graduated magna cum laude from Harvard University in 1975 and magna cum laude from Harvard Law School in 1978. He is married to Meryl Justin Chertoff and has two children. From 1979 to 1980 he clerked with U.S. Supreme Court justice William Brennan Jr. He made his name as prosecutor of the bosses of five Mafia families in New York. In 2005, Judge Chertoff was sworn in as the second secretary of the Department of Homeland Security after approval in the U.S. Senate by a 98–0 vote. He formerly had served as U.S. circuit judge for the Third Circuit Court of Appeals. Prior to his appointment as secretary of DHS, he served in the first George W. Bush administration as assistant attorney general and director of the Criminal Division of the Department of Justice, where he helped to trace the 9/11 terrorist attacks to the al-Qaeda network. He also worked to increase information sharing within the FBI and among state and local officials. Before joining the Bush administration, Michael Chertoff was a partner in a private law firm. From 1994 to 1996 he served as special counsel for the U.S. Senate Whitewater Committee. He spent more than a decade as a federal prosecutor, including service as U.S. attorney for the District of New Jersey and assistant U.S. attorney for the Southern District of New York. Chertoff investigated and prosecuted several significant cases involving political corruption, organized crime, and corporate fraud. He served as New York mayor Rudolph Giuliani's assistant when Giuliani was a federal prosecutor working on organized crime. As secretary of DHS, he oversees both divisions of the department that are concerned with illegal immigration matters and has been instrumental as an advocate for the renewal of the USA Patriot Act.

William Jefferson Clinton (b. 1946)

William Clinton entered Georgetown University in 1964 and clerked for Arkansas senator J. William Fulbright in 1966. He graduated from Georgetown in 1968 and went on to Oxford University as a Rhodes Scholar. In 1970 he entered Yale Law School and received his law degree there in 1973. He began teaching at the University of Arkansas Law School in 1973 and lost an election for the U.S. House of Representatives in 1974. He was elected Arkansas attorney general in 1976. He lost his first bid for governor of the state in 1980 but was elected to that office in 1982 and reelected in 1984. In 1986 he chaired the National Governors Association, and in 1988 he was reelected governor. Clinton was elected president in 1992. His most significant illegal-immigration policy role was shepherding the Personal Responsibility and Work Opportunity Reconciliation Act of 1996 through Congress and signing it into law. This welfare reform act had numerous and important immigration-related provisions, and it was soon followed by the Illegal Immigration Reform and Immigrant Responsibility Act of 1996. Clinton was reelected president in 1996. A 1998 sexual affair scandal led to his impeachment in 1998. He was acquitted by the U.S. Senate in 1999 and served out his term as president. After his term ended,

Clinton served with distinction in disaster relief efforts for the United Nations, most notably efforts to alleviate the devastation created by the Asian tsunami of 2004 and to aid refugees.

John Cornyn (b. 1952)

John Cornyn is the junior senator from Texas. He was born in Houston, Texas, and received his B.A. from Trinity University in 1973, his J.D. from St. Mary's Law School in 1977, and an L.L.M. degree from the University of Virginia in 1995. He served as the San Antonio District Court judge from 1984 to 1990; on the Texas Supreme Court from 1990 to 1997; and as Texas attorney general from 1998 to 2002. As attorney general, he argued that federal law bars public hospitals from giving illegal immigrants anything but emergency treatment, immunizations, and communicable disease treatment. He was elected to the U.S. Senate in 2002. He serves on the Armed Services Committee; on Budget, Environment and Public Works; on the Judiciary Committee and its subcommittees of Administrative Oversight and Courts, Constitution, Civil Rights, and Property Rights, of which he is chair; on Crime, Corrections and Victims' Rights; and on Immigration, Border Security, and Citizenship. He is the Senate cosponsor of the Comprehensive Enforcement and Immigration Control Act of 2005, a bill to reform illegal immigration policy that is a more conservative approach than the Kennedy-McCain bill.

Larry Craig (b. 1945)

Sen. Larry Craig is Idaho's senior senator. He received his B.A. from the University of Idaho in 1969 and served in the Army National Guard from 1970 to 1974. A rancher and farmer, he was elected to the Idaho Senate in 1974, the U.S. House of Representatives in 1980, and the U.S. Senate in 1990. He has compiled a staunchly conservative record. He serves as chairman of the Special Committee on Aging, on the Appropriations Committee, on Energy and Natural Resources, and, importantly for immigration matters, on the Senate Judiciary Committee and its subcommittee on Immigration, Border Security, and Citizenship. He also serves on the Veterans Affairs Committee. Sen.

Craig is also the chairman of the Republican Policy Committee. He sponsored the AgJobs bill in 2004 and 2005.

Tom Delay (b. 1947)

Tom Delay received a B.S. degree from the University of Texas in 1970. From 1973 to 1984 he owned and operated Albo Pest Control in Laredo, Texas. He served in the Texas House of Representatives from 1978 to 1984, and was elected to the U.S. House of Representatives in 1984. He served as the highly controversial majority whip and on the powerful Appropriations Committee. He was a House leader to impeach President Clinton. As to immigration matters, he was outspokenly in favor of very restricted immigration and was a leading proponent of the Homeland Security bill. Amid controversy over ethics violations, he resigned his House seat in 2006.

Dianne Feinstein (b. 1933)

Sen. Feinstein is California's senior senator. She was elected in 1992 and reelected in 2000. She received a B.A. from Stanford University in 1955. Prior to serving in the Senate, she served on California's Women's Parole Board, 1960–1966; on the San Francisco Board of Supervisors, 1970–1978; and as mayor of San Francisco, 1978–1988. Senator Feinstein serves on several committees important to immigration: the Appropriations Committee; Agriculture and Rural Development; Interior; Labor, Health and Human Services, Education, and Related Agencies; Judiciary; Immigration; and Technology, Terrorism and Government Information. A tough critic of the Immigration and Naturalization Service (INS) and now Immigration and Customs Enforcement (ICE), she has been notably involved in bills to strengthen the Border Patrol (1993), sponsored increased fees to fund the "fencing-in" pilot program in the San Diego area, and was instrumental in the legislative battles leading to the Department of Homeland Security. Sen. Feinstein is a sharp critic of some of the alleged abuses of civil liberties in the administration of the USA Patriot Act. Her most recent legislative proposal of note to illegal immigration is a bill to make it illegal to tunnel under a U.S. border.

Barney Frank (b. 1940)

Rep. Frank took his B.A. from Harvard in 1962 and received a J.D. from Harvard in 1977. He served in the Massachusetts House from 1972 to 1980, when he was elected to the U.S. House of Representatives. He served on Banking and Financial Services; Domestic and International Monetary Policy; Housing and Community Opportunity (RMM); Judiciary; Immigration and Claims. He serves on the Select Committee on Homeland Security and its subcommittees on Infrastructure and Border Security and Intelligence and Counterterrorism. He is an important advocate of civil rights and liberties and antidiscrimination measures on all immigration bills and was instrumental with key compromises on IRCA in 1986 and IMMACT in 1990.

Antonio O. Garza
(no birth date available)

President George W. Bush appointed Antonio O. Garza as ambassador extraordinary and plenipotentiary of the United States to Mexico. Garza was confirmed as an ambassador on November 12 and sworn into office on November 18, 2002. Antonio Garza is a graduate of the University of Texas and of Texas and Southern Methodist University School of Law. He began his public career as Cameron County judge after being elected in 1988 and re-elected in 1990. As CEO of Texas's tenth-largest county, he focused on various issues, including the construction of an international bridge. In 1994 he was appointed by then-governor George W. Bush as Texas's ninety-ninth secretary of state and senior adviser. He also served for three years as the state's head liaison on border and Mexican affairs, a position in which he worked on a diverse range of issues including the environment and border affairs. After his term as secretary of state of Texas, he joined a private Houston-based law firm as partner in their Austin office. In 1998 he was elected to the Texas Railroad Commission, the agency responsible for regulating the state's oil and gas industry (which generates $80 billion a year), and served as vice chairman of the Interstate Oil and Gas Compact Commission, representing thirty-seven oil and gas producing states. As ambassador to Mexico, he plays a key advisory role to the president on matters pertaining to any guest-worker program that may be enacted to allow for guest-workers from Mexico, and to legalize those illegal aliens from Mexico currently residing in the United States through the work authorization provisions of such an act and agreement with Mexico.

Robert Goldsborough (no birth date available)

Goldsborough founded the Americans for Immigration Control in 1982. He is a columnist for *Middle America News* and is a harsh critic of U.S. immigration policy, calling for drastically reduced legal immigration and stricter control over illegal immigration. He is especially critical of any legalization program and any guest-worker program. He is prominent in the English-only movement.

Alberto Gonzales (b. 1955)

Alberto Gonzales was sworn in as the eightieth U.S. attorney general on February 3, 2005. He was born in San Antonio, Texas, the second of eight children, and was raised in Houston. He is a graduate of Texas public schools, Rice University, and Harvard Law School. He served in the U.S. Air Force between 1973 and 1975 and attended the Air Force Academy between 1975 and 1977. He and his wife, Rebecca Turner Gonzales, have three sons. He received the President's Awards from the U.S. Hispanic Chamber of Commerce and the League of United Latin American Citizens, was recognized as a distinguished alumnus of Rice University, and also received the Harvard Law School Association Award. He was recognized as the 1999 Latino lawyer of the year by the Hispanic National Bar Association. He was a partner in a Houston, Texas, law firm, joining the firm in 1982. He also taught law as an adjunct professor at the University of Houston Law Center. Gonzales served as general counsel to Governor Bush from 1994 to 1997. He served as Texas secretary of state from December 1997 to January 10, 1999, and as such was the governor's lead liaison on Mexico and border issues, including illegal immigration matters. He served as justice of the Texas Supreme Court from 1999 to 2001. Gonzales was commissioned counsel to President George W. Bush in January 2001, a capacity in which he served until he was sworn in as attorney general in 2005. He became the first attorney general of Hispanic origin and the nation's top law enforcement official after being confirmed by a vote of 60 to 36. During his confirmation hearings before the Senate Judiciary Committee, Gonzales was unexpectedly opposed by all eight Democrats on the Judiciary Committee. He played a major role in the Bush administration's increased efforts to enforce expedited removal, the enactment of the USA Patriot Act, the creation of the Department of Homeland Security, and the creation of a law establishing the director of National Intelligence.

Bob Goodlatte (b. 1952)

Rep. Bob Goodlatte took his B.A. in 1974 from Bates College, and his J.D. from Washington and Lee Law School in 1977. He began his political career working for Congressman Caldwell Butler in 1977. He practiced law from 1970 until 1992, when he was first elected to the House. He serves on the Agriculture Committee, on the Judiciary Committee and its Crime, Terrorism and Homeland Security Subcommittee, and on the Select Committee on Homeland Security and its Subcommittee on Infrastructure and Border Security. He has sponsored a law imposing tougher penalties on commercial counterfeiters. He has compiled a conservative voting record. Most recently, he has sponsored a bill to end the visa lottery.

Chuck Hagel (b. 1946)

Chuck Hagel is the senior senator from Nebraska; he was elected to the Senate in 1996. Sen. Hagel received his B.A. from the University of Nebraska in 1971. He served with distinction in Vietnam, was a newscaster and talk show host, and worked as a lobbyist for Firestone. He began his career in politics serving as an aide to Congressman John McCollister. He served as a deputy administrator for the Department of Veterans Affairs and as a U.S. Deputy Commissioner General, World's Fair, and he also ran his own business. As a freshman in the U.S. Senate, Hagel served on the prestigious Foreign Relations Committee. He became a leading internationalist and has often cosponsored legislation with Democrats. On occasion, he has sharply differed with the Bush administration on foreign policy matters, particularly those relating to Iraq. He vigorously campaigned for Sen. John McCain for president. His committee assignments of note and of relation to illegal immigration and to national security matters include Banking, Housing and Urban Affairs; Foreign Relations; and Intelligence. His Intelligence Committee service has enabled him to be a key player on Patriot Acts I and II, and on the Department of Homeland Security legislation and the measure creating the director of National Intelligence.

J. D. Hayworth (b. 1958)

Rep. Hayworth was born and raised in North Carolina. Like former president Ronald Reagan, Hayworth made a career in local television as a sportscaster. He moved to Phoenix to work at a television station from 1987 to 1994. He was an insurance agent and PR consultant as well, and ran for and won his seat in Congress in 1994. He has a very conservative voting record and is known for his contentious partisanship. He serves on the Resources Committee and on the powerful Ways and Means Committee and its Social Security Subcommittee. He has sponsored legislation to increase border security and to build a border fence in Arizona.

Tamar Jacoby (b. 1954)

Born in New York, Tamar Jacoby took her degree from Yale University in 1976. She writes extensively on immigration and citizenship matters. She is a leading conservative voice in the news media in favor of immigration reform and works to organize a center-right position on immigration reform. She is the author of two books: *Someone Else's House* and *Reinventing the Melting Pot*, as well as numerous articles and essays. Before joining the Manhattan Institute, she was a senior writer and justice editor for *Newsweek*, and was deputy editor for the *New York Times* op-ed page and assistant to the editor of *The New York Review of Books*. She serves on the National Council on the Humanities and the advisory board of the National Endowment for the Humanities.

She is a graduate of Yale University and has taught at Yale, Cooper Union, and the New School University.

Lyndon Baines Johnson (1908–1973)

Born in Texas, Lyndon Johnson graduated from the Southwest Texas State Teachers College in 1927. He began teaching in Houston in 1930. He was named director of the National Youth Administration in Texas in 1935, and was elected to Congress in 1938. In 1941 he lost a U.S. Senate bid and went on to serve in the U.S. Navy before being sent to the Pacific by President Roosevelt to observe fighting conditions. He was elected to the Senate in 1948, served as Democratic whip in 1951, and became Senate minority leader in 1953. He became Senate majority leader after his reelection in 1954, directed passage of the 1957 Civil Rights Act, and was elected vice president in 1960. He became president upon John F. Kennedy's assassination in 1963 and was elected to the office in 1964. His most significant work in immigration policy was in successfully advocating for and signing the Immigration and Nationality Act of 1965. He chose not to run for reelection in 1968, retired to his ranch, and died on January 22, 1973.

Edward Kennedy (b. 1932)

Sen. Edward Kennedy received his B.A. from Harvard in 1956, attended The Hague International Law School in 1958, and took his LL.B. from the University of Virginia Law School in 1959. He worked on his brother's presidential bid in 1960; then as assistant district attorney for Suffolk County, in 1961–1962. He was elected to the U.S. Senate in 1962. He is without doubt the single most influential member of Congress on immigration matters. From the 1965 Immigration and Nationality Act (sometimes called the Kennedy Act) until today, every major bill dealing with immigration has born the Kennedy stamp. His most important immigration-related position is his role on the Judiciary Committee, Immigration, and the Joint Economic Committee. He has been one of the most outspoken critics of the Bush administration in the Senate with respect to civil rights and civil liberties issues as they are involved in the debates over how best to control illegal immigration. He is cosponsor of the McCain-

Kennedy bill to reform immigration policy with a comprehensive bill that includes a guest-worker program and an "earned legalization" provision.

John Fitzgerald Kennedy (1917–1963)

John Kennedy graduated from the Choate School Studies at the London School of Economics and also attended Princeton. He graduated from Harvard University in 1940, when he also wrote the award-winning *Why England Slept.* He served in the Pacific and was a war hero when his PT 109 was sunk by the Japanese. He was elected to the House of Representatives in 1946 and served there until his election to the Senate in 1952. In 1956 he published *Profiles in Courage*, which won the 1957 Pulitzer Prize. After being re-elected to the Senate in 1958, he also wrote *A Nation of Immigrants.* He was elected president of the United States in 1960 and inaugurated in 1961. In July 1963, he sent to Congress the bill that became the Immigration and Nationality Act of 1965. That law fundamentally altered legal immigration policy for the United States by replacing the quota system with the preference system. Among its many unanticipated consequences were dramatic shifts in the nations of origin from which legal immigrants came and huge backlogs in visas for legal permanent resident immigrants; the act also set the stage for the massive increase in the unauthorized immigration flow. Kennedy was assassinated in Dallas, Texas, on November 22, 1963. The Congress passed his legislation, in part to honor the "martyred" president, in October 1965.

Peter King (b. 1944)

Rep. King was born in Manhattan; his parents were Irish immigrants and Democrats; his father was an NYPD detective. He received a B.A. degree from St. Francis College in 1965 and took his J.D. degree from the University of Notre Dame in 1968. He served in the Army National Guard from 1968 to 1973. He practiced law from 1968 to 1972, worked as deputy attorney for Nassau County from 1972 to 1974, and was later both the executive assistant to the county executive and general counsel. He was elected to the Hempstead Town Council from 1977 to 1981 and served as Nassau County Comptroller in 1977. He was first elected to the

House in 1992. He has a moderately conservative voting record. King serves on the Financial Services Committee, on the International Relations Committee and its subcommittee on International Terrorism, and on the Select Committee on Homeland Security and its subcommittees on Emergency Preparedness and Response, and Intelligence and Counterterrorism. He has sponsored English-only legislation and generally opposes aid to illegal immigrants.

Mark Krikorian (b. 1961)

Mark Krikorian has a B.A. degree from Georgetown University and took a master's degree from the Fletcher School of Law and Diplomacy at Tufts University. He also studied for two years at Yerevian State University in the then-Soviet nation of Armenia. He has held various editorial and writing positions, and in 1995 he joined the Center for Immigration Studies in Washington, D.C. He frequently testifies before Congress and has published numerous articles in such periodicals as the *Washington Post*, the *New York Times*, *Commentary*, and the *National Review*. He has appeared on *60 Minutes*, *Nightline*, the *News Hour* with Jim Lehrer, CNN, National Public Radio, and similar television and radio programs.

Jon Kyl (b. 1942)

Sen. Jon Kyl was born in Oakland, Nebraska. He is the junior senator from Arizona; he was elected to that office in 1994 and reelected in 2000. He moved to Arizona and went to college and law school there, practiced law in Phoenix, and headed its chamber of commerce. He won the heavily Republican 4th District in 1986. In the House he became a leading Republican on missile defense and the balanced-budget amendment. He has a solidly conservative record and in the Senate has likewise become a major force on defense policy and a champion of the missile-defense system. Sen. Kyl serves on the Judiciary Committee and is cosponsor, with Sen. Dianne Feinstein, of a constitutional amendment on victim's rights. Before 9/11 Kyl and Feinstein also cosponsored a bill to prepare for attacks by terrorists with chemical and biological weapons. In 2001, the two introduced a bill to establish a comprehensive lookout database that would combine data from the CIA, FBI, and the State Department to make it available to the Border Patrol and consular officials. He has worked to beef up the Border Patrol and to track legal immigrants who overstay their visas; he supports cuts in legal immigration and new rules for family-based immigration. He has worked for more federal reimbursement of states and localities for the costs of hospitalizing and incarcerating illegal aliens. He is cosponsor of a limited guest-worker bill that competes with the more comprehensive Kennedy-McCain proposal. Of importance to illegal immigration matters, Sen. Kyl serves as chair of the Republican Policy Committee and on the Judiciary Committee and its subcommittees on Constitution, Civil Rights and Property Rights, and on Immigration, Border Security and Citizenship; he is also chair of the Subcommittee on Terrorism, Technology, and Homeland Security. He is cosponsor of the Cornyn/Kyle bill, the Comprehensive Enforcement and Immigration Control Act of 2005.

Richard Lamm (b. 1935)

Richard Lamm is a Democratic politician and lawyer who served three terms as governor of Colorado; he also ran for the Reform Party's nomination for president of the United States in 1996. He has a law degree from the University of California, Berkeley, and has taught at the University of Denver and led the movement to have Denver host the 1976 Winter Olympics. He has been an outspoken advocate of physician-assisted suicide, is a published novelist, and is a prominent voice on immigration reduction. He serves on the board of the anti-immigration group Federation for American Immigration Reform (FAIR) and on the board of directors of the Diversity Alliance for a Sustainable America, and is codirector of the Institute for Public Policy at the University of Denver.

Joseph I. Lieberman (b. 1942)

Sen. Lieberman took his B.A. from Yale University in 1964 and received an LL.B. from Yale in 1967. He was a practicing attorney from 1964 to 1980. In his political career, he served in the Connecticut state senate from 1970 to 1980, including serving as its majority leader from 1974 to 1980. He was attorney general of Connecticut from 1983 to 1988, at which time he was elected to the U.S. Senate. He rebuked President Bill Clinton during the Lewinski scandal but supported President Clinton during the impeachment process and the Senate's vote to acquit.

In 2000, Lieberman ran (with Al Gore) as the Democratic nominee for vice president and also for reelection to the U.S. Senate. He lost the former election but won the latter. In the Senate he serves on the Armed Services Committee, including as ranking minority member (RMM) of its subcommittee; on Environment and Public Works; on Small Business; and on Governmental Affairs (again as RMM). He serves as the chairman of the Democratic Leadership Council. In terms of illegal immigration policy reforms, he has been a leading spokesman for and the Senate sponsor of the Democratic alternative bill for the establishment of the Department of Homeland Security with its broad implications for restructuring the INS. He continues to be a vocal critic of the failures of the DHS in the post-Katrina disaster, particularly the record of FEMA.

Susan Forbes Martin (b. 1947)

Professor Martin serves as director of the Certification Program on Refugees and Humanitarian Emergencies. Prior to joining Georgetown University, she served as executive director of the U.S. Commission on Immigration Reform and as director of research and programs at the Refugee Policy Group. She has published numerous books and articles on refugee and immigration matters. Her most notable books, published by Lexington Books, are *Refugee Women; Beyond the Gateway: Immigrants in a Changing America;* and *The Uprooted: Improving Humanitarian Responses to Forced Migration.* She is the principal author of the 2004 surveys on women and development and on women and migration, both produced for the United Nations. She serves as a senior advisor to the Global Commission on International Migration and is on the advisory boards of the International Organization for Migration and the Comptroller General of the United States. She took her M.A. and Ph.D. in American studies from the University of Pennsylvania and her B.A. in history from Rutgers University, and has taught at both Rutgers University and the University of Pennsylvania.

John McCain (b. 1936)

John McCain, the senior senator from Arizona, was born in the Panama Canal Zone. A career naval officer from 1958 to 1980, he is the son and grandson of navy admirals and is a decorated navy pilot who was shot down in Vietnam and spent five years as a prisoner of war. In March 1973 McCain returned to the United States, where he served his final term in the navy as a Senate liaison. In 1980 he retired and moved to Arizona, ran in 1982 for a House seat, and won in both 1982 and 1984. In 1986 he ran and won a U.S. Senate seat. He strongly supported President Bush in the war on terrorism after 9/11. His independent and bi-partisan stands, and particularly his crusades for campaign finance regulation and against pork-barrel spending, have often made him unpopular among his colleagues. He brings to his work a strong sense of righteousness and conviction. His most notable legislative achievement was enactment of the McCain-Feingold campaign-finance law in 2001. He ran for president in 2000 but failed to get his party's nomination. After his failed presidential bid, he became more active in the Senate—increasingly allying with Democrats and opposing most Republican positions on campaign finance and on tobacco-related matters. He took a significant role in the post-9/11 legislative battles and called for government-run airport security. Sen. McCain chairs the Commerce, Science and Transportation Committee. He is cosponsor with Sen. Kennedy of Massachusetts of the most comprehensive bill to reform illegal immigration policy being considered in the Senate and proposes an extensive guest-worker/earned legalization program.

Candice Miller (b. 1954)

Rep. Miller was born in Detroit. She attended Macomb County Community College and Northwood University and served as secretary-treasurer of a marina. In elected offices, she served as trustee of the Harrison Township Board, as a Harrison Township supervisor, then as Macomb City treasurer before being elected Michigan's secretary of state, a position she held from 1994 to 2002. She was first elected to the House in 2002 and now serves on the Armed Services and Governmental Reform committees and is vice chair of the Intergovernmental Relations and Census subcommittee. She has a solidly conservative voting record and describes herself as a "Bush Republican"; she was very active in passage of NAFTA. She recently sponsored a constitutional amendment that would stipulate that only citizens be counted for the purpose of census data to determine representation to Congress.

Charles Norwood (b. 1941)

Rep. Charlie Norwood was born in Valdosta, Georgia. He took a B.S. degree from Georgia State University in 1964 and a D.D.S. degree from Georgetown University in 1967. He served in the army in Vietnam from 1967 to 1969. He practiced dentistry from 1969 to 1993 and was president of the Georgia Dental Association in 1983. He was first elected to the House in 1994. He serves on the Energy and Commerce Committee, the Education and Workforce Committee, is chair of its Workforce Protections Subcommittee, and is vice chair of the Energy and Commerce Committee's Health Subcommittee. Although he supported Bill Clinton's budget and tax packages, he won his district with comfortable margins and has an overall conservative voting record. He gained notice as one of the House's most influential members relating to the Patient Access to Responsible Care Act, which regulated HMOs, and cosponsored, with Democrat John Dingell, a bill on the patient's bill of rights. His most notable illegal immigration action is sponsorship of the CLEAR (Clear Law Enforcement for Criminal Alien Removal) Act, also known as the Homeland Security Enforcement Act, HR 3137.

Demetrios Papademetriou (b. 1946)

Demetrios Papdemetriou has published in the United States and abroad on immigration and refugee policies, with an emphasis on the labor market and developmental repercussions. He has taught at American University, the University of Maryland, and at Duke University, and is on the graduate faculty of the New School for Social Research. He has served as director of emigration policy and research at the U.S. Department of Labor and chaired the secretary of labor's Immigration Policy Task Force.

He also served as U.S. representative to the Migration Committee of the Organisation for Economic Cooperation and Development (OECD). Before his governmental service, he was executive editor of the *International Migration Review* and directed the research activities of the Center for Migration Studies in New York. Papademetriou now directs the Endowment's International Migration Policy Program and also serves as chair of the OECD Migration Committee. He concentrates on U.S. immigration policies and practices, the migration politics and practices of advanced industrial societies, and the role of multilateral institutions in developing and coordinating collective responses to voluntary and involuntary international population movements.

Nancy Pelosi (b. 1940)

Nancy Pelosi was first elected to the House in 1987. She was born in Baltimore, Maryland, and now resides in San Francisco. She took her B.A. from Trinity College in 1962. She was a PR executive from 1986 to 1987 and served as California Democratic Party northern chairman from 1977 to 1981; she was state chair from 1981 to 1983, and served as the DSCC finance chair from 1985 to 1987. She serves as the minority leader in the House of Representatives and has an almost perfect liberal voting record. She has been elected and reelected by huge margins. As minority leader she has taken very vocal stances against the Bush administration and its positions on immigration and the guest-worker programs. She joined with Sen. Feinstein on bills to increase border security along the California-Mexico border.

Richard Pombo (b. 1961)

Mr. Pombo attended the California Polytechnic Institute from 1979 to 1982. He is a cattle rancher and cofounder of the Citizens Land Alliance in 1986. He served on the Tracy City Council from 1990 to 1992 and was elected to the U.S. Congress in 1992. He serves on the Agriculture Committee and on its Resources Committee. His most notable effort concerning immigration issues was his cosponsorship of the 1998 guest-worker bill. He continues to support such a program and is currently backing the Bush administration's proposal and position on the matter.

Ronald Reagan (1911–2004)

President Reagan was born in Illinois. He graduated from Eureka College in 1932 and began a career as a sports announcer before he signed a movie contract with Warner Brothers Studio in 1939. In 1947 he was elected president of the Screen Actors Guild, and in 1954 he hosted the *General Electric Theater* television show. In 1960 he campaigned for Richard Nixon for president. In 1963 he hosted the popular television show *Death Valley Days*, and in 1966 he was elected governor of California. He was reelected in 1970 but lost a bid for the Republican presidential nomination in 1976 before being elected president in 1980. His contributions to illegal-immigration policy center on his establishment of a presidential task force on immigration that helped shape the debate over the Immigration Reform and Control Act (IRCA) in 1986. After his reelection in 1984, he signed IRCA into law. In doing so, he established the employer-sanctions approach. He retired from the presidency in 1989. In 1994 he announced that he suffered from Alzheimer's disease; the much-revered former president died on June 6, 2004.

Silvestre Reyes (b. 1944)

Rep. Reyes was first elected to the House in 1996. He was born in Canutillo, just north of El Paso. He received his A.A. degree in 1977 from El Paso Community College. A Vietnam veteran, he served in the army from 1966 to 1968. He was elected to and served on the Canutillo School Board from 1968 to 1970 and was a Border Patrol agent from 1965 to 1995. He serves on the Armed Services Committee; on the Permanent Select Committee on Intelligence and its Terrorism and Homeland Security Subcommittee; and on the Veteran Affairs Committee. As a Border Patrol agent, he worked in four cities in Texas and in Glynco, Georgia. In 1993 he began its Operation Hold the Line, which positioned 400 agents on the border and dramatically reduced the flow of illegal migrants—by more than 50 percent. His voting record places him among the House's moderate Democrats. He has advocated economic stabilization for Mexico as the most sensible and permanent solution for problems along the border. He backed NAFTA, and after 9/11 he blamed flaws in U.S. intelligence for the attacks. He was critical of the Bush administration's plan to invade Iraq, citing no evidence of a link between Iraq and al-Qaeda terrorists, and he opposed the use of force in Iraq. In 2001 he became chairman of the Hispanic Caucus. He ran unopposed in 2002 and has won by comfortable margins in other elections. He briefly considered a run for the U.S. Senate in 2002.

Charles E. Schumer (b. 1950)

Now the senior senator from New York, Charles Schumer took his B.A. from Harvard in 1971 and his J.D. from there in 1974. He served in the New York Assembly from 1974 to 1980; then in the U.S. House from 1980 to 1998. He was elected to the Senate in 1998. He was critically important in crafting compromises making possible the passage of the Immigration Reform and Control Act of 1986 and has continued to play a critical role in all immigration-related bills since then. In the Senate he serves on several committees including Banking, Housing and Urban Affairs; International Trade and Finance; Judiciary and its subcommittees of Administrative Oversight and the Courts; Criminal Justice Oversight; Immigration (where he is the ranking minority member, or RMM); and Rules and Administration.

James Sensenbrenner (b. 1943)

Rep. Sensenbrenner was first elected to the House in 1978. He was born in Chicago. He received an A.B. degree from Stanford University in 1965 and his J.D. degree from the University of Wisconsin in 1968. He practiced law from 1968 to 1969 and was elected to the Wisconsin assembly (1968–1974) and the Wisconsin senate (1974–1978). He was staff assistant to Congressman Arthur Younger in 1965. He serves as the chair of the powerful Judiciary Committee in the House and on the Select Committee on Homeland Security. He staunchly supported the use of force in Iraq and creation of the Department of Homeland Security but was critical of Attorney General Ashcroft's possible violations of civil liberties and calls for additional investigative powers for law enforcement. Sensenbrenner insisted on sunset provisions (which would expire after four years) for the USA Patriot Act. He sponsored a bill to split the INS into two separate agencies, and when these agencies were moved to the new Department of Homeland Security he expressed strong concerns that internal problems would remain unresolved. He has long opposed racial quotas and preferences and was vocal in his support of Milwaukee's school-choice program. He has won election and reelection by wide margins and has often been unopposed in the general election. His most notable recent legislation concerning illegal immigration is his sponsorship of the REAL ID Act.

Frank Sharry (no birth date available)

Frank Sharry directs one of the nation's leading immigration policy organizations and is an advocate of upholding America's tradition as a nation of immigrants. He is a leading spokesperson for proimmigration policies and frequently appears in print and on television. Prior to joining the National Immigration Forum (NIF), he was executive director of the Centro Presente, which helps Central American refugees. He helped found the Massachusetts Immigration and Refugee Advocacy Coalition and led efforts to resettle refugees from Vietnam and Cuba; he also led the campaign against passage of California's Proposition 187.

Christopher H. Smith (b. 1953)

Rep. Christopher Smith received a B.S. from Trenton State College in 1975. He was a sales executive in a family-owned sporting goods business from 1975 to 1980. He served as executive director of New Jersey Right to Life from 1976 to 1978. He was elected to the U.S. House of Representatives in 1980. He serves on the International Relations Committee and chairs its subcommittee on International Operations and Human Rights, Western Hemisphere. He also holds vice chair positions on the Veterans Affairs Committee and on the Health Committee. His most notable immigration reform measure was sponsoring the Trafficking Victims Protection Act.

Gordon H. Smith (b. 1952)

Sen. Gordon Smith took his B.A. from Brigham Young University in 1976. He received his J.D. degree from Southwestern University in 1979. He then served as a law clerk to the New Mexico

Supreme Court until 1980. He practiced law from 1980 to 1981 and served as president of Smith Frozen Foods from 1980 to 1996. Smith was elected to the U.S. Senate in 1996. His principal assignments are on the Budget Committee, the Energy and Natural Resources Committee, and the Foreign Relations Committee, where he is a member of the East Asian and Pacific Affairs Subcommittee, the Near Eastern and South Asian Affairs Subcommittee, and the European Affairs Subcommittee (of which he is chair). His most notable immigration-related activity was his 1998 cosponsorship of the guest-worker bill.

Lamar S. Smith (b. 1947)

Rep. Smith was born in San Antonio. He took a B.A. from Yale in 1969 and his J.D. from Southern Methodist University in 1975. He worked for the U.S. Small Business Administration from 1969 to 1970 and was a business writer for the *Christian Science Monitor* from 1970 to 1972. He practiced law from 1975 to 1976. He was elected to the Texas House of Representatives from 1981 to 1982. He served on the Bexar County Committee from 1982 to 1985 and was elected to the U.S. House of Representatives in 1986. Rep. Smith serves on the Judiciary Committee, where he is chair of its Immigration and Claims Subcommittee; on the Science Committee; and on the Standards of Official Conduct Committee, which he also chairs. Since his arrival in the House, he has been an outspoken critic of immigration policy and is one of the House's strongest advocates for restricted immigration, illegal-immigration reform, strengthening of the Border Patrol, and opposition to amnesty proposals.

Arlen Specter (b. 1930)

Arlen Specter is the senior senator from Pennsylvania. He was born in Wichita, Kansas. One of the nation's most durable career politicians, he has held public office and been an important national figure for four decades. His father was an immigrant who worked as a tailor and sent four children through college. Specter came to Philadelphia at seventeen to attend the University of Pennsylvania, and he went on to serve in the U.S. Air Force from 1951 to 1953. He went to Yale Law School and practiced law in

Philadelphia. In 1964 he became a top staffer for the Warren Commission. He often bolts party lines to vote with Democrats on issues of conscience. He serves on the Homeland Security Committee and on Governmental Affairs and its subcommittee on Budget and International Security. As chair of the Judiciary Committee, he also serves on its Terrorism, Technology and Homeland Security Subcommittee. He has been supportive of President Bush's proposal for a guest-worker program.

John E. Sununu (b. 1964)

Sen. John Sununu is the junior senator from New Hampshire. When he was elected to the Senate in 2002, he was its youngest member. He is the son of John H. Sununu, who was a three-term governor and served as the White House chief of staff from 1989 to 1991. John E. Sununu graduated from M.I.T. and took an M.B.A. from Harvard. Before entering politics, he worked as an engineer for a microwave manufacturer, and he also worked for a high-tech consulting firm, for the automation systems company Teletrol, and as a consultant for JHS Associates. He first entered politics by running for the House in 1996. He compiled a conservative voting record and served on the Appropriations and Budget committees. He was reelected in 1998. He ran for and won the Senate seat in 2002. His committee assignments include Banking, Housing and Urban Affairs; Foreign Relations; Government Affairs; and the Joint Economic Committee. Important to illegal immigration matters, on the Government Affairs Committee he serves on its subcommittee on Budget and International Security. He took a key role in proposing some civil liberty provisions that enabled the enactment of the USA Patriot Act II in March 2006. Elected at age thirty-eight from a predominantly Republican state, John Sununu is likely to have a long Senate career ahead of him.

Roberto Suro (no birth date available)

Roberto Suro is the founding director of the Pew Hispanic Center, a Washington-based research and policy-analysis organization that he founded in 2001. He was born in Washington, D.C., to Puerto Rican and Ecuadorian parents, and has chronicled Hispanic and related issues as a journalist for some thirty years. He began a career in journalism in Chicago in 1974. During his career as a journalist, he researched and wrote about Latinos for the *Washington Post*. He has also worked as a foreign correspondent for *Time Magazine* and the *New York Times* in Latin America, Europe, and the Middle East. He was bureau chief for the *New York Times* in Rome, Italy. He is author of *Strangers among Us: Latino Lives in a Changing America* (1999), and he is author of two Twentieth Century Fund papers on immigration matters: "Remembering the American Dream" and "National Policy and Watching America's Door: The Immigration Backlash and the New Policy Debate." He is a graduate of Yale University, where he took his B.A. in 1973, and Columbia University, where he received an M.S. degree in 1974. He lives in Washington, D.C.

Tom Tancredo (b. 1945)

Rep. Tancredo was elected to the House in 1998 and is now serving his fourth term. Born in Denver, he took his B.A. degree from the University of Northern Colorado in 1968. He was a junior high school teacher from 1968 to 1981; was regional representative of the U.S. Department of Education from 1981 to 1993; and was president of the Independence Institute, a libertarian think tank located in Golden, Colorado, from 1993 to 1998. He served in the Colorado House of Representatives from 1967 to 1981. He serves on the Budget Committee, the International Relations Committee, and on the Resources Committee. He staunchly supported the use of force in Iraq and the creation of the Department of Homeland Security. A self-described religious-right Republican, he has won elections by comfortable margins, although he gained notoriety as an extreme-right and fiercely partisan campaigner who often "shoots from the hip." He is the only Colorado member of the House to vote for the NRA's bills, and he won passage, by a voice vote, of a bill to establish school-violence hotlines across the nation after the Columbine High School shooting incident. He has emerged as the House's most ardent crusader on immigration reform, calling for dramatically reduced legal immigration and strong control measures against illegal immigration. He has crusaded for stricter border control and against the Bush administration's guest-worker plan, which he labels as an obstacle to immigration reform and an "open door" policy. His views have made him very controversial, but he has won reelection by overwhelming margins.

John H. Tanton
(no birth date available)

John Tanton is a widely recognized leader in the anti-immigration and "official English" movements in the United States. Tanton cofounded the Federation for American Immigration Reform and NumbersUSA in 1996, founded Pro-English in 1993, founded the Center for Immigration Studies in 1985, and cofounded and became chair of U.S. English in 1982. Tanton played a central role in mobilizing neoconservatives, the New Right, and the Christian Right against center-left politics in the United States, and he mobilized backlash sentiment against immigrants. He co-organized E Pluribus Unum in 1992, the Emergency Committee on Puerto Rican Statehood in 1990, and he became founder and chairman of U.S., Inc. in 1982. He has worked with the Sierra Club, the National Audubon Society, and Zero Population Growth, and he is founder and publisher of Social Contract Press, which publishes books that shape a nationalist ideology and focus on the perceived threat of immigration to the white, English-speaking population. He is a retired eye surgeon, and a graduate of Michigan State University and the University of Michigan Medical School. He is coauthor, with Wayne Lutton, of *The Immigration Invasion.*

Georges Vernez (b. 1939)

Dr. Vernez took his Ph.D. in Urban and Regional Development from the University of California, Berkeley. He has directed and conducted studies on a broad range of immigration issues, including most notably a comprehensive assessment of the implementation of the Immigration Reform and Control Act of 1986, with particular focus on its effects on undocumented immigration, the supply of labor, and relations between the United States and Mexico. He has analyzed issues related to the effects of immigration on the demand for state and local services and on labor markets, and issues related to the social and economic adjustments of immigrants in the United States. He has also made comparative studies of policies on immigration and refugee movements and their outcomes in Western nations, and he has recently completed a comprehensive assessment of the demographic, economic, institutional, and distributional effects of thirty years of immigration in California. He is currently conducting a study of the performance of immigrant women in the U.S. labor market and a study of the social benefits from increasing the educational attainments of Hispanics. In 1991 he became the founding director of the RAND Institute on Education and Training, which examines all forms of education and training.

Ron Wyden (b. 1949)

Sen. Ron Wyden took his B.A. from Stanford University in 1971, and his J.D. from the University of Oregon in 1974. He served as the codirector and cofounder of the Oregon Gray Panthers from 1974 to 1980; then as director of Oregon's Legal Services for the Elderly, 1977 to 1979. He was also professor of gerontology at the University of Oregon, 1976, and at Portland State University of Oregon, 1980. He served in the U.S. House of Representatives from 1980 to 1996, when he was elected to the U.S. Senate. His Senate committees of note are Aging; Budget; Commerce, Science and Transportation; Energy and Natural Resources; and Environment and Public Works. His most notable action on the immigration issue was his cosponsorship, with Sen. Gordon Smith, of the 1998 guest-worker bill. As senator from a state near the Canadian border, immigration matters continue to be a major focus of his legislative agenda. He continues to be an important advocate of a guest-worker program and of the earned legalization provision accompanying it.

References

Anderson, James. 1979. *Public Policy Making.* New York: Holt, Rinehart and Winston.

Barone, Michael, Grant Ujifusa, and Eleanor Evans, eds. 1972. *The Almanac of American Politics.* Washington, DC: National Journal.

_____. 1976. *The Almanac of American Politics.* Washington, DC: National Journal.

_____. 1978. *The Almanac of American Politics.* Washington, DC: National Journal.

_____. 1986. *The Almanac of American Politics.* Washington, DC: National Journal.

_____. 1990. *The Almanac of American Politics.* Washington, DC: National Journal.

_____. 1994. *The Almanac of American Politics.* Washington, DC: National Journal.

_____. 1996. *The Almanac of American Politics.* Washington, DC: National Journal.

_____. 2000. *The Almanac of American Politics.* Washington, DC: National Journal.

_____. 2004. *The Almanac of American Politics.* Washington, DC: National Journal.

Diller, Daniel C., and Stephen L. Robertson. 2001. *The Presidents, First Ladies, and Vice Presidents: White House Biographies, 1789–2001.* Washington, DC: Congressional Quarterly Press.

Graff, Henry A., ed. 1997. *The Presidents: A Reference History.* New York: Charles Scribner's Sons.

Hamilton, Neil A. 2001. *Presidents: A Biographical Dictionary.* New York: Facts on File.

Jacobson, Doranne. *Presidents and First Ladies of the United States.* New York: Smithmack, 1995.

U.S. Citizenship and Immigration Services. 2006. http://www.uscis.gov/.htm.

U.S. Department of Justice. 2006. http://www.usdoj.gov.

6

Data and Documents

Introduction

Public policy has been defined as "a purposive course of action followed by an actor or set of actors in dealing with a problem or matter of concern" (Anderson, 1979: 3). Chapter 5 presented biographical sketches of the major actors involved. In its first section, this chapter presents data on illegal immigration–related trends in table and graphic formats. In its second section it presents summaries of the "actions"—some key legislative and judicial decisions. These laws and cases, taken together, constitute the "course" of immigration policy and its frequent reforms aimed at controlling illegal immigration.

Tables and Figures

Table 6.1 presents the distribution of immigrants from Mexico to specific states within the United States. For these states, termed "gateway states," the table shows the percentage distribution of Mexican immigrants by state of residence, from 1940 to 2000. The dominance of their residing in these five gateway states is evident, as is their growing dispersal to more states after enactment of the IRCA in 1986.

Table 6.2 shows how the trend to dispersal continues since 2000. It presents immigrants by state and by share of the population for immigrants (legal and illegal) arriving since 2000.

TABLE 6.1
Distribution of Mexican Immigrants
by State of Residency, 1940–2000

Gateway States	1940	1950	1960	1970	1980	1990	2000
Arizona	7.2	6.7	6.3	4.5	3.3	3.7	2.6
California	35.6	34.0	41.9	52.7	57.0	62.9	35.4
Illinois	2.5	2.6	4.8	6.2	7.7	4.9	6.1
New Mexico	4.2	2.1	1.8	0.8	0.8	0.9	0.8
Texas	39.5	44.5	35.9	26.5	22.6	14.9	16.4
All Other States	11.1	10.2	9.4	9.4	8.5	12.8	35.3

Source: Table by author. Based on data in Tables 1.1, 1.2, and 1.3 in Zuniga and Hernandez-Leon, eds. *New Destinations: Mexican Immigration in the United States.* (New York: Russell Sage, 2005), 5, 10, 14.

TABLE 6.2
Immigration by State, by Share of Population,
and Arrival since 2000

State	Immigrants	Share of Population	Arrivals
California	9,984,000	27.8	1,809,000
New York	3,900,000	20.5	707,000
New Jersey	1,620,000	18.7	312,000
Florida	3,203,000	18.3	648,000
Hawaii	215,000	17.2	22,000
Nevada	408.000	17.1	90,000
Texas	3,379,000	15.1	948,000
Arizona	851,000	14.8	198,000
Massachusetts	880,000	13.8	201,000
Washington, D.C.	74,000	13.5	24,000
Maryland	725,000	13.1	212,000
Rhode Island	126,000	11.9	24,000
Illinois	1,417.000	11.3	286,000
Washington	650,000	10.6	137,000
Connecticut	363,000	10.4	67,000
Colorado	443,000	9.8	117,000
Virginia	719,000	9.7	188,000

Continued on next page

Table 6.2 — *Continued*
Immigration by State, by Share of Population,
and Arrival since 2000

State	Immigrants	Share of Population	Arrivals
New Mexico	177,000	9.3	57,000
Georgia	762,000	8.8	248,000
Oregon	303,000	8.5	64,000
Delaware	67,000	8.1	26,000
Alaska	48,000	7.4	10,000
Minnesota	374,000	7.3	99,000
North Carolina	590,000	7.0	243,000
Utah	150,000	6.3	35,000
Idaho	82,000	6.0	21,000
Michigan	593,000	5.9	160,000
Nebraska	93,000	5.4	27,000
Iowa	148,000	5.1	49,000
Kansas	129,000	4.8	36,000
Wisconsin	251,000	4.6	64,000
Tennessee	264,000	4.5	142,000
New Hampshire	58,000	4.5	13,000
Pennsylvania	534,000	4.4	174,000
Oklahoma	153,000	4.4	39,000
Ohio	371,000	3.3	115,000
Louisiana	145,000	3.3	30,000
Kentucky	127,000	3.1	56,000
Indiana	184,000	3.0	60,000
South Carolina	116,000	2.8	27,000
Vermont	17,000	2.8	3,000
Maine	34,000	2.6	6,000
Missouri	138,000	2.5	36,000
Mississippi	72,000	2.5	26,000
Arkansas	65,000	2.4	7,000
South Dakota	18,000	2.4	6,000
Alabama	99,000	2.2	48,000
Wyoming	10,000	2.0	3,000
North Dakota	12,000	1.9	5,000
Montana	7,000	0.8	less than 1,000
West Virginia	8,000	0.4	2,000

Source: Center for Immigration Studies. Analysis of Census Bureau's. Current Population Survey (March 2005).

TABLE 6.3
Coping with Illegal Immigration (2002)

Australia	Dominican Republic	Iran	Philippines
Austria	European Union	Italy	Portugal
Basotho	Fiji	Japan	Russia
Botswana	France	Lethoso	Saudi Arabia
Brunei	Gambia	Malaysia	South Africa
Burma	Germany	Malta	South Korea
Cambodia	Georgia	Mexico	Spain
Canada	Greece	Morocco	Switzerland
Caribbean	Guatemala	Netherlands	Taiwan
China	Hong Kong	New Zealand	Turkey
Costa Rica	India	Norway	Uganda
Croatia	Indonesia	Pakistan	UAE
Cyprus	Ireland	Panama	UK
Demark	Isreal	Peru	Zambia

Source: Table by author.

Table 6.3 offers insight into the global pattern of illegal immigration. It presents a listing, from A to Z, of those countries currently coping with illegal immigration.

Table 6.4 shows the refugees, as of 2002, in various host countries, and the number of refugees or asylees, returned refugees, or internally displaced, according to the UN High Commissioner for Refugees. Similarly, Table 6.5 offers the number of applications for asylum of the twenty-eight most industrialized countries submitted from January 2001 to June 2002, according to the UNHCR, and the nation of origin from the top twenty source nations of refugees/aslyees.

TABLE 6.4
Refugees/Asylees by Host Country

Host Country: Number of Refugees/Asylees/Returned Refugees/ Internally Displaced					
Afghanistan	1,226,098	Germany	988,533	Thailand	111,059
Algeria	169,497	Guinea	179,318	Turkmenistan	200,518
Angola	228,280	India	169,756	UK	187,950

Continued on next page

TABLE 6.4— *Continued*
Refugees/Asylees by Host Country

Host Country: Number of Refugees/Asylees/Returned Refugees/ Internally Displaced

Armenia	264,339	Iraq	130,503	Tanzania	691,438
Azerbaijan	587,317	Iran	1,868,011	United States	911,730
Bosnia/ Herzegovina	570,221	Kazakhstan	119,543	Yugoslavia F.	777,104
Burundi	125,775	Kenya	251,816	Zimbawe	284,671
Canada	175,028	Kuwait	139,335		
China	295,326	Liberia	253,414		
Colombia	720,389	Nepal	130,957		
Congo	122,251	Netherlands	230,888		
Cote d'Ivoire	128,363	Pakistan	2,199,379		
D. R. of Congo	366,917	Russia	1,139,842		
Ethiopia	161,922	Saudi Arabia	345,502		
France	166,152	Sierra Leone	103,105		
FYR Macedonia	168,953	Sri Lanka	683,347		
Georgia	272,214	Sweden	164,091		

Source: UNHCR. 2002 UNHCR Statistical Yearbook. UNHCR. http://www.unhcr.org/statistics/STATISTICS/ 41373cca4.pdf

TABLE 6.5A
Asylum Applications, 28 Industrialized Countries,
January 2001–June 2002

Country of Asylum	January–June 2001	July–Dececmber 2001	January–June 2002
Austria	14,991	15,144	17,075
Belgium	12,372	12,176	9,029
Bulgaria	1,090	1,337	2,055
Czech Republic	8,907	9,130	4,622
Denmark	5,856	6,547	3,310
Finland	733	878	1,400
France	23,258	24,005	24,761
Germany	40,786	47,577	38,259
Hungary	3,842	3,712	3,120
Ireland	4,769	5,555	5,085

Continued on next page

TABLE 6.5A — *Continued*
Asylum Applications, 28 Industrialized Countries, January 2001–June 2002

Country of Asylum	January–June 2001	July–December 2001	January–June 2002
Liechtenstein	39	73	35
Luxemburg	321	368	394
Netherlands	17,137	15,442	11,135
Norway	4,050	10,734	8,153
Poland	2,195	2,338	1,789
Portugal	116	118	117
Romania	1,292	1,008	609
Slovakia	2,417	5,734	3,351
Slovenia	1,057	451	258
Spain	4,342	4,877	3,798
Sweden	8,753	14,760	14,607
Switzerland	9,308	11,450	11,854
U.K.	14,800	47,500	51,500
Canada	20,954	21,792	15,633
U.S.	32,078	29,632	32,441
Australia	7,138	5,228	3,284

Source: UNHCR. "Asylum Applications Submitted in 28 Mostly Industrialized Countries." UNHCR.
http://www.unhcr.org/statistics/STATISTICS/3d7dfc985.pdf

TABLE 6.5B
Asylum Seekers, Top-Twenty Nations of Origin

Origin	Number of Applications	Origin	Number of Applications
Iraq	22,833	Nigeria	5,956
Afghanistan	15,514	Iran (Islamic Republic of)	5,405
Turkey	14,540	Somalia	5,322
F. R. of Yugoslavia	14,522	Algeria	5,301
China	13,024	Sri Lanka	5,191
Russian Federation	8,398	Pakistan	5,172
Colombia	7,104	Armenia	4,713
Mexico	6,448	Angola	4,503
Dem. Rep. of Congo	6,422	Georgia	4,150
India	6,027	Bosnia/Herzegovina	3,910

Source: UNHCR. "Asylum Applications Submitted in 28 Mostly Industrialized Countries." UNHCR.
http://www.unhcr.org/statistics/STATISTICS/3d7dfc985.pdf

Important data as to illegal immigration trends are presented in the following fourteen figures.

Figure 6.1 shows the number of apprehensions at U.S. Borders between 1960 and 1988. Note the bar for 1986, the year in which IRCA was enacted, is at the highest level. There is a dropoff in 1987 and 1988. Figure 6.2, a line graph, presents much the same image, but shows alien apprehensions at the border for fiscal years 1951 through 1991. Note that after the dip in the years immediately following enactment of IRCA, the apprehensions begin climbing back up to pre-IRCA levels.

Figure 6.3 is a bar graph indicating the total number of estimated unauthorized immigrants in the United States (that is, unauthorized entrants and visa overstayers) in the post-IRCA years, 1986 to 2002. By 2002 their numbers were approaching 10 million per year and have returned to the highest levels of the immediate pre-IRCA years. The graph demonstrates dramatically that the employer sanctions approach enacted by IRCA, at least

Figure 6.1 INS Apprehensions at U.S. Borders, 1960–1988

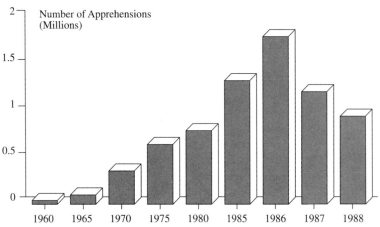

Source: Adapted from graph and data in GAO, "Immigration Reform: Status of Implementing Employer Sanctions after One Year" (Washington D.C.: U.S. Government Printing Office, 1987), 8, with data for 1987–1988 added from the U.S. Department of Justice, "INS Reporter" (Washington D.C.: U.S. Government Printing Office, 1988), 21; and updated by further INS data cited in "Border Attacks Worry INS Agents," *Washington Post,* October 16, 1988: A-18.

Figure 6.2 Aliens Apprehended, FY 1951–1991

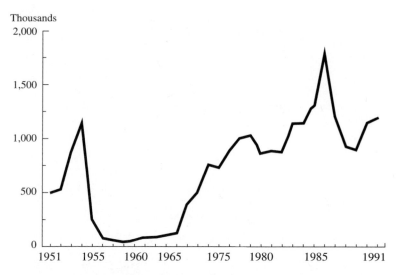

Source: Adapted from graphs and data from the U.S. Department of Justice, "INS Reporter" (Washington D.C.: U.S. Government Printing Office, 1992), 144.

in terms of how the policy was implemented, had little or no effect on the levels of unauthorized immigration. Figure 6.4 is a pie chart showing the regions of origin of the unauthorized immigrants in 1986 and 2002. Note that about two-thirds (69 percent and 57 percent, respectively) came from Mexico, and that other Latin American countries account for nearly another third. In short, 85 to 92 percent came from "south of the border."

Figure 6.5 shows that most of the unauthorized immigrants in the United States as of 2004 have arrived since 1990, and that since 2000 have been significantly moving away from the big six settlement states (the gateway states discussed earlier) to more states in the interior and to states that traditionally had few illegal aliens. This distribution trend has fueled the political movement for illegal immigration policy reform as more and more states experience significant levels of the problem.

Figure 6.6 gives an overall depiction of the legal status of immigrants in the United States as of 2004, then estimated at 10.4 million. That estimated number had climbed to between 11 and

Figure 6.3 Estimates of Unauthorized Aliens Residing in the United States, 1986–2002

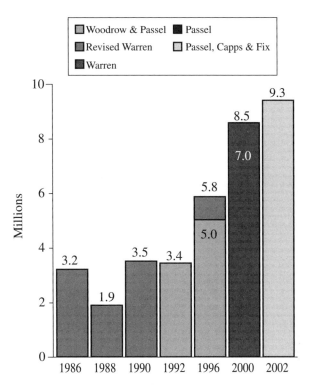

Source: Adapted from graphs and data from the U.S. Department of Justice, "INS Reporter" (Washington D.C.: U.S. Government Printing Office, 1992), 144.

12 million by 2006. The pie chart distinguishes between legal permanent resident aliens and unauthorized immigrants, the number of naturalized citizens, and those in the United States as refugees or as temporary legal resident aliens.

The recent trend in high levels of annual immigration to the United States is presented in Figure 6.7, which shows that annual migration peaked in FY1999–2000, dipped after 2001, but began climbing again since 2004.

Figures 6.8 and 6.9 show two significant aspects of the trends. Figure 6.8 shows that legal permanent resident aliens are now exceeded in numbers by unauthorized immigrants (both

Figure 6.4 Unauthorized Alien Residents by Region of Origin,
1986 and 2002

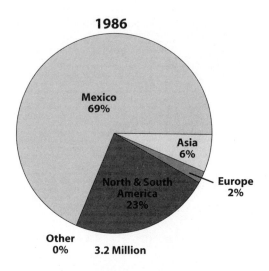

1986

Mexico
69%

Asia
6%

North & South
America
23%

Europe
2%

Other
0%   3.2 Million

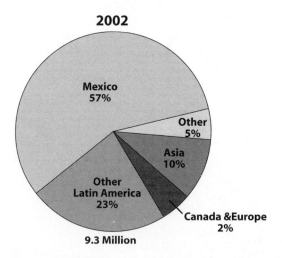

2002

Mexico
57%

Other
5%

Asia
10%

Other
Latin America
23%

Canada &Europe
2%

9.3 Million

Source: Ruth E. Wasem, "Figure 2. Unauthorized Alien Residents by Region
of Origin, 1986 and 2002," in "Unauthorized Aliens in the United States:
Estimates since 1986," Congressional Research Service, Library
of Congress, September 15, 2004, at http://www.immigration.org/
documents/crs/CRS_undocumented_2004.pdf (accessed March 2005)

Figure 6.5 Unauthorized Alien Residents, Arrivals and Redistribution

Most Unauthorized Arrived Since 1990

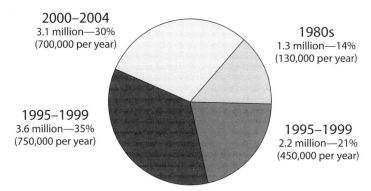

2000–2004
3.1 million—30%
(700,000 per year)

1980s
1.3 million—14%
(130,000 per year)

1995–1999
3.6 million—35%
(750,000 per year)

1995–1999
2.2 million—21%
(450,000 per year)

10.3 Million Unauthorized in March 2004
(Demographic estimates based on March 2004 CPS
with allowance for omissions)

Major Redistribution Away from Big Six Settlement States

Percent of Total Unauthorized Migrant Population

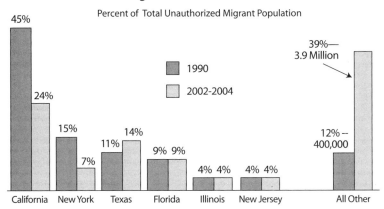

Source: Roberto Suro, Pew Hispanic Center, Presentation at the Regional Conference on Illegal Immigration, NCLS, Denver, Colorado, December 12, 2005

Figure 6.6 Legal Status of Immigrants, 2004

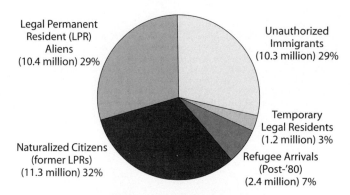

Legal Permanent
Resident (LPR)
Aliens
(10.4 million) 29%

Unauthorized
Immigrants
(10.3 million) 29%

Temporary
Legal Residents
(1.2 million) 3%

Naturalized Citizens
(former LPRs)
(11.3 million) 32%

Refugee Arrivals
(Post-'80)
(2.4 million) 7%

35.7 Million Foreign-Born in 2004
(Demographic estimates based on March 2004 CPS
with allowance for omissions)

Source: Roberto Suro, Pew Hispanic Center, Presentation at the Regional
Conference on Illegal Immigration, NCLS, Denver, Colorado, December 12,
2005

Figure 6.7 Annual Migration to the U.S.—Peaked in 1999–2000

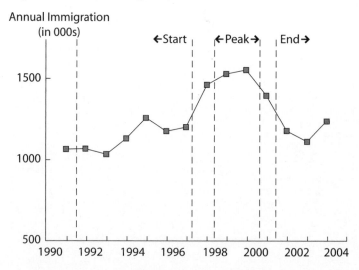

Annual Immigration
(in 000s)

←Start   ←Peak→   End→

1500

1000

500

1990   1992   1994   1996   1998   2000   2002   2004

Source: Roberto Suro, Pew Hispanic Center, Presentation at the Regional
Conference on Illegal Immigration, NCLS, Denver, Colorado, December 12,
2005

Figure 6.8 Trend Down for LPRs; Unauthorized Exceed LPRs

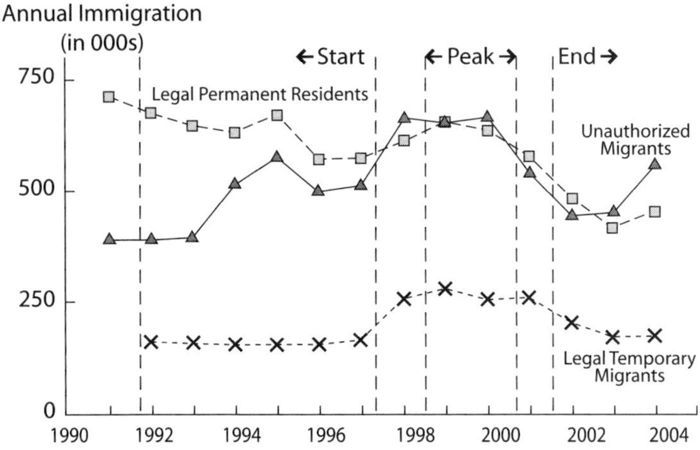

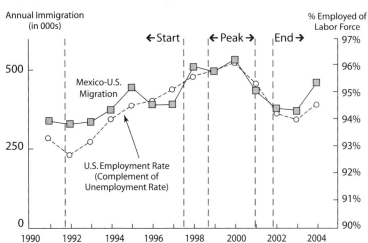

Source: Roberto Suro, Pew Hispanic Center, Presentation at the Regional
Conference on Illegal Immigration, NCLS, Denver, Colorado, December 12,
2005

**Figure 6.9 Mexican Migration Follows Trends in U.S.
Employment Rate**

Source: Roberto Suro, Pew Hispanic Center, Presentation at the Regional
Conference on Illegal Immigration, NCLS, Denver, Colorado, December 12,
2005

Figure 6.10 Rapid Growth of Mexicans in U.S.

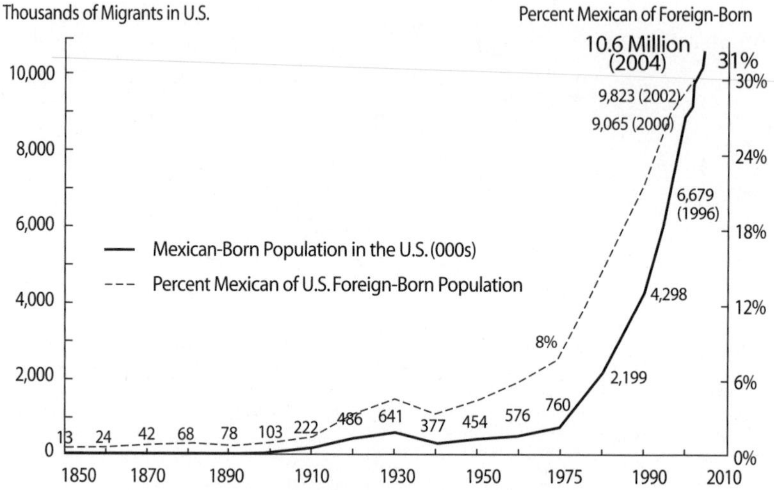

Thousands of Migrants in U.S.   Percent Mexican of Foreign-Born

Source: Roberto Suro, Pew Hispanic Center, Presentation at the Regional Conference on Illegal Immigration, NCLS, Denver, Colorado, December 12, 2005

those who came without documents and those who overstayed their visas). Figure 6.9 demonstrates graphically and dramatically that the compelling force underlying the illegal immigration trend is U.S. employment. It compares immigration trends from Mexico with the rate of employment in the United States. The close parallel between the two trends graphically depicts that the U.S. labor market is the single most important driving force compelling the high levels of illegal immigration to the United States.

The result of the trends shown in Figures 6.8 and 6.9 are dramatically evident in the line graph presented in Figure 6.10. It shows the remarkably rapid growth in the Mexican population residing within the United States, which climbed exponentially after 1970 with the effects of the 1964 law ending the Bracero Program and the 1965 Immigration and Naturalization law, which reduced legal immigration to the United States from Mexico so drastically that the illegal immigration trend replaced and soon greatly outstripped the legal flow.

Figure 6.11 Country Groups Show Similar Trends: Rise, Peak, and Decline

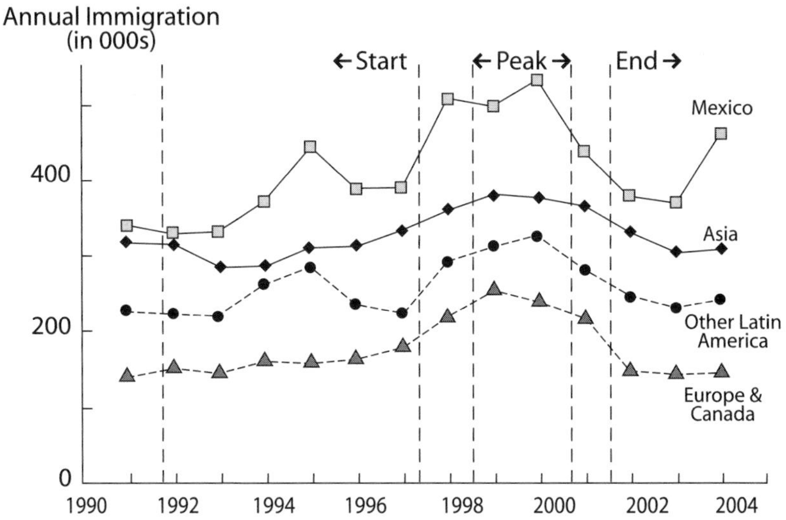

Source: Roberto Suro, Pew Hispanic Center, Presentation at the Regional Conference on Illegal Immigration, NCLS, Denver, Colorado, December 12, 2005

Immigration from all sources (regions of origin) clearly respond to U.S. economic and labor market conditions more so than to any other factor. Figure 6.11 shows that groups from Mexico, Asia, other Latin American countries, Europe, and Canada rose, peaked, and declined in remarkably similar, indeed, nearly the same, trends from 1990 through 2004.

Figure 6.12 presents a map of the United States, showing the sectors of the U.S. Border Patrol as of 2003 (that is, post–9/11/2001 and the establishment of the DHS).

Figure 6.13 shows the organizational chart of the new Department of Homeland Security and its bureaus of concern to immigration and to illegal immigration matters.

Finally, Figure 6.14 is a pie chart that gives a bit of the global perspective on the issue. It depicts UNHCR data on the nearly 20 million refugees, asylees, and others of concern to the UNHCR as of the end of 2004, indicating their regions of origin as well as their categories of UNHCR status.

Figure 6.12 Border Patrol Sectors

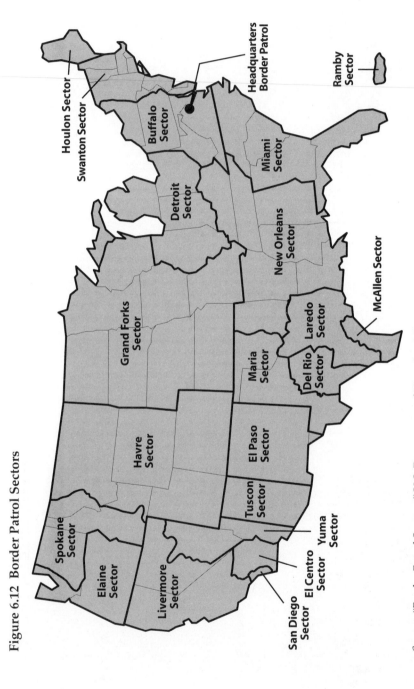

Source: "Border Patrol Sectors," U.S. Department of Homeland Security,
http://www.ebp.gov/xp/cgov/enforcement/border_patrol/border_patrol_sectors/ (accessed April 6, 2003)

Figure 6.13 Department of Homeland Security

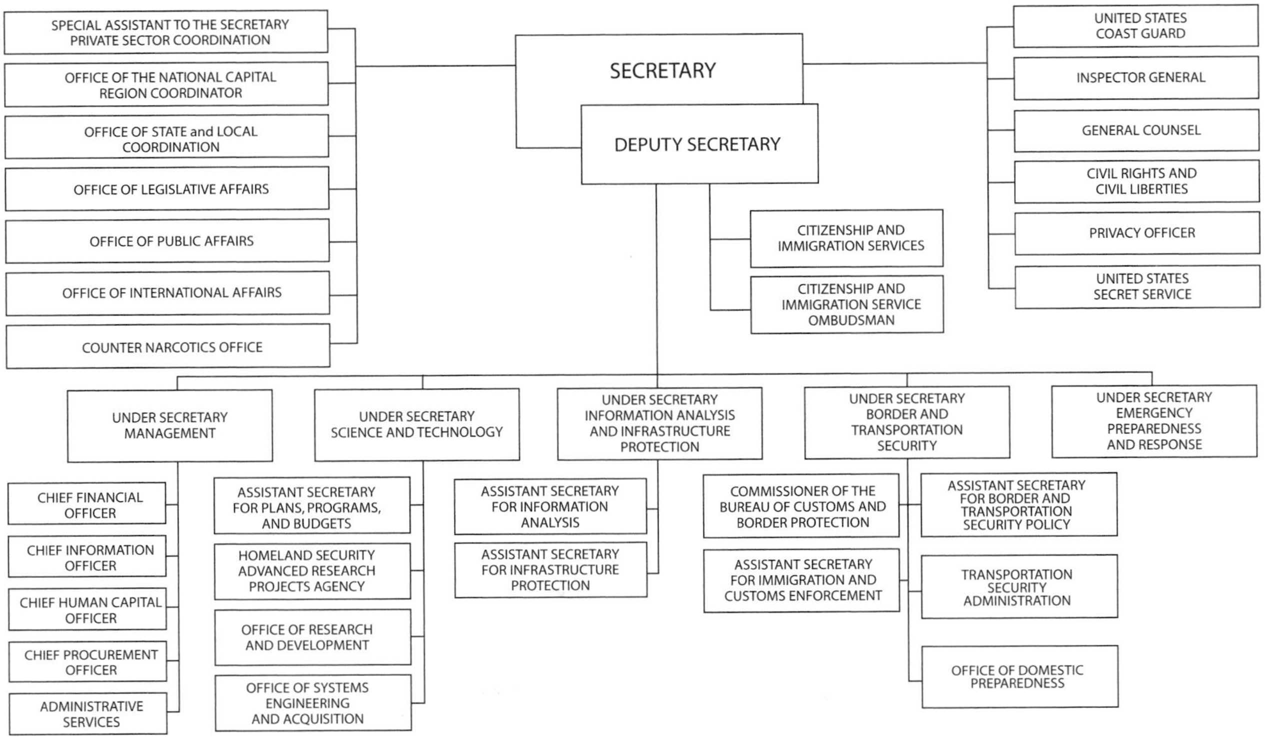

Source: U.S. Government Manual, 2004. http://www.dhs.gov/ (accessed 11/29/04).

Figure 6.14 Refugees, Asylum-Seekers, and Others of Concern
to UNHCR before 2004 (Total: 19.2 million)

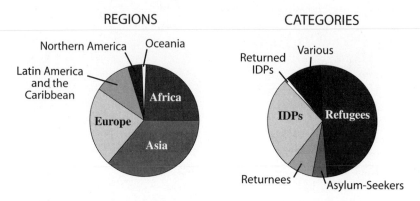

Source: adapted from UNHCR
http://www.unhcr.org/cgi-bin/texis/vtx/home?page=statistics

Key Legislative Actions, 1965–2006

On October 3, 1965, the Immigration and Nationality Act of 1965
was signed into law. It dramatically changed the immigration
flow, increasing markedly the total number of immigrants and al-
tering the composition from Northwestern Europe to Latin
America and Asia. Of equal significance, it was amended to impose the first ceiling on immigration from the Western Hemisphere, with the preference system extended to that migration
eleven years later. These limits fueled the illegal immigration
trend, as Mexicans and Central Americans who had come as
Bracero Program workers and those who wanted to continue to
work in the United States but were no longer able to come legally
chose to arrive illegally. Moreover, prior trends in legal immigration (including those who came as temporary workers through
the Bracero Program) forged the chain migration network that
readily enabled them to do so.

Consistent with the spirit of the Civil Rights Act of 1964, the
1965 act reasserted the nation's liberal tradition in immigration. It

set up individual rather than group criteria for granting immigration visas. It sought to balance a number of goals: (1) preserving family unity and reuniting separated families; (2) meeting a need for some highly skilled aliens; (3) easing pressures created by emergencies, such as political upheavals, communist aggression, and natural disasters; (4) assisting cross-national exchange programs; (5) barring from the United States aliens who could present problems of adjustment because of their physical or mental health, past criminal history, dependency, or for national security reasons; (6) standardizing admission procedures; and (7) establishing for the first time limits for the Americas. It replaced the national origins quota system with a seven-category system of preferences. It abolished the national origins system and emphasized other terms than quota and nonquota immigrants. Prospective immigrants either were nonpreference or met one of the preferences, or they were not subject to new per country limits because they were immediate relatives of U.S. citizens or were special immigrants.

Summary of the Immigration and Nationality Act of 1965 (79 Stat. 911, October 3, 1965)

The law amends the Immigration and Nationality Act of 1952 as follows:

1. Exclusive of special immigrants defined in section 101 (a) (27), and of the immediate relatives of United States citizens, the number of aliens who may be issued immigrant visas was limited to a total of 170,000.

(a) "Immediate relatives" were defined to mean the children, spouses, and parents of a citizen of the United States, provided that in the case of parents, such citizen must be at least twenty-one years of age.

(b) The immigration pool and the quota areas were terminated as of June 30, 1968.

(c) No person shall receive any preference or priority or be discriminated against in the issuance of an immigrant visa because of his race, sex, nationality, place of birth, or place of residence, but the total number of immigrant visas and the number of conditional entries made available to natives of any single foreign state was not to exceed 20,000 in any fiscal year.

(d) Each independent country, self-governing dominion, mandated territory, and territory under the international trusteeship of the United Nations, other than the United States and its outlying possessions, shall be treated as a separate foreign state for the purposes of the numerical limitation

2. **Sec. 203** covered aliens subject to the numerical limitations, setting up preference categories as follows:

(1) Visas shall be first made available, in a number not to exceed 20 per centum, of the number specified in section 201 (170,000) to qualified immigrants who are the unmarried sons or daughters of citizens of the United States.

(2) Visas shall next be made available, in a number not to exceed 20 per centum, of the number specified in section 201 to qualified immigrants who are spouses, unmarried sons, or unmarried daughters of an alien admitted for permanent residence.

(3) Visas shall next be made available, in a number not to exceed 10 per centum, to qualified immigrants who are members of the professions, or who because of their exceptional ability in the sciences or arts will substantially benefit prospectively the national economy, cultural interests, or welfare of the United States.

(4) Visas shall next be made available, in a number not to exceed 10 per centum, to qualified immigrants who are the married sons or married daughters of citizens of the United States.

(5) Visas shall next be made available, in a number not to exceed 24 per centum, to qualified immigrants who are the brothers or sisters of citizens of the United States.

(6) Visas shall next be made available, in a number not to exceed 10 per centum of the number specified, to qualified immigrants who are capable of performing specified skilled or unskilled labor, not of a temporary or seasonal nature, for which a shortage of employable and willing persons exists in the United States.

(7) Conditional entries shall next be made available by the Attorney General, pursuant to such regulations as he may prescribe and in a number not to exceed 6 per centum, to aliens who satisfy an Immigration and Naturalization Service officer that because of persecution or fear of persecution on account of race, religion, or political opinion they have fled their country of origin and are unable or unwilling to return to such country or area on account of race, religion, or political opinion, and are not nationals of the countries or areas in which their application for conditional entry is made; or that they are persons uprooted by catastrophic natural calamity as defined [by] the President who are unable to return to their usual place of abode.

(8) Visas authorized in any fiscal year shall be made available to other qualified immigrants strictly in the chronological order in which they qualify. Waiting lists of applicants shall be maintained

in accordance with regulations prescribed by the Secretary of State. No immigrant visa shall be issued to a non-preference immigrant under this paragraph, or to an immigrant with a preference under paragraph (3) or (6) of this subsection, until the consular officer is in receipt of a determination made by the Secretary of Labor.

Every immigrant shall be presumed to be a nonpreference immigrant until he establishes to the satisfaction of the consular officer and the immigration officer that he is entitled to a preference status.

3. **Sec. 10** amends the Immigration and Nationality Act as follows:

(a) Aliens seeking to enter the United States, for the purpose of performing skilled or unskilled labor, unless the Secretary of Labor has determined and certified to the Secretary of State and to the Attorney General that there are not sufficient workers in the United States who are able, willing, qualified, and available at the time of the application for a visa and admission to the United States and at the place to which the alien is destined to perform such skilled or unskilled labor, and the employment of such aliens will not adversely affect the wages and working conditions of the workers in the United States similarly employed. . . .

4. **Sec. 21** establishes a Select Commission of Western Hemisphere Immigration to study:

(1) Prevailing and projected demographic, technological, and economic trends as they pertain to the Western Hemisphere;

(2) Present and projected unemployment in the United States, by occupations, industries, geographic areas, and other factors in relation to immigration from the Western Hemisphere;

(3) The interrelationships between immigration, present and future, and existing and contemplated national and international programs and projects of Western Hemisphere nations, including programs and projects for economic and social development;

(4) The operation of immigration laws of the United States as they pertain to Western Hemisphere nations, including adjustment of status for Cuban refugees. . . .

(5) The implications of the foregoing with respect to the security and international relations of Western Hemisphere nations; and

(6) Any other matters which the Commission believes to be germane to the purposes for which it was established.

The plight of the Cuban refugees was recognized and responded to by the Congress. In November 1966, Congress passed a special act to adjust their status to permanent residence.

Act of November 2, 1966 (80 Stat. 1161) to Adjust the Status of Cuban Refugees

The status of any alien who is a native or citizen of Cuba and who has been inspected and admitted or paroled into the United States subsequent to January 1, 1959, and has been physically present in the United States for at least two years may be adjusted by the Attorney General, in his discretion and under such regulations as he may prescribe, to that of an alien lawfully admitted for permanent residence if the alien makes application for such adjustment, and the alien is eligible to receive an immigrant visa and is admissible to the United States for permanent residence. Upon approval of such application for adjustment of status, the Attorney General shall create a record of the alien's admission for permanent residence as of the date thirty months prior to the filing of such an application or the date of his last arrival into the United States, whichever date is later. The provisions of this Act shall be applicable to the spouse and child of any alien described in this subsection, regardless of their citizenship and place of birth, who are residing with such alien in the United States.

During the final weeks of the congressional session of 1976, the Congress passed a law to amend the Immigration Act of 1965 to deal with a perceived problem created by that law. The result of the 1965 law was that all would-be immigrants from the Western Hemisphere were required to apply for visas on a first-come, first-served basis, including those who were close relatives of U.S. citizens and skilled foreign workers, which were groups that received preferences in the system as it was in effect for the Eastern Hemisphere. By the mid-1970s the waiting period for immigrant visas in the Western Hemisphere stretched in excess of two years. This waiting period caused hardships for those who would otherwise have qualified for a preferred status and gained much faster entry into the United States. It induced family members wanting to be reunited to attempt to enter illegally. To rectify these problems, the 1976 amendment law extended the preference system to the Western Hemisphere nations. It was expected that the amendment would cut the waiting period for immigrants from Mexico, for example, in half. The next document presents a summary of the law's key provisions.

Act of October 20, 1976, to Amend the 1965 Immigration Act

The 1976 amendments had several important effects. They:

1. Retained the annual hemispheric immigration ceilings of 170,000 for the Eastern Hemisphere and 120,000 for the Western Hemisphere.

2. Extended the seven immigration preference systems to visa applicants from the Western Hemisphere calculated as percentum of the 120,000 ceiling.

3. Established a country-by-country triggering mechanism for the hemispheric visa percentage allotments for the various preference categories to become applicable within a given country whenever immigration from that country reaches its 20,000 limit in a preceding year, in order to assure that visas in lower preference categories would be available.

4. Retained the labor certification requirement for all third, sixth, and nonpreference immigrants who intended to work in the United States.

5. Required the Secretary of Labor to certify that equally qualified American professionals are available before denying labor certification for teachers or other immigrants with exceptional skills in the arts and sciences.

6. Recommended establishment of a special advisory group of experts to advise the Secretary of Labor in difficult cases involving visa applicants with exceptional professional skills.

7. Provided that Cuban refugees present in the U.S. prior to the enactment of the bill who change their status to permanent resident will not be charged to the annual ceiling for Western Hemisphere visas.

8. Allowed Western Hemisphere migrants to adjust their status from nonimmigrant to permanent resident without first returning to their home countries. This provision had formerly applied only to the Eastern Hemisphere. It set a precedent relative to proposed guest-worker provisions currently under consideration by the Congress.

9. Prohibited aliens who are not immediate relatives of either U.S. citizens or permanent residents from receiving an adjustment

in status to permanent resident after accepting unauthorized employment in the United States.

10. Prohibited aliens who were admitted to the United States in transit without visas from receiving an adjustment in status to permanent resident.

Source: Summary by author.

In 1980, Congress dealt most specifically with the problem of refugee admissions. Older refugee laws tended to deal with the refugee as a single individual "escaping" communism, for example. But the 1960s and 1970s evidenced refugee flows in which they were arriving in mass asylum movements, in the tens to even hundreds of thousands each. The Refugee Act of 1980, in an effort to systematize refugee policy, used the UN definition of a refugee and initially allowed for 50,000 persons annually who had a "well-founded fear of persecution" on account of race, religion, nationality, or membership in a social group or political movement to enter as refugees, and stipulated that the president could notify Congress if he determined that it was warranted to increase their number. After fiscal year 1982, he would have the responsibility of presenting Congress with a recommended total annual figure.

Act of March 17, 1980 (94 Stat. 102)— The Refugee Act of 1980

Sec. 101 declares that it is the historic policy of the United States to respond to the urgent needs of persons subject to persecution in their homelands, including humanitarian assistance for their care and maintenance in asylum areas, efforts to promote opportunities for resettlement or voluntary repatriation, aid for necessary transportation and processing, admission to this country of refugees for special humanitarian concern to the United States, and transitional assistance to refugees in the United States, and to encourage all nations to provide assistance and resettlement opportunities to refugees to the fullest extent possible.

Among its provisions, the act amends the Immigration and Nationality Act, defining a "refugee" to be as follows: (A) any person who is outside any country of such person's nationality or, in the case of a person having no nationality, is outside any country in which such person last habitually resided, and who is unable or unwilling to return to, and unable or unwilling to avail himself or herself of the protection of, that country because of persecution or a well-founded fear of persecution on account of race, religion, nationality, membership in a particular social group, or political opinion, or (B) in such special circumstances as the President after appropriate consultation . . . may specify. Excluded from the status of "refugee" is any person who ordered, incited, assisted, or otherwise participated in the persecution of any person on account of race, religion, nationality, membership in a particular social group, or political opinion.

Sec. 207 sets the number of refugees who may be admitted under this section in fiscal years 1980, 1981, or 1982, not to exceed 50,000 unless the President determines, before the beginning of the fiscal year and after appropriate consultation . . . that admission of a specific number of refugees in excess of such number is justified by humanitarian concerns or is otherwise in the national interest; and sets the number of refugees who may be admitted under this section in any fiscal year after fiscal year 1982 . . . as the President determines, before the beginning of the fiscal year and after appropriate consultation, [as] justified by humanitarian concerns or [as] otherwise in the national interest; and that admissions under this subsection shall be allocated among refugees of special humanitarian concern to the United States in accordance with a determination made by the President after appropriate consultation.

If the President determines, after appropriate consultation, that (1) an unforeseen emergency refugee situation exists, (2) the admission of certain refugees in response to the emergency refugee situation is justified by grave humanitarian concern or is otherwise in the national interest, and (3) the admission to the United States of these refugees cannot be accomplished under subsection (a), the President may fix a number of refugees to be admitted to the United States during the succeeding period (not to exceed twelve months) in response to the emergency refugee situation, and such admissions shall be allocated among refugees of special humanitarian concern to the United States in accordance with a determination made by the President after the appropriate consultation provided under this subsection. . . .

The refugee status of any alien (and of the spouse or child of the alien) may be terminated by the Attorney General pursuant to such regulations as the Attorney General may prescribe if the Attorney General determines that alien was not in fact a refugee within the meaning of subsection 101 at the time of the alien's admission.

Before the start of each fiscal year the President shall report to the Committees of the Judiciary of the House of Representatives and of the Senate regarding the foreseeable number of refugees who will be in need of resettlement during the fiscal year and the anticipated allocation of refugee admissions during the fiscal year. . . .

Sec. 208 stipulates that the Attorney General shall establish a procedure for an alien physically present in the United States or at a land border or port of entry to apply for asylum, and the alien may be granted asylum in the discretion of the Attorney General if the Attorney General determines that such alien is a refugee within the meaning of section 101.

Sec. 209 states that not more than 5,000 of the refugee admissions authorized under section 207(a) in any fiscal year may be made available by the Attorney General.

Exclusive of special immigrants in section 101(a)(27), immediate relatives specified in subsection (b) of this section, and aliens who are admitted or granted asylum under section 207 or 208, the number of aliens born in any foreign country or dependent area who may be issued immigrant visas or who may otherwise acquire the status of an alien lawfully admitted to the United States for permanent residence, shall not in any of the first three-quarters of any fiscal year exceed 72,000 and shall not in any fiscal year exceed 270,000.

The Attorney General shall not deport or return any alien (other than an alien described in section 241(a)(19)) to a country if the Attorney General determines that such alien's life or freedom would be threatened in such country on account of race, religion, nationality, membership in a particular social group, or political opinion.

Sec. 204 goes on to stipulate that the Attorney General establish the asylum procedure referred to in section 208 no later than June 1, 1980.

Sec. 301 states that the President shall appoint, by and with the advice and consent of the Senate, a U.S. Coordinator for Refugee Affairs with the rank of Ambassador-at-Large.

Of great importance to the reform of immigration policy was the report of the Select Commission on Immigration and Refugee Policy (SCIRP). The commission was a joint presidential and congressionally appointed commission that began its work in the final days of the Carter administration in 1979. It thoroughly studied immigration law and more particularly the problem of illegal immigration. It issued its final report in 1981, and its recommendations formed the basis of subsequent legislative action by the Congress throughout the 1980s and even into the 1990s. The next document presents some of the major recommendations of the SCIRP's final report.

Executive Summary Recommendations of the Select Commission on Immigration and Refugee Policy, 1981

The Select Commission recommends:

1. The United States work with other nations and principal international organizations to collect information and research on migratory flows and treatment of international migration.

2. The United States expand bilateral consultation with other governments, especially Mexico and other regional neighbors, regarding migration.

3. Border patrol funding levels be raised to provide for a substantial increase in the number and training of personnel, replacement sensor systems . . . and other needed equipment.

4. That regional border enforcement posts be established to coordinate work with the INS, the U.S. Customs Service, the DEA, and the U.S. Coast Guard in the interdiction of both undocumented/illegal migrants and illicit goods, specifically narcotics.

5. That high priority be given to the training of INS officers to familiarize them with the rights of aliens and U.S. citizens and to help them deal with persons of other cultural backgrounds.

6. That legislation be passed making it illegal for employers to hire undocumented workers.

7. That a program to legalize illegal/undocumented aliens now in the United States be adopted.

8. That eligibility for legalization be determined by interrelated measurements of residence—date of entry and length of continuous residence—and by specified groups of excludability that are appropriate to the legalization program.

9. That voluntary agencies and community organizations be given a significant role in the legalization program

10. An annual ceiling of 350,000 numerically limited immigrant visas with an additional 100,000 visas available for the first five years to . . . allow backlogs to be cleared.

11. That a substantial number of visas be set aside for reunifying spouses and unmarried sons and daughters, and it should be given top priority in the numerically limited family reunification. . . .

12. That country ceilings apply to all numerically limited family reunification preferences. . . .

13. That "special" immigrants remain a numerically exempt group but be placed within the independent category.

14. Creation of a small, numerically limited subcategory within the independent category to provide for the immigration of certain investors.

15. That specific labor market criteria be established by the selection of independent immigrants. . . .

16. A fixed percentage limit to the independent immigration from any one country.

17. That U.S. allocation of refugee numbers include both geographic considerations and specific refugee characteristics. . . .

18. That state and local governments be involved in planning for initial refugee resettlement and that . . . a federal program of impact aid [be established] to minimize the financial impact of refugees on local services. . . .

19. That refugee achievement of self-sufficiency and adjustment to living in the United States be reaffirmed as the goal of resettlement.

Source: The Select Commission on Immigration and Refugee Policy, *Final Report* (Washington, D.C.: U.S. Government Printing Office, March 1, 1981), xv–xxxii. Summary by author.

In 1983 the U.S. Supreme Court rendered a decision in an immigration case that had importance beyond the immediate issue of immigration law: *INS v. Chadha et al.* In that case a class action suit was filed against the INS over its deportation proceedings. The Court ruled that the use by the House of Representatives of the "legislative veto" of executive branch (the INS) rules and regulations was unconstitutional. The following is a summary of that decision.

INS v. Chadha et al.
(462 U.S. 919), 1983

Decision: One-house congressional veto provision in 244(c)(2) of Immigration and Nationality Act held unconstitutional.

Summary: An immigration judge suspended an alien's deportation pursuant to 244(c)(1) of the Immigration and Nationality Act (8 USCS 1254(c)(1)). The U.S. House of Representatives passed a resolution vetoing the suspension pursuant to 244(c)(2) of the Act (8 USCS 1254(c)(2)), which authorizes one House of Congress to invalidate the decision of the executive branch to allow a particular deportable alien to remain in the United States. The immigration judge reopened the deportation proceedings to implement the House order, and the alien was ordered deported. The Board of Immigration Appeals dismissed the alien's appeal, holding that it had no power to declare unconstitutional an Act of Congress. The U.S. Court of Appeals for the Ninth Circuit held that the House was without constitutional authority to order the alien's deportation and that 244(c)(2) violated the constitutional doctrine of separation of powers (634 F2nd 408).

On appeal, the U.S. Supreme Court affirmed. In an opinion by Chief Justice Burger, joined by Justices Brennan, Marshall, Blackmun, Stevens, and O'Connor, it was held that the legislative veto provision in 244(c)(2) was unconstitutional since the one-house veto was legislative in purpose and effect and subject to the procedures set out in Article I of the Constitution requiring passage by a majority of both Houses and presentment to the President.

Justice Powell, concurring in the judgment, expressed the view that the case should be decided on a narrower ground and declared that when Congress finds that a particular person does not satisfy the statutory criteria for permanent residence it has assumed a judicial function in violation of the principle of separation of powers.

Justice White dissented, expressing the view that the legislative veto is an important if not indispensable political invention and that neither Article I nor the doctrine of separation of powers is violated by this mechanism. Justice Rehnquist joined by Justice

White, dissenting, expressed the view that 244(c)(2) was not severable from the rest of the statute.

Source: U.S. Supreme Court Reports, 77 L. Ed 2nd, Briefs of Counsel, p. 1516, infra: 317–318

In 1985, another class action suit against the INS reached the Supreme Court. This case, *Jean et al. v. Nelson,* concerned the denial by the INS of parole to undocumented Haitian aliens who were ruled as "economic refugees" and therefore excluded from parole status. A federal district court ruled in favor of the Haitians on the basis that the decision by the INS to detain the aliens without parole was on the basis of race and national origin and thus in violation of the equal protection clause of the Fifth Amendment to the Constitution. The Supreme Court affirmed the judgment of the appeals court, which although rejecting the constitutional claim accorded relief on the basis of INS regulation, remanding the case to the district court to ensure that the INS exercised its discretion in parole decisions in a nondiscriminatory manner. The next document presents a summary of the case and decision of the Supreme Court.

Jean et al. v. Nelson **(472 U.S. 846), 1985**

Decision: Court of Appeals held to have improperly reached constitutional issue in deciding case challenging denial by the INS of parole to undocumented Haitian aliens.

Summary: The named representatives of a class of undocumented and unadmitted aliens from Haiti brought suit against the Commissioner of the Immigration and Naturalization Service (INS) in a federal district court, alleging in part that they had been detained without parole by INS officials on the basis of race and national origin, in violation of the equal protection guarantee of the Fifth Amendment to the U.S. Constitution. The district court rejected the constitutional claim (544 F Supp 973), but a panel of the U.S. Court of Appeals for the Eleventh Circuit held that the Fifth Amendment's equal protection guarantee applied to the parole of unadmitted aliens (711 F2nd 1455). After a rehearing en banc, the Court of Appeals held that the Fifth Amendment did not apply to the consideration of unadmitted aliens for parole. Although rejecting the constitutional claim, the Court of Appeals accorded relief based on the applicable INS regulation (8 CFR 212.5), remanding to the district court to ensure that the INS exercised its discretion in making parole decisions in an individualized and nondiscriminatory manner (727 F2d 957).

On certiorari, the U.S. Supreme Court affirmed the judgment remanding the case to the District Court. In the opinion of Justice Rehnquist, and joined by Justices White, Blackmun, Powell, Stevens, and O'Connor, it was held that the Court of Appeals should not have reached and decided the parole question on constitutional grounds, since the applicable statute and regulations were facially neutral, and since the parole discretion of the INS thereunder did not extend to considerations of race or national origin.

Justice Marshall, joined by Justice Brennan, dissented, expressing the view that there was no principled way to avoid reaching the constitutional issue and that aliens have a Fifth Amendment right to parole decisions free from invidious discrimination based on race or national origin.

Source: U.S. Supreme Court Reports, Briefs of Counsel, p. 826 infra., 86 L Ed 2nd: 664–665.

The Immigration Reform and Control Act of 1986, commonly known as IRCA, had a lengthy and tangled history. In 1986 a joint Conference Committee finally agreed on a package that could be enacted into law. The next document offers portions of the major provisions of IRCA.

Act of November 6, 1986 (100 Stat. 3360)— The Immigration Reform and Control Act of 1986

Title I — Control of Illegal Immigration

Sec. 101. Control of Unlawful Employment of Aliens

In General, It is unlawful for a person or other entity to hire, or to recruit or refer for a fee, for employment in the United States—

(A) an alien, knowing the alien is an unauthorized alien . . .

(B) an individual without complying with the requirements of subsection (b).

Continuing employment—It is unlawful for a person or other entity, after hiring an alien for employment in accordance with paragraph (1), to continue to employ the alien in the United States knowing the alien is (or has become) an unauthorized alien with respect to such employment.

Defense—A person or entity that establishes that it has complied in good faith with the requirements of subsection (b) with respect to the hiring, recruiting, or referral for employment of an alien in the United States has established an affirmative defense that the person or entity has not violated paragraph (1)(A) with respect to such hiring, recruiting, or referral.

Use of Labor through Contract— A person or other entity who uses a contract, subcontract, or exchange, entered into, renegotiated, or extended after the date of the enactment of this section, to obtain the labor of an alien in the United States knowing that the alien is an unauthorized alien, with respect to performing such labor, shall be considered to have hired the alien for employment in the United States in violation of paragraph (1)(A).

Use of State Employment Agency Documentation — A person or entity shall be deemed to have complied with the requirements of subsection (b) with respect to the hiring of an individual who was referred for such employment by a State employment agency.

Employment Verification System—The requirements referred to [above] are, in the case of a person or other entity hiring, recruiting, or referring an individual for employment in the United States, the requirements specified in the following three paragraphs:

(1)   Attestation after Examination of Documentation—

(A) In General—The person or entity must attest, under penalty of perjury and on a form established by the Attorney General by regulation, that it has verified that the individual is not an unauthorized alien by examining—

(i) a document described in subparagraph (B), or

(ii) a document described in subparagraph (C) and (D).

(B) Documents Establishing Both Employment Authorization and Identity—A document described in this subparagraph is an individual's—

(i) United States passport;

(ii) certificate of United States Citizenship;

(iii) certificate of naturalization;

(iv) unexpired foreign passport, if the passport has an appropriate, unexpired endorsement of the Attorney General authorizing the individual's employment in the United States; or

(v) resident alien card or other alien registration, if said card contains a photograph of the individual, and is evidence of authorization of employment in the United States.

(C) Documents Evidencing Employment Authorization —A document described [above] is

(i) a social security account number card;

(ii) certificate of birth in the United States or establishing United States nationality at birth;

(iii) other documents evidencing authorization of employment in the United States which the Attorney General finds, by regulation, to be acceptable for the purposes of this section.

(D) Documents Establishing Identity of an Individual— A document described in this subparagraph is an individual's

(i) driver's license or similar document issued for the purpose of identification by a State, if it contains a photograph of the individual;

(ii) in the case of individuals under 16 years of age or in a State which does not provide for issuance of an identification document,

(iii) documentation of personal identity of such type as the Attorney General finds, by regulation, provides a reliable means of identification. . . .

(3) Definition of Unauthorized Alien— the term "unauthorized alien" means, with respect to the employment of an alien at a particular time, that the alien is not at that time either (A) an alien lawfully admitted for permanent residence, or (B) authorized to be so employed by this Act or by the Attorney General.

Deferral of Enforcement with Respect to Seasonal Agricultural Services—

(A) In General—it is unlawful for a person or entity (including a farm labor contractor) or an agent of such a person or entity, to recruit an unauthorized alien (other than an alien described in clause [ii]) who is outside the United States to enter the United States to perform seasonal agricultural services.

(ii) Exception—Clause (i) shall not apply to an alien who the person or entity reasonably believes to meet the requirements of section 210(a)(2) of this Act (relating to the performance of seasonal agricultural services).

General Accounting Office Reports—

In General—
Beginning one year after the date of enactment of this Act, and at intervals of one year thereafter for a period of three years after such date, the Comptroller General of the United States shall prepare and transmit to the Congress and to the task force established under subsection (k) a report describing the results of a

review of the implementation and enforcement of this section during the preceding twelve-month period, for the purpose of determining if—

(A) such provisions have been carried out satisfactorily;

(B) a pattern of discrimination has resulted against citizens or nationals of the United States or against eligible workers seeking employment; and

(C) an unnecessary regulatory burden has been created for employers hiring such workers.

Review by Task Force—

(1) Establishment of Task Force—The Attorney General, jointly with the Chairman of the Commission on Civil Rights and the Chairman of the Equal Employment Opportunity Commission, shall establish a task force to review each report of the Comptroller General.

(2) Recommendations to Congress—If the report transmitted includes a determination that the implementation of this section has resulted in a pattern of discrimination in employment (against other than unauthorized aliens) on the basis of national origin, the task force shall, taking into consideration any recommendations in the report, report to Congress recommendations for such legislation as may be appropriate to deter or remedy such discrimination. . . .

Termination Date for Employer Sanctions—

(1) If Report of Widespread Discrimination and Congressional Approval—The provisions of this section shall terminate 30 days after receipt of the last report required to be transmitted under subsection (j), if—

(A) the Comptroller General determines, and so reports . . . that a widespread pattern of discrimination has resulted against citizens or nationals of the United States or against eligible workers seeking employment solely from the implementation of this section; and

(B) there is enacted, within such period of 30 calendar days, a joint resolution stating in substance that the Congress approves the findings of the Comptroller General contained in such report.

(2) Senate Procedures for Consideration—Any joint resolution referred to in clause (B) of paragraph (1) shall be considered in the Senate in accordance with subsection (n). . . .

Increased Authorization of Appropriations for INS and EOIR—
In addition to any other amounts authorized to be appropriated, in order to carry out this Act, there are authorized to be appropriated to the Department of Justice—

(1) for the [INS], for FY 1987, $12,000,000, and for FY 1988, $15,000,000 . . . to provide for an increase in the border patrol personnel . . . so that the average level of such personnel in each fiscal year 1987 and 1988 is at least 50 per cent higher than such level for fiscal year 1986.

Title II—Legalization
Sec. 201. Legalization of Status.

Temporary Resident Status—
The Attorney General shall adjust the status of an alien to that of an alien lawfully admitted for temporary residence if the alien meets the following requirements:
(1) Timely Application—
(A) During Application Period—Except as provided in subparagraph (B), the alien must apply for such adjustment during the 12-month period beginning on a date (not later than 180 days after the date of enactment of this section) designated by the Attorney General. . . .
(2) Continuous Lawful Residence Since 1982—
(A) In General—The alien must establish that he entered the United States before January 1, 1982, and that he has resided continuously in the United States in an unlawful status since such date and through the date the application is filed under this subsection.
(B) Nonimmigrants—In the case of an alien who entered the United States as a nonimmigrant before January 1, 1982, the alien must establish that the alien's period of authorized stay as a nonimmigrant expired before such date through the passage of time or the alien's unlawful status was known to the Government as of such date.

Subsequent Adjustment to Permanent Residence and Nature of Temporary Resident Status—
(1) Adjustment to Permanent Residence—The Attorney General shall adjust the status of any alien provided lawful temporary resident status under subsection (a) to that of an alien lawfully admitted for permanent residence if the alien meets the following requirements:
(A) Timely Application After One Year's Residence—The alien must apply for such adjustment during the one-year period beginning with the nineteenth month that begins after the date the alien was granted such temporary status.
(B) Continuous Residence—the alien must establish that he has continuously resided in the United States since the date the alien was granted such temporary resident status.

(C) Admissible as Immigrant—The alien must establish that he or she—

(i) is admissible to the United States as an immigrant . . . and

(ii) has not been convicted of any felony or three or more misdemeanors committed in the United States.

Basic Citizenship Skills—The alien must demonstrate that he or she either—

(I) meets the requirements of section 312 (relating to minimal understanding of ordinary English and a knowledge and understanding of the history and government of the United States), or (II) is satisfactorily pursuing a course of study (recognized by the Attorney General) to achieve an understanding of English and such knowledge and understanding of the history and government of the United States. . . .

Temporary Disqualification of Newly Legalized Aliens from Receiving Certain Public Welfare Assistance—

(1) In General—During the five-year period beginning on the date an alien was granted lawful temporary resident status under subsection (a) except as provided in paragraphs (2) and (3), the alien is not eligible for—

(i) any program of financial assistance furnished under Federal law;

(ii) medical assistance under a State plan approved under Title XIX of the Social Security Act; and

(iii) assistance under the Food Stamp Act of 1977; and State or political subdivision therein may, to the extent consistent with paragraph (A) and paragraphs (2) and (3), provide that an alien is not eligible for the programs of financial assistance or for medical assistance described in subparagraph (A) (ii) furnished under the law of that State or political subdivision. . . .

Title III—Reform of Legal Immigration
Part A—Temporary Agricultural Workers

Sec. 301. H-2A Agricultural Workers

(a) Providing New "H-2A" Nonimmigrant Classification for Temporary Agricultural Labor— Paragraph (15) (H) of section 101 (a) (8 USC 1101(a)) is amended by striking out "to perform temporary services or labor," in clause (ii) and inserting in lieu thereof, "(a) to perform agricultural labor or services, as defined by the Secretary of Labor in regulations and including agricultural labor defined in section 3121(g) of the Internal Revenue Code of 1954 and agriculture as defined in section 3(f) of the Fair Labor Standards Act of 1938 . . . or a temporary or seasonal nature, or (b) to perform other temporary service or labor."

(b) Involvement of Departments of Labor and Agriculture in H-2A Program—Section 214(c) (8 USC 1184(c)) is amended by adding to the end the following: "For purposes of this subsection with respect to nonimmigrants described in section 101(a)(15)(H)(ii)(a), the term 'appropriate agencies of Government' means the Department of Labor and includes the Department of Agriculture. The provisions of section 216 shall apply to the question of importing any alien as nonimmigrant under section 101(a)(15)(H)(ii)(a)."

Despite the national legislation intended to curb illegal immigration, the size of that flow, as we have seen, continued unabated. The political pressure to do more increased during the 1990s. States that received the largest number of legal and illegal immigrants—for example, California, Florida, and Texas—sued the federal government in their respective federal district courts for the estimated billions of dollars that they were paying in extra costs for prisons, in education, and for health care for illegal immigrants and for their children. California also made legislative attempts to reduce the draw of its economy and services, and to "send a message to Congress" by passing, in 1994, an anti-immigration initiative commonly referred to as Proposition 187, presented in the next document.

California's Proposition 187— The "Save Our State" Initiative

Section 1. The People of California find and declare as follows:

That they have suffered and are suffering economic hardship by the presence of illegal aliens in the state. That they have suffered and are suffering personal injury and damage by the criminal conduct of illegal aliens in the state. That they have a right to the protection of their government from any person or persons entering this country unlawfully.

Therefore, the People of California declare their intention to provide for cooperation between their agencies of state and local government with the federal government, and to establish a system of required notification by and between such agencies to prevent illegal aliens in the United States from receiving benefits or public services in the State of California.

Section 2. Manufacture, Distribution or Sale of False Citizenship or Resident Alien Documents: Crime and Punishment.

Section 113. Is added to the Penal Code, to read: Any person who manufactures, distributes or sells false documents to conceal the true citizenship or resident alien status of another is guilty of a felony and shall be punished by imprisonment in the state prison for five years or by a fine of seventy-five thousand dollars.

Section 3. Use of False Citizenship or Resident Alien Documents: Crime and Punishment.

Section 114. Is added to the Penal Code, to read: Any person who uses false documents to conceal his or her true citizenship or resident alien status is guilty of a felony, and shall be punished by imprisonment in a state prison for five years or by a fine of twenty-five thousand dollars.

Section 4. Law Enforcement Cooperation with INS.

Section 834b. Is added to the Penal Code, to read: Every law enforcement agency in California shall fully cooperate with the United States Immigration and Naturalization Service regarding any person who is arrested if he or she is suspected of being present in the United States in violation of federal immigration laws.

(b) With respect to any such person who is arrested, and suspected of being present in the United States in violation of federal immigration laws, every law enforcement agency shall do the following:

(1) Attempt to verify the legal status of such person as a citizen of the United States, an alien lawfully admitted as a permanent resident, an alien lawfully admitted for a temporary period of time or as an alien who is present in the United States in violation of immigration laws. The verification process may include, but shall not be limited to, questioning the person regarding his or her date and place of birth and entry into the United States, and demanding documentation to indicate his or her legal status.

(2) Notify the person of his or her apparent status as an alien who is present in the United States in violation of federal immigration laws and inform him or her that, apart from any criminal justice proceedings he or she must obtain legal status or leave the United States.

(3) Notify the Attorney General of California and the United States INS of the apparent illegal status and provide any additional information that may be requested by any other public entity.

(c) Any legislative, administrative, or other action by a city, county, or other legally authorized local governmental entity with jurisdictional boundaries, or by a law enforcement agency, to prevent or limit the cooperation required by subdivision (a) is expressly prohibited.

Section 5. Exclusion of Illegal Aliens from Public Social Services.

Section 10001.5. Is added to the Welfare and Institutions Code, to read: In order to carry out the intention of the People of California that only citizens of the United States and aliens lawfully admitted to the United States may receive the benefits of public social services and to ensure that all persons employed in the providing of those services shall diligently protect public funds from misuse, the provisions of this section are adopted.

(b) A person shall not receive any public social services to which he or she may not otherwise be entitled until the legal status of that person has been verified as one of the following:

(1) A citizen of the United States.

(2) An alien lawfully admitted as a permanent resident.

(3) An alien lawfully admitted for a temporary period of time.

(c) If any public entity in this state to whom a person has applied for public social services determines or reasonably suspects, based upon the information provided to it, that the person is an alien in the United States in violation of federal law, the following procedures shall be followed by the public entity:

(1) The entity shall not provide the person with benefits or services.

(2) The entity shall, in writing, notify the person of his or her apparent illegal immigration status, and that the person must either obtain legal status or leave the United States.

(3) The entity shall also notify the State Director of Social Services, the Attorney General of California and the United States Immigration and Naturalization Service of the appar-

ent illegal status, and shall provide any additional information that may be requested by any other public entity.

Section 6. Exclusion of Illegal Aliens from Publicly Funded Health Care.

Chapter 1.3 (commencing with Section 130) is added to Part 1 of Division 1 of the Health and Safety Code to read: In order to carry out the intention of the People of California that, excepting emergency medical care as required by federal law, only citizens of the United States and aliens lawfully admitted to the United States may receive the benefits of publicly-funded health care, and to ensure that all persons employed in the providing of those services shall diligently protect public funds from misuse, the provisions of this section are adopted.

(b) A person shall not receive any health care service from a publicly-funded health care facility to which he or she is otherwise entitled until the legal status of that person has been verified as one of the following:

(1) A citizen of the United States.

(2) An alien lawfully admitted as a permanent resident.

(3) An alien lawfully admitted for a temporary period of time.

(c) If any publicly-funded health care facility in this state from whom a person seeks health care services, other than emergency medical care as required by federal law, determines or reasonably suspects, based on the information provided it, that the person is an alien in the United States in violation of the federal law, the following procedures shall be followed by the facility:

(1) The facility shall not provide the person with services.

(2) The facility shall, in writing, notify the person of his or her apparent illegal immigration status, and that the person must either obtain legal status or leave the United States.

(3) The facility shall also notify the State Director of Social Services, the Attorney General of California and the United States Immigration and Naturalization Service of the apparent illegal status, and shall provide any additional information that may be requested by any other public entity.

(d) For purposes of this section "publicly-funded health care facility" shall be defined as specified in Section 1200 and 1250 of the Health and Safety Code as of January 1, 1993.

Section 7. Exclusion of Illegal Aliens from Public Elementary and Secondary Schools.

Section 48215. Is added to the Education Code to read: No public elementary or secondary school shall admit, or permit the attendance of, any child who is not a citizen of the United States, an alien lawfully admitted as a permanent resident, or a person who is otherwise authorized under federal law to be present.

(b) Commencing January 1, 1995, each school district shall verify the legal status of each child enrolling in the school district for the first time in order to ensure the enrollment or attendance only of citizens, aliens lawfully admitted as permanent residents, or persons who are otherwise authorized under federal law to be present in the United States.

(d) By January 1, 1996, each school district shall also have verified the legal status of each parent or guardian of each child referred to in subdivision (b) and (c) above, to determine whether such parent or guardian is one of the following:

(1) A citizen of the United States.

(2) An alien lawfully admitted as a permanent resident.

(3) An alien admitted lawfully for a temporary period of time.

(e) Each school district shall provide information to the State Superintendent of Public Instruction, the Attorney General of California and the United States INS regarding any enrollee or pupil, or parent or guardian, attending a public elementary or secondary school in the school district determined or reasonably suspected to be in violation of federal immigration laws within forty-five days after becoming aware of an apparent violation. The notice shall also be provided to the parent or legal guardian of the enrollee or pupil, and shall state that an existing pupil may not continue attending school after ninety calendar days from the date of the notice unless legal status is established.

(f) For each child who cannot establish legal status in the United States, each school district shall continue to provide education for a period of ninety days from the date of the notice. Such ninety day period shall be utilized to accomplish an orderly transition to a school in the child's country of origin. Each school district shall cooperate in this transition effort to ensure that the educational needs of the child are best served for that period of time.

Section 8. Exclusion of Illegal Aliens from Public Postsecondary Educational Institutions.

Section 66010.8. Is added to the Education Code to read: No public institution of postsecondary education shall admit, enroll, or permit the attendance of any person who is not a citizen of the United States, an alien lawfully admitted as a permanent resident in the United States, or a person who is otherwise authorized under federal law to be present in the United States.

(c) Commencing with the first term or semester that begins after January 1, 1996, and at the end of each term or semester thereafter, each public postsecondary educational institution shall verify the status of each person enrolled or in attendance at that institution in order to ensure the enrollment or attendance only of United States citizens, aliens lawfully admitted as permanent residents in the United States, and persons who are otherwise authorized under federal law to be present in the United States.

(c) No later than 45 days after the admission officer of a public postsecondary educational institution becomes aware of the application, enrollment, or attendance of a person determined to be, or who is under reasonable suspicion of being, in the United States in violation of federal immigration laws, that officer shall provide that information to the State Superintendent of Public Instruction, the Attorney General of California and the United States Immigration and Naturalization Service. The information shall be provided to the applicant, enrollee, or person admitted.

Section 9. Attorney General Cooperation with the INS.

Section 53609.65. Is added to the Government Code, to read: Whenever the state or a city, or a county, or any other legally authorized local government entity with jurisdictional boundaries reports the presence of a person who is suspected of being present in the United States in violation of federal immigration laws to the Attorney General of California, that report shall be transmitted to the United States Immigration and Naturalization Service. The Attorney General shall be responsible for maintaining on-going and accurate records of such reports, and shall provide any additional information that may be requested by any other government entity.

Section 10. Amendment and Severability.
The statutory provisions contained in this measure may not be amended by the Legislature except to further its purposes by statute passed in each house by a roll call vote entered in the journal, two-thirds of the membership concurring, or by a statute that become[s] effective only when approved by the voters. In the event that any portion of this act or the application thereof to any person or circumstances is held invalid, that invalidity shall not affect any other provision or application of the act, which can be

given effect without the invalid provision or application, and to that end the provisions of this act are severable.

Source: LULAC v. Wilson, 908 F.Supp. 755 (C.D.Cal. 1995): 787–791. Summarized by author.

The last provision of Proposition 187 anticipated a federal court challenge as to the law's constitutionality. Indeed, it was immediately brought to court by the League of United Latin American Citizens, and the federal district court did rule that most of the law was unconstitutional. The next document presents the summary judgment of the federal court decision on the initiative measure that granted an injunction to bar the state from enforcing Proposition 187.

LULAC et al. v. Pete Wilson et al. (908 F. Supp. 755 [C.D. Cal. 1995])

Public interest groups and individual citizens, in consolidated actions, brought suit for declaratory and injunctive relief to bar California Governor, Attorney General and other state actors from enforcing provisions of voter-approved California initiative measure requiring state personnel to verify immigration status of persons with whom they come into contact, report persons in United States unlawfully to state and federal officials, and deny those persons social services, health care, and education benefits. On plaintiff's motions for summary judgment, the District Court, Pfaelzer, J., held that: (1) classification, notification, cooperation and reporting provisions of the measure had direct and substantial effect on immigration, so as to be preempted by federal immigration law; (2) initiative's denial of public benefits based on federal determinations of immigration status was not impermissible regulation of immigration; (3) provision excluding illegal aliens from public elementary and secondary schools was preempted by federal law as being prohibited by equal protection clause of Fourteenth Amendment; (4) verification components of measure prohibiting public postsecondary education to persons not authorized under federal law to be in the United States were permissible; (5) provisions of measure criminalizing making and using false documents to conceal true citizenship or resident alien status were legitimate exercise of state's police power; (6) provisions denying public social services to illegal immigrants as applied to federally funded programs administered by state that awarded benefits regardless of immigration status conflicted with and were preempted by federal law; (7) provisions of measure prohibiting public postsecondary educational institutions from admitting, enrolling or permitting attendance of persons not authorized under federal law to be present in the United States were not preempted by federal law; and (8) criminal penalties contemplated by provision criminalizing manufacture, distribution, sale or use of false documents to conceal immigration status were not preempted by federal law.

Source: 908 Federal Supplement: 755–756. Summary by author.

The highly popular voter approval of Proposition 187 and Governor Pete Wilson's easy margin of victory in his reelection bid did not pass unheeded by the U.S. Congress. Even though much of Proposition 187 was overturned by the federal district court decision, the Congress moved to enact national legislation that essentially enforced those portions of 187 that were ruled unconstitutional as state infringements of the national government's sole authority to enact immigration law or state actions preempted by existing federal law. In 1996 the Congress passed and President Clinton signed into law two measures that essentially enacted the provisions of Proposition 187. Congress enacted a welfare reform act that contained several legal and illegal immigrant–related provisions with aspects similar to those in Proposition 187. The illegal immigration provisions are shown in the next document.

Welfare Reform Act of 1996 (HR 3734—PL 104-193)

Immigration Provisions of the Welfare Reform Act

The welfare reform law imposed restrictions on both legal and illegal immigrants, including provisions to:

Illegal Aliens

Restrictions. Restrict the federal benefits for which illegal aliens and legal nonimmigrants, such as travelers and students, could qualify. The benefits denied were those provided by a federal agency or federal funds for:

- Any grant, contract, loan, professional license or commercial license.

• Any retirement, welfare, health, disability, food assistance or unemployment benefit.

Exceptions. Allow illegal aliens and legal nonimmigrants to receive:

• Emergency medical services under Medicaid, but denied coverage for prenatal or delivery assistance that was not an emergency, and short-term, noncash emergency disaster relief.
• Immunizations and testing for treatment for the symptoms of communicable diseases.
• Noncash programs identified by the attorney general that were delivered by community agencies such as soup kitchens, counseling, and short-term shelter that were not conditioned on the individual's income or resources and were necessary for the protection of life and safety.
• Certain housing benefits (for existing recipients only).
• Licenses and benefits directly related to work for which a nonimmigrant had been authorized to enter the United States.
• Certain Social Security retirement benefits protected by treaty or statute.

State and local programs. Prohibit states from providing state or local benefits to most illegal aliens, unless a state law was enacted after August 22, 1996, the day the bill was enacted, that explicitly made illegal aliens eligible for the aid. However, illegal aliens were entitled to receive a school lunch and/or breakfast if they were eligible for a free public education under state or local law and a state could opt to provide certain other benefits related to child nutrition and emergency food assistance.

Source: Summary by author.

From 1994 through 1996, Congress grappled with bills that would have reformed immigration law more generally—not just dealing with problems of illegal immigration. A sufficient consensus to enact broad-scale legal immigration reform could not be reached. Congress cleared a measure to restrict illegal immigration only after folding its provisions into the omnibus fiscal 1997 spending bill (HR 3610—PL 104-208) that President Clinton signed into law on September 30, 1996. The full measure is over 200 pages long. The next document summarizes the illegal immigration section of the omnibus spending bill.

Act of September 30, 1996 (HR 3610—PL 104-208)
Illegal Immigration Provisions of the Omnibus Spending Bill

Border Controls.   Authorized funding to increase the number of Border Patrol agents by 1,000 per year through fiscal 2001, doubling the total force from 5,000 to 10,000, and to increase the number of clerical workers and other support personnel at the border by 300 per year through fiscal 2001. The law ordered the INS to relocate as many agents as possible to border areas with the largest number of illegal immigrants, and to coordinate relocation plans with local law enforcement agencies. The INS was required to report to Congress on these activities within six months of enactment.

Authorized funding of 900 additional INS agents to investigate and prosecute cases of smuggling, harboring or employing illegal aliens; and 300 new agents to investigate people who overstay their visas.

Authorized $12 million for the second and third tiers of a triple fence along a 14-mile strip at the U.S.-Mexico border south of San Diego, and for roads surrounding the fence. The project was exempt from the strictures of the 1973 Endangered Species Act and the 1969 Environmental Policy Act if either would prevent expeditious construction and allowed the attorney general to acquire land for the fence.

Required the INS to develop alien identification cards that include a biometric identifier, such as a fingerprint, that could be read by machine, and for future cards that could use such devices as retina scanners.

Created a penalty up to five years in prison for fleeing through an INS checkpoint, and deportation of those convicted.

Ordered the attorney general, within two years, to create a data base of information gathered from the documents people filled out as they legally entered and left the country which would allow the INS to match entry and exit records to identify people who overstayed their visas.

Required the INS to establish "preinspection" stations at five of the ten foreign airports that were the departure points for the largest number of inadmissible immigrants to screen people who did not have proper documents.

Allowed the INS to enter into agreements with state and local governments for help in investigating, arresting, detaining, and transporting illegal immigrants.

Document Fraud and Alien Smuggling.   Granted wiretap authority to the criminal division of the Justice Department for investigating cases of immigration document fraud.

Created felonies for alien smuggling for up to ten years in prison for the first and second offenses, and fifteen years for subsequent offenses; and making it a crime with up to five years in prison for employers who knowingly hired ten people or more who were smuggled into the United States.

Created twenty-five positions for assistant U.S. attorneys to prosecute cases of alien smuggling and document fraud.

Granted broad authority for the INS to conduct undercover operations to track organized illegal immigration rings that allowed the INS to create or acquire companies, deposit funds in bank accounts without regard to federal regulations, and use profits from such front companies.

Increased the penalty for document fraud from five years to ten or fifteen years in most cases; and if fraud was used in facilitating a drug trafficking crime, a new penalty of twenty years in prison, and if involving terrorism, a new penalty of twenty-five years.

Created a civil penalty for hiring someone to make a false application for public benefits such as food stamps, and created a criminal penalty for "knowingly and willfully" failing to disclose it, punishable by up to fifteen years.

Created a criminal penalty of up to five years in prison for falsely claiming U.S. citizenship.

Created a criminal penalty for up to one year in prison for unlawfully voting in a federal election.

Allowed courts, in imposing sentences against violators of immigration statutes, to seize vehicles, boats, airplanes, and real estate if they were used in the commission of a crime or profit from the proceeds of a crime.

Increased the penalty from five years in prison to ten years for employers who kept workers in a state of involuntary servitude.

Allowed INS agents to subpoena witnesses and to videotape testimony at deportation proceedings.

Detention and Deportation.   Barred any alien who had been deported from reentry into the United States for five years; and up to ten years if the alien left while deportation proceedings were in progress or attempted to reenter the country unlawfully; and barred repeat offenders for two years, and people convicted of aggravated felonies.

Denied legal status to anyone who resided in the United States unlawfully for at least 180 days; and persons so convicted could not gain legal status for three years. People in the country illegally for a year or more could not become legal for ten years, except for minors or persons with a pending application for asylum, or were battered women and children, or were people granted protection under the family unity provision of the 1990 Act, or spouses and minor children granted amnesty under the Immigration Reform and Control Act of 1986 to stay in the United States even if they entered illegally, while their application for legal status was pending.

Allowed people who arrived in the United States without legitimate documentation to be detained and deported without hearing unless they could demonstrate a credible fear of persecution back home. An asylum officer was to screen each case and if decided there was no credible fear, could summarily deport the applicant. The applicant could request a review by an immigration judge within seven days, during which time the applicant had to remain in detention.

Required the detention of most illegal aliens serving criminal sentences after their prison terms were completed. The attorney general could release certain illegal immigrants from detention centers if there was insufficient space and if he determined their release did not pose a security risk or a risk of fleeing, or who came from countries that would not take them back.

Streamlined deportation by replacing multiple proceedings with one, allowing proceedings by telephone or teleconference after ten-day notice of a hearing.

Required aliens be deported within ninety days of a deportation order, with mandatory detention during that period. Violent criminals would have to complete their prison terms before being deported; some nonviolent criminal aliens could be deported before their term was up.

Limited judicial review of deportation orders. The state department could discontinue all visas for countries that declined to take back their deported nationals.

Authorized $5 million for a criminal alien tracking center using criminal alien data base authorized in the 1994 crime law (PL 103-322) to be used to assist local governments in identifying criminals who might be deportable.

Advised the president to negotiate bilateral prisoner transfer treaties to allow criminals to serve their terms in their home countries. The secretary of state and attorney general were to report to Congress by April 1, 1997, on the potential for such treaties.

Made a potential immigrant who did not have proof of proper vaccinations inadmissible.

Added stalking, domestic violence, and child abuse to the crimes that made someone deportable.

Permanently barred from entry anyone who renounced his or her citizenship to avoid taxes.

Allowed the attorney general to authorize local law enforcement officials to perform the duties of an immigration officer in the event of a mass influx of immigrants.

Broadened authority of judges to issue deportation orders; allowing someone deported as part of probation or a plea agreement.

Created a pilot program on the use of closed military bases as INS detention centers.

Employee Verification.   Ordered the attorney general to set up three pilot programs—a basic pilot program, a Citizen Attestation Program, and a Machine-Readable Document Pilot Program—to test the effectiveness of workplace verification systems. Participation in the pilot programs by employers would be voluntary; and the attorney general was to choose the states where each program would be tested, though in some cases employers in nonselected states could participate. All federal departments and agencies within the chosen states were required to participate in the program.

Allowed participating employers to contact the INS via telephone, fax, or e-mail, to check job applicant's immigration status. INS was to maintain a database of names, Social Security numbers, and other information useful to verify an applicant's eligibility to work; and the INS was to respond to inquiries within three days, and if the tentative response was that the person was not legal, the INS had ten days to confirm that determination. The program was to be tested in five of the seven states with the largest number of illegal immigrants.

Created a similar program that would allow applicants to bypass the check if they attested that they were U.S. citizens. The penalty for false claims of such was set at five years in prison.

Allowed employers to scan a card into a machine to verify the owner's Social Security number with the INS data base. These were to be placed in states selected by the attorney general in which driver's licenses or other state documents included Social Security numbers that could be read by machine.

Made it harder for the government to sue employers who used immigration laws to discriminate against certain workers, job applicants, or other individuals by placing the burden on the government to show that the employer "acted for the purpose, or with the intent to discriminate" against the individual.

Public Benefits.   Allowed any consular agent to deny an immigrant visa on the basis that the person was likely to become a public charge.

Allowed states to create pilot programs to explore the feasibility of denying driver's licenses to illegal immigrants. The attorney general was to report to Congress on such after three years.

Clarified that Social Security benefits were not to be paid to illegal immigrants.

Ordered the General Accounting Office to study the use of student aid by illegal immigrants and to report on such to Congress within one year of enactment.

Required the GAO to report to Congress within 180 days on the unlawful use of means-tested benefits—such as food stamps and cash welfare—by illegal immigrants.

Amended the new welfare law to permit certain illegal immigrants who were victims of domestic violence to qualify for public benefits.

Amended the welfare law so that nonprofit charitable organizations were no longer required to verify the immigration status of applicants to determine their eligibility for benefits.

Allowed judges to double the monetary penalty and triple the prison terms for anyone who forged or counterfeited any U.S. seal to make a false application for public benefits.

Allowed reimbursement to states and localities for emergency medical care of illegal immigrants, if the care was not already reimbursed via existing federal programs.

Required the secretary of Housing and Urban Development to deny financial assistance through subsidized housing programs to families in which all members were illegal immigrants. If families were split between legal and illegal immigrants, HUD could adjust the size of the benefit to match the percentage of family members who were in the United States legally.

Other Provisions.   Created a crime punishable by prison for performing female genital mutilation.

Required "international matchmaking organizations" to disseminate to their clients information about U.S. immigration laws under penalty of a $20,000 fine for failure to do so; and requiring the attorney general to prepare a report to Congress on the mail-order bride business within a year of enactment.

Required the INS to report by the end of 1996 whether or not the United States had an adequate number of temporary agricultural workers.

Set national standards for birth certificates, driver's licenses, and other identification documents. The Department of Transportation was to set standards for IDs, which had to include Social Security numbers, and agencies issuing them had to keep those numbers on file and confirm their accuracy with the Social Security Administration. The standards were intended to make such documents more tamper-resistant; were to be issued within one year; and to be complied with by October 1, 2000.

Required the Social Security Administration to develop a prototype tamperproof identity card.

Source: Summary by author.

In response to the international terrorist attacks on the New York City World Trade Center and on the Pentagon in Washington, D.C., Congress passed the USA Patriot Act. It was a lengthy bill of 288 pages. Its key immigration-related provisions broadened the definition of terrorism, expanded grounds for inadmissibility to include aliens suspected of terrorist activity or who publicly endorsed such, and required the attorney general to detain aliens whom he certified as threats to national security.

USA Patriot Act of 2001— HR 3162, October 24, 2001

Sec. 102. Sense of Congress Condemning Discrimination against Arab and Muslim Americans.

(a) Congress makes the following findings:

(1) Arab Americans, Muslim Americans, and Americans from South Asia play a vital role and are entitled to nothing less than the full rights of every American.

(2) The acts of violence taken against [them] since September 11, 2001, should be condemned by all Americans who value freedom.

It is the sense of Congress that—

(1) the civil rights and civil liberties of all Americans, including Arab Americans, Muslim Americans, and Americans from South Asia, must be protected, and that every effort made to preserve their safety.

(2) any acts of violence or discrimination against any Americans be condemned;

(3) the Nation is called upon to recognize the patriotism of fellow citizens of all ethnic, racial, and religious backgrounds.

Title IV—Protecting the Border.
This title goes on to the following sections:

Subtitle A—Protecting the Northern Border
Sec. 401—Ensures adequate personnel on the northern border.
Sec. 403—Grants access by the Department of State and the INS to certain identifying records of visa applicants and applicants for admission to the United States.
Sec. 405—Establishes an integrated automated fingerprint identification system for ports of entry and overseas consular posts.

Subtitle B—Enhanced Immigration Provisions
Sec. 411—Defines new definitions relating to terrorism.
Sec. 412—Mandates detention of suspected terrorists; suspends habeas corpus under certain conditions; and limits judicial review.
Sec. 413—Ensures multilateral cooperation against terrorists.
Sec. 414—Provides for increased integrity and security of visas.
Sec. 415—Mandates the participation of the Office of Homeland Security on the Entry-Exit Task Force.
Sec. 416—Establishes a foreign student monitoring program.
Sec. 417—Calls for machine-readable passports.

Subtitle C—Preservation of Immigration Benefits for Victims of Terrorism
Sec. 421—Grants special immigrant status to victims of the 9/11 attacks.
Sec. 423—Grants humanitarian relief for certain surviving spouses and children.
Sec. 427—Denies such benefits to terrorists or family members of terrorists.

Title X—Miscellaneous
Sec. 1006—Provides for the inadmissibility of aliens engaged in money laundering.

Source: http://www.epic.org/privacy/terrorism/hr3162/html.

About a year later, on November 19, 2002, Congress passed the Department of Homeland Security (DHS) Act of 2002. It is a massive law, in excess of 400 printed pages. It merged twenty-two federal agencies and resulted in the most extensive reorganization of the federal bureaucracy since creation of the Department of Defense after World War II. It creates within DHS two bureaus (called directorates), each headed by an undersecretary. The Directorate of Border and Transportation Security is headed by an undersecretary for Border and Transportation Security; and the Bureau of Citizenship and Immigration Services is headed by the undersecretary for Citizenship and Immigration Services. Some key provisions from Title IV of the Act are highlighted below.

H.R. 5005—Homeland Security Act of November 19, 2002

Title IV—Border and Transportation Security.
Subtitle A—General Provisions

Sec. 401. Creates the Under Secretary for Border and Transportation Security.

Sec. 402. Responsibilities —Transfers functions of the INS to the DHS.

The Secretary, acting through the Under Secretary for Border and Transportation Security, shall be responsible for the following:

(1) Preventing the entry of terrorists and the instruments of terrorism into the U.S.

(2) Securing the borders, territorial waters, ports, terminals, waterways, and air, land and sea transportation systems of the United States, including managing and coordinating those functions transferred to the Department at ports of entry.

(3) Carrying out the immigration enforcement functions vested by statute in, or performed by, the Commissioner of Immigration and Naturalization (or any officer, employee, or component of the Immigration and Naturalization Service) immediately before the date on which the transfer of functions specified under section 441 takes effect [March 1, 2003].

(4) Establishing and administering rules, in accordance with section 428, governing the granting of visas or other forms of permissions, including parole, to enter the United States to individuals who are not a citizen or an alien lawfully admitted for permanent residence in the United States.

(5) Establishing national immigration enforcement policies and priorities.

Subtitle B—Immigration and Nationality Functions

Chapter 1 — Immigration Enforcement
Sec. 411. Details the transfer of functions of the Border Patrol, INS, to the Under Secretary for Border and Transportation Security in the DHS.
Sec. 412. Establishes a Bureau of Border Security headed by a Director.
Sec. 415. Calls for a report to Congress on improving enforcement functions.

Chapter 2 — Citizenship and Immigration Services
Subchapter A—Transfer of Functions
Sec. 421. Establishes a Bureau of Citizenship and Immigration Services headed by a Director
Sec. 422. Establishes a Citizenship and Immigration Services Ombudsman office.
Sec. 425. Establishes an Office of Immigration Statistics within Bureau of Justice Statistics.
Sec. 426. Concerns preservation of the Attorney General's authority.
Subchapter B — Other Provisions
Sec. 431. Concerns funding for citizenship and immigration services.
Sec. 432. Calls for elimination of backlogs.
Sec. 433. Requires a report to Congress on efforts at improving immigration services.
Sec. 435. Calls for the application of Internet-based technologies.

Chapter 3—General Provisions
Sec. 41. Abolishes the INS as of March 1, 2003.
Sec. 45. Requires reports and implementation plans to Congress.
Sec. 46. Details immigration functions.

Source: Summary by author.

References

Anderson, James. 1979. *Public Policy Making.* New York: Holt, Rinehart and Winston.

Information Plus. 2001. *Immigration and Illegal Aliens: Burden or Blessing?* Wylie, TX: Information Plus.

_____. 2006. *Immigration and Illegal Aliens: Burden or Blessing?* Detroit: Thomson/Gale.

LeMay, Michael. 2004. *U.S. Immigration: A Reference Handbook.* Santa Barbara, CA: ABC-CLIO.

LeMay, Michael, and Elliott Robert Barkan. 1999. *U.S. Immigration and Naturalization Laws and Issues: A Documentary History.* Westport, CT: Greenwood.

7

Directory of Organizations and Government Agencies

This chapter lists and briefly discusses the major agencies and organizations involved in immigration policy and particularly those concerned with illegal immigration policy reforms. It discusses national domestic government agencies first.

The domestic government section is followed by a list of some of the more important international organizations active in the global scene, with particular emphasis on those involved in refugee issues and concerns. It lists some exemplary organizations found in several of the most significant immigration and refugee receiving nations.

In addition to governmental agencies and organizations, there are numerous important nongovernmental organizations involved (often known as NGOs). This chapter discusses those most active in advocacy for or against immigration and illegal immigration matters. For each organization, it discusses their positions on immigration reform. Finally, the chapter lists and discusses scholarly organizations involved in the policy arena of immigration reform. These are presented as examples of so-called immigration-related "think tanks" or centers for the study of immigration and immigration policy. The chapter provides specific contact information for each organization discussed herein.

National Government Agencies and Organizations

There are many federal agencies involved in the administration and implementation of U.S. immigration policy. They are all involved in immigration policy reform affairs as well, and they have an impact on illegal-immigration reform, either through attempts to control or mitigate illegal immigration, or by indirectly providing service to illegal immigrants. The principal federal agencies are the following:

United States Census Bureau
1100 Vermont Ave., N.W.
Washington, DC 20005
(202) 728–6829
Fax: (301) 457–3620
http://www.census.gov

The bureau collects and does analysis of statistical data on the population, including immigrants. Its data form the basis for the most accurate information available to project or analyze the level and distribution of illegal immigrants throughout the United States and to track trends in the illegal immigration flow over time. Its numerous statistical studies and reports make possible the tracking of all immigrants. Their reports provide demographic data as to the gradual incorporation of immigrants into the major institutions of society.

United States Commission on Civil Rights
1121 Vermont Ave., N.W.
Washington, DC 20425
(202) 376–8177
E-mail: publications@usccr.gov
http://www.admin@usccr.gov.

The commission is an independent, bipartisan, fact-finding agency of the executive branch established under the Civil Rights Act of 1957. It investigates complaints as to discrimination; appraises federal laws and policies with respect to discrimination because of race, color, religion, sex, age, disability, or national origin; studies and collects information relating to such discrimination; serves as a clearinghouse for such information; and submits reports, findings, and recommendations to the president and the Congress, many of which concern rights of immigrants and refugees, the problems generated by the illegal immigration flow, and civil rights guaranteed to all persons, including illegal immigrants, as basic human rights.

United States Commission on Immigration Reform
2430 E Street South Building
Washington, DC 20037
(202) 776–8400; Fax: (202) 776–8635

The commission was a Bipartisan U.S. Commission on Immigration Reform authorized by the Immigration Act of 1990 that was mandated to review and evaluate implementation and impact of U.S. immigration policy and to transmit reports of its findings and recommendations to the U.S. Congress. It issued its first interim report on September 30, 1994, its second interim report in 1995, and two final reports in 1997: *U.S. Refugee Policy: Taking Leadership;* and *Becoming an American: Immigration and Immigration Policy.* Like the SCIRP Commission report of the 1980s, the recommendations contained in these two reports formed the basis for several legislative proposals aimed at better coping with the illegal immigration problem.

United States Department of Agriculture
1400 Independence Ave., S.W.
Washington, DC 20250–7600
Fax: (202) 720–1031
E-mail: IraHobbs@usda.gov
http://www.ocio.usda.gov/

The department's immigration role is largely supportive of other departments and agencies. Given the importance of illegal immigrants to the agricultural sector, particularly the seasonal agricultural workers flow, the Department of Agriculture plays a crucial role in supplying information and data on the need for temporary agricultural workers. It assists immigrants through programs such as its Food and Nutrition Service. Although legally and technically it cannot provide such service to illegal aliens, given the poor quality of documentation control, the department undoubtedly does help, if inadvertently, to provide services to illegal as well as legal immigrants.

United States Department of Education
400 Maryland Ave., S.W.
Washington, DC 20202–5130
(800) USA-LEARN, or (202) 401–2000

Fax: (202) 401–0689
E-mail: customerservice@inet.ed.gov

The department is the agency of the federal government that establishes policy for, administers, and coordinates most federal assistance to education. The immigration role of the department is to assist, supplement, and complement the efforts of states, the local school systems and other state agencies, the private sector, public and private educational institutions, public and private nonprofit educational research institutions, and community-based organizations to serve the educational needs of immigrants, particularly in the educational aspects of the naturalization process. By federal law and especially as the result of several critical court decisions, education must be provided to the children of illegal immigrants despite the status of the parents. Federal programs that assist local school districts, in providing health services or school lunch programs, for example, are therefore extended to the children of illegal immigrants as well as to those whose parents are in the United States as permanent legal residents.

United States Department of Health and Human Services
Office of Refugee Resettlement
370 L'Enfant Promenade, S.W.
Washington, DC 20447
(202) 401–9246
Fax (202) 401–5487
http://www.acf.dhhs.gov/programs/orr

HHS impacts immigration and refugee policy through their administration of such programs as the Administration for Children and Families; Health Care Financing Administration; Division of State Legalization Assistance; Financial Support Administration; U.S. Public Health Service Office of Refugee Health; and Office of Planning, Research and Evaluation. Their intergovernmental role is significant in coping with illegal immigration. They were important actors involved with the implementation of IRCA and its program, SLIAG, aimed particularly at the legalization programs of IRCA. Should some sort of guest-worker program involving the "earned legalization" proposals of that legislation be in fact enacted into law, HHS would undoubtedly again have a major role in its implementation.

United States Department of Homeland Security
425 I Street, N.W.
Washington, DC 20536
(202) 514–1900; Fax (202) 514–3296
http://www.usdhs.gov

Established in 2002 and in the process of merging the functions of many federal agencies into this newest cabinet-level department of the federal bureaucracy, the new DHS, as of March 1, 2003, is now the principal agency to administer immigration-related policy. Its immigration-related functions are implemented by two bureaus headed by an undersecretary: a Bureau of Border and Transportation Security, and a Bureau of Citizenship and Immigration Services.

The Department of HS deals with all visa, passport, and citizenship matters; monitors all U.S. borders; ensures mass transit security and provides airport and seaport security. It supervises the U.S. Border Patrol operations, the principal agency charged with controlling the illegal immigration flow and problem. Its antiterrorism responsibilities also involve monitoring the illegal immigration flow for suspected terrorist and terrorist cells. It has newly established policy related to bioterrorism, as well, that overlaps its illegal immigration control functions.

United States Department of Housing and Urban Development
451 7th Street, S.W.
Washington, DC 20410
(202) 708–1112; Fax: (202) 708–1455
E-mail: CA_Webmanager@hud.gov
http://www.hud.gov

HUD's mission is to promote a decent, safe, sanitary, and suitable home environment for every American. Its impact on immigration matters is primarily through programs designed to assist low-income persons, to create, rehabilitate and maintain the nation's affordable housing, to enforce fair housing laws, to help the homeless, to spur economic growth in distressed neighborhoods, and to help local communities meet their development needs. Federal law specifically bans the provisions of HUD aid to illegal aliens, but the extensiveness of document fraud in the matter likely results in their providing some benefits to persons who are in fact in the United States illegally.

United States Department of Labor
Bureau of International Labor Affairs
200 Constitution Ave., NW
Room S-2235
Washington, DC 20210
(202) 693–4770
http://www.dol.gov/dol/ilab

The department oversees all labor-related policy and law, including matters related to temporary labor. Other agencies within the department with immigration-related policy roles are its Office of Federal Contract Compliance Program and its Wage and Hour Division. Its role related to the implementation of IRCA, to date the most directly related federal program attempting to control and decrease illegal immigration, was significant. Strict enforcement of U.S. labor laws may be one of the more effective ways to discourage employers from using the "cheap" labor source of undocumented workers. The department also plays a role in informing Congress or in certifying the need for temporary workers. It would play an important role in any new guest-worker program. Its data collection has helped certify the extent of discrimination against workers who are or were suspected of being undocumented workers.

United States Department of State
Bureau of Population, Refugees, and Migration
2401 E Street, N.W., Suite L-505, SA-1
Washington, DC 20522–0105
(202) 647–8472
E-mail: askpublicaffairs@state.gov
http://www.state.gov/prm
See also: Bureau of Migration and Refugee Affairs; and their Bureau of Consular Affairs.

The Department of State is primarily involved in legal immigration, of course, but its consular affairs division, which issues visas, has a role in illegal immigration mostly related to visa overstayers. It has occasionally been embroiled in scandals in which "sting operations" have led to consular officials who have been caught selling visas and work certification cards (green cards) to illegal aliens, allowing them to enter the country with false documents or work authorizations.

United States Equal Employment Opportunity Commission
1801 L Street, N.W.
Washington, DC 20507
(202) 663–4900; Fax: (202) 663–4494
http://www.eeoc.gov

Housed within the Department of Health and Human Services, the EEOC administers three basic programs: an affirmative employment program; special emphasis/diversity programs; and the discrimination complaint program. They attempt to promote and ensure equal opportunity for all employees and foster a culture and environment free from discrimination. They impact illegal immigration primarily through their antidiscrimination program and monitor the employer sanctions provisions of current policy.

United States Government Accountability Office
441 G Street, N.W.
Washington, DC 20548
(202) 512–5400; Fax: (202) 512–6000
E-mail: gao.gov
http://www.gao.gov

The Government Accountability Office is an agency that works for the U.S. Congress and the American people. Congress asks GAO to study the programs and expenditures of the federal government. The GAO is commonly called the investigative arm of Congress or the congressional watchdog. It is independent and nonpartisan. It studies how the federal government spends taxpayer dollars, and advises Congress and the heads of executive departments about ways to make government more effective and responsive. It evaluates federal programs, audits federal expenditures, and issues legal opinions, many of which over recent years have focused on the INS and the DOJ's efforts and programs related to illegal immigration law and policy. Its reports are among the most reliable estimates of the size, nature, and impact of illegal immigration on the economy, on state and local government finances and services, and on society more generally. A number of their reports directly linked to the illegal immigration problem are listed in the print sources of Chapter Eight.

United States House Committee on the Judiciary
Subcommittee on Immigration, Border Security and Claims
B370B Rayburn House Office Building
Washington, DC 20515
(202) 225–5727
http://www.house.gov/judiciary

This standing committee of the U.S. House of Representatives deals with all bills introduced to the Congress that concern immigration law and policy matters. Its members have become leading voices in efforts to reform policy to deal with illegal immigration and border control and security issues particularly.

United States Senate Committee on the Judiciary
Subcommittee on Immigration, Border Security and Citizenship
Room SD-323
Dirksen Senate Office Building
Washington, DC 20510
(202) 224–6098
http://www.senate.gov/~judiciary

This standing committee of the U.S. Senate deals with all legislative matters concerning immigration policy and law. Like its counterpart in the House, its members and staff become principal actors in the illegal immigration reform effort. While both the House and the Senate committees are strongly supportive of efforts to beef up the Border Patrol and increase border security at airports and seaports, the Senate Judiciary Subcommittee has been notably more amenable to a guest-worker program than has its counterpart in the House.

United States Social Security Administration
Office of Public Inquiries
Windsor Park Building
6401 Security Blvd.
Baltimore, MD 21235
(800) 772–1213; Fax: (800) 325–0778
E-mail: webmaster@ssa.gov
http://www.ssa.gov/reach.htm

The SSA's role in immigration policy matters is also supportive of other agencies. Its data bank is used to verify a person's identity and to guard against fraud, waste, abuse, and mismanagement in administration of the benefit programs based upon contributory financing of social insurance programs to ensure that protection was available as a matter of right as contrasted with a public assistance approach whereby only those persons in need would be eligible for benefits, whether natural-born citizens, naturalized citizens, or legal resident aliens who had worked and contributed into the system. As a system, it collects benefit payments from all workers, including illegal aliens, who pay into the system. The large number of illegal workers who pay into the system yet who do not withdraw benefits from it results in a net benefit estimated to be in the billions of dollars annually. Given the increasing age of the citizen workforce, the illegal aliens, who generally are much younger and therefore work longer and pay into the system for longer periods of time, are significant in filling the gap or shortfall between income and payments out of the system. In no small measure, these estimated billions of dollars in contributions from illegal workers help to keep the Social Security system solvent. Although they are only a stopgap factor in the financial strength of the Social Security system, their impact is nonetheless important. If policy designed to cut off that illegal alien flow were to be efficient, the Social Security system would suffer a noticeable decrease of considerable size.

International Agencies and Organizations

Amnesty International
5 Penn Plaza
New York, NY 10001
(212) 807–8400
http://www.amnestyusa.org

Founded in London in 1961, Amnesty International is now a Nobel Prize–winning grassroots activist organization with nearly 2 million members worldwide. Amnesty International supports research and grassroots action focused on preventing and ending grave abuses of the rights to physical and mental integrity, freedom of conscience and expression, and freedom from discrimination, within the context of its work to promote all human rights. Amnesty International USA is the U.S. section of Amnesty International.

Human Rights Watch
350 Fifth Ave., 34th Floor
New York, NY 10118–3299
(212) 290–4700; Fax: (212) 736–1300
E-mail: hrwnyc@hrw.org
http://www.hrw.org

An organization dedicated to protecting human rights of people around the world, it stands with victims and activists to prevent discrimination, to uphold political freedom, and to protect people from inhumane conduct in wartime and bring offenders to justice. It investigates and exposes human rights violations and holds abusers accountable, challenging governments to respect international human rights laws. It is an independent, nongovernmental organization supported by private individuals and foundations worldwide. It plays a critical role in providing information on the exploitation of illegal immigrant workers in many countries around the world. It has been critical in the past of procedures of the United States dealing with expedited removal and with the way in which claims of "fears of persecution" have been handled with respect to persons applying for refugee status; it strongly criticized the manner in which Haitian refugees were detained and processed.

Inter-American Development Bank
1300 New York Ave., N.W.
Washington, DC 20577
(202) 623–3096; Fax: (202) 623–3096
http://www.iadb.org/

The Inter-American Development Bank is a long-standing initiative of various Latin American countries first established in 1959. It has become the model of development institutions having issued novel mandates and tools. It lends technical cooperation programs for economic and social development projects that go beyond mere financing of economic projects. Its innovations became the model on which virtually all other regional and subregional multilateral development institutions were created. It is the oldest and largest regional development bank and a major source of multilateral financing for economic, social, and institutional development, as well as trade and regional integration programs in Latin America and the Caribbean region. To the extent that its developmental projects are successful, it helps to lessen the push factors compelling international migration, particularly illegal immigration. Likewise, its failures or shortcomings help to fuel the mass migration north to the United States.

International Committee of the Red Cross
801 Second Ave., 18th Floor
New York, NY 10017
(212) 599–6021; Fax: (212) 599–6009.
[For United States and Canada]:
2100 Pennsylvania Ave., N.W., Suite 545
Washington, DC 20037
(202) 239–9340
E-mail: washington.was@icrc.com
http://www.icrc.org

Established in 1863, the ICRC is an impartial, neutral, and independent organization whose exclusively humanitarian mission is to protect the lives and dignity of victims of war and internal violence and to provide them with assistance. It also directs and coordinates the international relief activities of the Red Crescent Movement in situations of conflict. It endeavors to prevent suffering by promoting and strengthening humanitarian law and universal humanitarian principles. It plays an especially important role in dealing with refugees. In the post-Tsunami and post-Katrina natural disasters, it provided relief to survivors without regard to their legal status as residents.

International Immigrants Foundation
1435 Broadway, 2nd Floor
New York, NY 10018–1909
(212) 302–2222; Fax: (212) 221–7206

E-mail: info@10.org
http://www.10.org

Founded in 1973, the IIF has consultative status with the UN Economic and Social Affairs Council, and is associated with the Department of Public Information as a charitable, nongovernmental, nonpolitical, nonprofit tax-exempt organization. Its stated mission is to help immigrant families and children to achieve their aspirations for a better life in the United States. It does so without regard to and without checking on the legal status of the immigrant. The organization addresses its mission by providing support to promote positive intercultural relations. It supports family reunification goals of legal immigration policy and supports legalization programs as a more effective way to bring illegal immigrants out of the shadow of illegality.

UN Department of Humanitarian Affairs
UN Headquarters
New York, NY 10017
(212) 963–4832; Fax: (202) 963–1388

The UN Department of Humanitarian Affairs, established by the General Assembly, was created to "mobilize and coordinate the collective efforts of the international community, in particular those of the UN system, to meet in a coherent and timely manner the needs of those exposed to human suffering and material destruction in disasters and emergencies. This involves reducing vulnerability, promoting solutions to root causes and facilitating the smooth transition from relief to rehabilitation and development."

UN High Commissioner for Refugees
1775 K Street, N.W., Suite 300
Washington, DC 20006–1502
(202) 296–5191; Fax: (202) 296–5660
E-mail: usawa@unhcr.ch
http://www.unhcr.ch

The UN agency responsible for all matters relating to refugees, it leads and coordinates international action for the worldwide protection of refugees and the resolution of refugee problems. Its primary purpose is to safeguard the rights and well-being of refugees, the right to asylum and safe refuge in another state, and the right to return home voluntarily. It was established by the 1951 UN Convention relating to the Status of Refugees and its 1967 protocol. It seeks to reduce situations of forced displacement by encouraging states and other institutions to create conditions that are conducive to the protection of human rights and the peaceful resolution of disputes, assists the reintegration of returning refugees into their country of origin, and offers protection and assistance to refugees and others in an impartial manner, on the basis of their need irrespective of their race, religion, political opinion, gender, or legal status in the host nation. It pays particular attention to the needs of children and seeks to promote the equal rights of women and girls. See also the related agencies: UN Relief and Works Agency for Palestine; International Organization for Migration; World Food Programme.

Domestic Advocacy Agencies and Organizations

American Bar Association
750 N. Lake Shore Drive/740 15th Street, N.W.
Chicago, IL 60611/Washington, DC 20005–1019
Chicago: (312) 988–5000/DC: (202) 662–1000
E-mail: askaba@abanet.org
http://www.abanet.org/about/home.html

The ABA claims to be the largest voluntary professional association in the world, with more than 400,000 members. It provides law school accreditation, promotes education and information about the law, offers programs of assistance to lawyers and judges in their work, and sponsors initiatives to improve the legal system for the public. Its members defend refugees and persons charged with being in the national illegally. It advocates for legalization programs as a more fair, sensible, and effective policy to deal with the illegal immigration problem.

American Civil Liberties Union
125 Broad St., 18th Floor
New York, NY 10004
(212) 549–2500
E-mail: aclu@aclu.org
http://www.aclu.org

The ACLU works nationally and with local chapters to protect the civil rights of citizens as guaranteed in the U.S. Constitution. It annually publishes many policy statements, pamphlets, studies, and reports on civil rights issues. Its newsletter, *Civil Liberties Alert*, is published semiannually. It has been a leading coalition partner in efforts to reform or amend the USA Patriot Act, and to rectify what it determines are civil rights abuses in procedural matters dealing with the process to remove illegal aliens in an expedited manner. It has been an active member of the coalition to promote a guest-worker program and legalization proposals more generally.

American Conservative Union
Cameron Street
Alexandria, VA 22314
(703) 836–8602
Fax: (703) 836–8606
http://www.conservative.org

The American Conservative Union is the oldest and largest of the numerous conservative lobbying organizations. Its purpose is to communicate effectively and advance the goals and principles of conservatism through one multi-issue, umbrella organization. ACU supports capitalism, belief in the doctrine of original intent of the framers of the Constitution, confidence in traditional moral values, and commitment to a strong national defense. Since 1994 it has sponsored "town meetings" to spearhead the conservative response to the health care reform issue, and since then has used the approach to support issues such as military protection, defending the homeland, and against more liberal immigration policy reforms. It rates the members of Congress according to their votes on issues of concern to conservatives; those ratings are used in a host of almanac and reference guides across the political spectrum. Its rating system has been copied by many other organizations. It publishes a significant amount of print, audio, and video material and television documentaries to promote public opinion on its issues of concern. Since 1974 it has hosted the Conservative Political Action Conference, where thousands of conservative activists and leaders from across the country discuss current issues and controversies.

American Immigration Control Foundation
P.O. Box 525
Monterey, VA 24465
(540) 468–2022
Fax: (540) 468–2024
E-mail: aicfndn@cfw.com
http://www.aicfoundation.com/index.htm

The AIC Foundation is a nonprofit research and educational organization whose stated primary goal is to inform Americans about the need for a reasonable immigration policy based on the nation's interests and needs. It is a large publisher of publications on America's immigration crisis. Founded in 1983, it is a prominent national voice for immigration control and is committed to educating citizens on the disastrous effects of uncontrolled immigration, and most particularly advocates for reform to better control illegal immigration. Besides its lobbying activity for immigration control, AIC conducts public education campaigns to influence public opinion of the issue, campaigning through direct mail, paid advertisements, opinion surveys, and public appearances by its spokesmen on radio and television. Its president is Robert Goldsborough, who also is a columnist with *Middle America News.*

American Immigration Law Foundation
918 F Street, N.W.
Washington, DC 20004
(202) 742–5600
Fax: (202) 742–5619
E-mail: info@ailf.org
http://www.ailf.org/about.htm

Founded in 1987 as a tax-exempt, not-for-profit educational and service organization, its stated mission is to promote understanding among the general public of immigration law and policy through education, policy analysis, and support to litigators. It has three core program areas: the Legal Action Center, the Public Education Program, and an Exchange Visitor Program.

American Immigration Lawyers Association
1400 I Street, N.W., Suite 1200
Washington, DC 2005
(202) 371–9377
Fax: (202) 371–9449
E-mail: webmaster@aila.org
http://www.aila.org

The American Immigration Lawyers Association is the national association of immigration lawyers established to promote justice, advocate for fair and reasonable immigration law and policy, advance the quality of immigration and nationality law and practice, and enhance the professional development of its members. Its members defend individuals charged with being in the United States illegally and in deportation hearings. It advocates against what it considers unfair or anti–civil liberty provisions in immigration law, particularly the USA Patriot Act and the Department of Homeland Security Act.

American Library Association
50 E. Huron
Chicago, IL 60611
(800) 545–2433
T.D.D.: (888) 814–7692
e-mail: library@ala.org
http://www.ala.org/

ALA is the oldest and largest library association in the world, with more than 64,000 members. Its stated mission is to promote the highest quality library and information service and public access to information. ALA offers professional services and publications to members and nonmembers. It recently entered the fray by joining in coalition with other organizations attempting to amend the USA Patriot Act.

American Refugee Committee International
Headquarters USA
430 Oak Grove St., Suite 204
Minneapolis, MN 55404
(612) 872–7060

Fax: (612) 872–4309
E-mail: archq@archq.org
http://www.archq.org/

Begun in 1978, the ARC's stated mission is to work for the survival, health, and well-being of refugees, displaced persons, and those at risk, and its seeks to enable them to rebuild productive lives of dignity and purpose, striving always to respect the values of those served. ARC is an international, nonprofit, and nonsectarian organization that has provided multisectoral humanitarian assistance and training to millions of beneficiaries for more than twenty years.

Border Sanctuary
Scalabrinian Missionaries
Father Richard Zanotti
Our Lady of the Holy Rosary Church
Via Calandrelli, 42–00153 Roma
Rome, Italy 7800
Phone: 06.58.33.11.35
Fax: 06.580.38.08
http://www.scalabrini.org

Run by the Scalabrini Order of the Roman Catholic Church, Border Sanctuary manages the Casa del Migrantes (Immigrants' House) in Tijuana, Mexico, where migrants can find a bed and three meals per day on their journey toward or away from the United States. The shelter welcomes all migrant men and is used primarily by Mexicans and other Latin Americans leaving the United States or trying to make their way—legally or illegally—into the United States. In 2002, Casa del Migrantes housed 4,700 men, about half of whom were deported from the United States. The Scalabrini Order is the only order within the Catholic Church devoted exclusively to immigrants and migrants. It has a worldwide presence with about 600 priests in more than twenty countries. Founded in 1886 in Italy when there was mass migration to the United States, the priests went where the Italians were migrating to provide spiritual and practical support. In the 1960s, the order changed its focus to include all migrants, not only Italians. The priests do not seek information from individuals as to their legal status, helping those in need, often with people arriving who have only the clothes on their backs. They provide food, shelter, and clothing; help the men find temporary work; and provide medical attention, legal assistance, and spiritual guidance.

Business Roundtable
1615 L Street, N.W., Suite 1100
Washington, DC 20036
(202) 872–1260
http://www.brtable.org/newsroom_about.htm

The Business Roundtable is the association of chief executive officers of leading U.S. corporations with a combined workforce of more than 10 million employees in the United States. It is committed to advocating public policies that foster vigorous economic growth, a dynamic global economy, and a well-trained and productive U.S. workforce essential for future competitiveness. The Roundtable is selective in the issues it studies; a principal criterion is the impact the problem will have on the economic well-being of the nation. Working in task forces on specific issues, it directs research, supervises the preparation of position papers, recommends policy, and lobbies Congress and the administration on selected issues. It supports proposals to establish a guest-worker program, including "earned legalization" provisions.

Catholic Charities USA
1731 King Street
Alexandria, VA 22314
(703) 549–1390
Fax: (703) 549–1656
http://www.catholiccharitiesusa.org/who/index/htm

Catholic Charities USA is a membership organization based in Alexandria, Virginia. It provides leadership, technical assistance, training, and other resources to enable local agencies to better devote their own resources to serving their communities. It promotes innovative strategies that address human needs and social injustices. It advocates policies that aim to reduce poverty, improve the lives of children and families, and strengthen communities. One of its major service programs involves refugee and immigration assistance.

Center for the Applied Study of Prejudice and Ethnoviolence
Stephens Hall Annex
Towson State University
Towson, MD 21204–7097

The Center examines responses to violence and intimidation based on prejudice—racial, ethnic, and so on. It issues a quarterly newsletter, *Forum,* as well as periodic reports and study papers. It is critical of efforts to control illegal immigration that it sees as often resulting from racial and ethnic prejudice against "undesirable" aliens.

Center for Democracy and Technology
1634 I Street, N.W., Suite 1100
Washington, DC 20006
(202) 637–9800
Fax: (202) 637–0968
http://www.cdt.org/

The Center for Democracy and Technology works to promote democratic values and constitutional liberties in the digital age. With expertise in law, technology, and policy, the CDT seeks practical solutions to enhance free expression and privacy in global communications technologies. CDT states that it is dedicated to building a consensus among all parties interested in the future of the Internet and other new communications media. It has become a lobbying organization on the issue and has joined in coalition with other organizations concerned with civil liberty issues around the DHS, the USA Patriot Act, and Patriot Act II.

Center for Human Rights and Constitutional Law
256 S. Occidental Blvd.
Los Angeles, CA
(213) 388–8693
http://www.reachout.org/losangeles/children/center.html

The CFHRCL Homeless Youth Project is the organization that helps homeless twelve to seventeen-year-old inner-city youth to find an alternative to life on the streets. It provides case management, job assistance, individual counseling, placement assistance, school placement, legal and medical referrals, life skills training, and aftercare. Of particular importance to immigrants, it assists in ESL classes, tutoring, clerical, recreation, outdoor activities, art, gardening, and a variety of other assignments. It does so without regard to the legal status of the immigrant being so served.

Center for the Study of Hate Crimes and Extremism
California State University–San Bernardino
5500 University Parkway
San Bernardino, CA 92407–2397
(909) 880–7711
Fax: (909) 880-7025

A nonpartisan, domestic research and policy center that examines bigotry on both the regional and national levels, methods used to advocate extremism, and the use of terrorism to deny civil or human rights to people on the basis of race, ethnicity, religion, gender, sexual orientation, disability, or other relevant status characteristic. It sponsors public conferences, collaborates with international news media, and maintains an Internet site with information about and in cooperation with government organizations, human relations organizations, nonprofit organizations, and law enforcement.

Central American Resource Center
91 N. Franklin St., Suite 211
Hempstead, NY 11550
(516) 489-8330

A nonprofit immigration and human rights organization serving the refugee community on Long Island and throughout the southern portion of the state of New York. Founded in 1983, it works to protect the civil rights of immigrants, increase understanding between the native-born and newcomer communities, and raise awareness of the interaction of human rights disasters and immigration. It provides its services to persons without regard to their legal status.

Church World Service
28606 Phillips St.
P.O. Box 968
Elkhart, IN 46515
(800) 297–1516; Fax: (219) 262–0966

E-mail: cws@nccusa.org
http://www.churchworldservice.org

Founded in 1946, the CWS is the relief, development, and refugee assistance ministry of thirty-six Protestant, Orthodox, and Anglican denominations in the United States. Working with indigenous organizations in more than eighty countries, it works worldwide to meet human needs and to foster self-reliance for all whose way is hard. One of its major programs is Immigration and Refugee Services. It advocates for more liberalized immigration policy and provides relief assistance to individuals without regard to their legal status. It supports "sanctuary" programs and provides emergency medical assistance to illegal immigrants. Critics allege that its sanctuary programs in fact promote and encourage illegal immigration. It works in coalition with other organizations to reform immigration law in a more fair and humanitarian way.

Colorado Alliance for Immigration Reform
http://www.cairoco.org/

This organization, largely a website to organize a coalition of groups and persons concerned about illegal immigration, is a nonprofit, Colorado-based organization that developed in response to the growing number of immigrants, and particularly illegal immigrants, who have dispersed to states beyond the traditional "gateway states." It is exemplary of similar coalitions that have sprung up in many states newly experiencing significant immigration influxes. CAIR promotes a proactive national policy to stabilize the population and conserve natural resources by insisting that Congress limit legal immigration (not to exceed 100,000 per year) and to crack down firmly on illegal immigration. It considers that both major political parties are supporting an "open borders" policy, which it adamantly opposes. It organizes protests and anti-immigration rallies focusing on the negative impacts of illegal immigration. It has been a leading supporter of Colorado congressman Tom Tancredo. It sponsors "Defend Colorado Now"—a ballot initiative that would amend Colorado's constitution to require that persons who are trying to access certain public services be required to show that they are present in the United States legally—a Colorado version of California's Proposition 187. It advocates an immigration moratorium, no more amnesty programs, strict enforcement of immigration laws both at the borders and in the interior, enhanced employer sanctions, and, through the ballot-initiative process, ending government-sponsored benefits and entitlements for illegal immigrants. It promotes a U.S. constitutional amendment that would deny citizenship to children of illegal immigrants born in the United States. It has launched educational billboard campaigns and, most recently, the Colorado Alliance News, an all-volunteer news service, to promote its views on the immigration issue. Among its more notable directors is former Colorado governor Richard Lamm.

Episcopal Migration Ministries
Episcopal Church Center
815 Second Ave.
New York, NY 10017
(212) 867–8400; (800) 334–7626
E-mail: jbutterfield@episcopalchurch.org
http://www.ecusa.anglican.org/emm

The EMM serves as the organizational arm of the Episcopal Church in all matters related to immigration and migration relief and assistance, and works in close consultation and coalition with other churches in pursuing humanitarian immigration policy and providing assistance and even sanctuary to persons accused of or suspected of being in the United States illegally.

Essential Worker Immigration Coalition
1615 H Street, N.W.
Washington, DC 20062
(202) 463–5931

Supported by the U.S. Chamber of Commerce, the EWIC is a coalition of business groups, trade associations, and other organizations nationwide and across the industrial spectrum concerned about the shortage of both skilled and less skilled ("essential worker") labor. It lobbies the administration and the Congress to push forward immigration reform issues. It supports policies that facilitate the employment of essential workers by U.S. companies and organizations—that is, a guest-worker program. It advocates reforming U.S. immigration policy to facilitate a sustainable workforce for the national economy while ensuring national security and prosperity.

Ethiopian Community Development Council
1038 South Highland St.
Arlington, VA 22204
(703) 685–0510
Fax: (703) 685–0529
E-mail: ecdc@erols.com
http://www.ecdcinternational.org

The ECDC's stated mission is to resettle refugees, promote cultural, educational, and socioeconomic development in the refugee and immigrant community in the United States, and conduct humanitarian and development programs in the Horn of Africa. It provides programs and services to assist newcomers to the United States to become productive members of their community; conducts outreach and educational activities to increase public awareness of refugee and immigrant issues; promotes civic participation by newcomers in the decision-making processes of local, state, and national levels; provides cross-cultural training to service providers; and assists in educational development and cultural preservation of the Ethiopian community. It does so without regard to the legal status of the immigrant or refugee being served.

Federal Immigration Reform and Enforcement Coalition
http://www.firecoalition.com/
info@firecoalition.com

Largely a website approach to coalition building, FIRE is an offshoot of AIC. It claims to be a nationwide coalition of individuals and groups dedicated to influencing federal, state, and local law to stop the flood of immigration and to promote policies to limit and control legal immigration. It pushes government to vigorous enforcement of immigration laws, the repatriation of illegal immigrants, and the removal of all incentives for individuals to illegally cross the borders through the enforcement and strengthening of existing laws penalizing those who employ or harbor illegal immigrants, and to inform public opinion as to the consequences of illegal immigration. It describes itself as a nonpartisan, direct-action, public education, and political campaigning coalition.

Federation for American Immigration Reform
Ira Mehlman, FAIR Spokesman
1666 Connecticut Ave., N.W., Suite 400
Washington, DC
(202) 328–7004;
Fax: (202) 386–3447
E-mail: info@fairus.org
http://www.fairus.org/

Founded in 1979, FAIR is a national, nonpartisan, nonprofit, public-interest membership organization of concerned citizens who share a common belief that the unforeseen mass immigration that has occurred over the past thirty years should be curtailed. It advocates a moratorium on all immigration except for spouses and minor children of U.S. citizens, and a limited number of refugees. In its view, a workable immigration policy is one that allows time to regain control of the U.S. borders and reduce overall levels of immigration to more traditional levels of about 300,000 a year. It believes that the United States can and must have an immigration policy that is nondiscriminatory while at the same time is designed to serve the social, economic, and environmental needs of the U.S.

Free Congress Foundation
717 Second St., N.E.
Washington, DC 20002
(202) 546–3000
Fax: (202) 543–5605
http://www.freecongress.org/

Free Congress is a politically conservative, culturally conservative "think tank" that is more of an advocacy organization that promotes the "Culture War" and advocates returning the nation and its policies to the traditional, Judeo-Christian, Western cultural heritage by stopping what it calls the long slide into the moral and cultural decay of "political correctness." It is strenuously opposed to illegal immigration and to any amnesty or legalization policy; favors strict enforcement of immigration law and English-only policy; and rejects multiculturalism.

Freedom Works
1775 Pennsylvania Ave., N.W., 11th Floor
Washington, DC 2006–5805

(202) 783–3870
Fax: (202) 942–7649
Toll free: (888) 564–6273
http://www.freedomworks.org

Founded in 1984, Freedom Works has full-time staffed offices in ten states. It claims to be a coalition of some 700,000 volunteers nationwide. The organization is chaired by former U.S. House majority leader Dick Armey. It fights for lower taxes, less government, and more freedom. It has strongly backed a private business–based approach to a guest-worker program developed by the Krieble Foundation.

Hebrew Immigrant Aid Society
337 7th Ave., 17th Floor
New York, NY 10001
(212) 967–4100; Fax: (212) 967–4483
E-mail: info@hias.org
http://www.hias.org

Founded in 1881, HIAS has assisted more than 4.5 million people in their quest for freedom, including the million Jewish refugees it helped to migrate to Israel and the thousands it helped resettle in Canada, Latin America, Australia, New Zealand, and elsewhere. As the oldest international migration and refugee resettlement agency in the United States, HIAS played a major role in the rescue and relocation of Jewish survivors of the Holocaust and Jews from Morocco, Ethiopia, Egypt, and the communist countries of Eastern Europe. It advocates on behalf of refugees and migrants on the international, national, and community level. It provides its services without regard to the legal status of the immigrant being assisted. It works in coalition with other church organizations of immigrant/refugee assistance and has lobbied on behalf of legislation aimed at reforming immigration law in a more liberal approach. It favors legalization and guest-worker programs.

Heritage Foundation
241 Massachusetts Ave., N.E.
Washington, DC 20002–4999
(202) 546–4400
Fax: (202) 546–8328
http://www.heritage.org

The Heritage Foundation was founded in 1973 as a research and educational institute—one of the early "think tanks." Its stated mission is to formulate and propose conservative public policies that are based upon the principles of free enterprise, limited government, individual freedom, traditional American values, and a strong national defense. On the illegal immigration issue, it promotes immigration reform that lessens total legal immigration levels, strengthens the enforcement of laws against illegal immigration, opposes amnesty, and increases border control to better secure the homeland against international terrorism.

Humane Borders
740 E. Speed Blvd.
Tucson, AZ 85719
(520) 628–7753
E-mail: info@humaneborders.org
http://www.humaneborders.org/

The mission statement of Humane Borders describes it as an organization of people motivated by faith and committed to work to create a just and humane border environment. Its members respond with humanitarian assistance to those who are risking their lives and safety crossing the U.S. border with Mexico. It encourages the creation of public policies toward a humane, nonmilitarized border with legalized work opportunities for migrants in the United States and legitimate economic opportunities in migrants' countries of origin. It favors legalization and guest-worker programs. It lobbies and advocates in coalition with other organizations promoting more liberalized immigration policy.

Jesuit Relief Service/USA
1616 P Street, N.W., Suite 400
Washington, DC 20036
(202) 462–5200; Fax: (202) 462–7009
Jesuit Relief Services International
C.P. 6139
I-00195 Roma Prati, Italy
Tel.: 39–066977386

Fax: 39–066806418
E-mail: international@jrs.net
http://www.jrsref.org/refugee/jrs.htm

The Jesuit Refugee Service is an international Catholic organization working in more than forty countries to accompany, serve, and defend the rights of refugees and forcibly displaced people. It embraces all who are driven from their homes by conflict, humanitarian disaster, or violation of human rights, following Catholic social teaching, which applies the expression "de facto refugee" to many categories of people. It does so without regard to the legal status of the immigrant or refugee being served.

League of United Latin American Citizens (LULAC)
201 East Main Drive, Suite 605
El Paso, TX 79901
(915) 577–0726
Fax: (915) 577–0914
http://www.lulac.org/About/Creeds/html

LULAC is organized to promote the democratic principle of individual political and religious freedom, the right of equality of social and economic opportunity, and in the cooperative endeavor toward the development of a U.S. society wherein the cultural resources, integrity, and dignity of every individual and group constitute basic assets of the American way of life. Among its goals are to be a service organization to actively promote and establish cooperative relations with civic and governmental institutions and agencies in the field of public service, to uphold the rights guaranteed to every individual by state and national laws, to ensure justice and equal treatment under those laws, and to oppose any infringement upon the constitutional political rights of an individual to vote and or be voted upon at local, state, and national levels. It brought the court case that overturned as unconstitutional many of the provisions of California's Proposition 187. It works in coalition with other organizations to oppose renewal of the USA Patriot Act without amending some of its more egregious civil rights infringements. It favors legalization and a guest-worker program such as that contained in the Kennedy/McCain proposal.

Lutheran Immigration and Refugee Service
700 Light St.
Baltimore, MD 21230
(410) 230–2700
Fax: (410) 230–2890
E-mail: lirs@lirs.org
http://www.lirs.org/

The LIRS states as its mission to welcome the stranger, bringing new hope and new life through ministries and justice. It mobilizes action on behalf of uprooted people and sees that they receive fair and equal treatment, regardless of national origin, race, religion, culture, or legal status. They advocate for just and humane solutions to migration crises and their root causes, both national and international; work to turn solutions into reality; and encourage citizens to take part in shaping just and fair public policies, practices, and law. They work in coalition with other mostly church-based immigration and refugee service organizations and lobby to enact immigration reform that is more liberal. They favor legalization and a guest-worker provision. Some of the organization's member churches have supported the sanctuary movement.

Mexican American Legal Defense Fund (MALDEF)
926 J Street, Suite 408
Sacramento, CA 95814
(916) 443–7531
Fax: (916) 443–1541
http://www.maldef.org/about/index.htm

Founded in 1968 in San Antonio, Texas, MALDEF is a leading nonprofit Latino litigation, advocacy, and educational outreach institution whose stated mission is to foster sound public policies, laws, and programs to safeguard the civil rights of the 40 million Latinos living in the United States and to empower the Latino community to fully participate in society. It advocates in coalition with other organizations to promote legalization, favors a guest-worker program, and is highly critical of what it holds are the civil rights infringements of the Patriot Act. It strongly opposed state initiatives like California's Proposition 187 and the congressional acts of 1996, which it held were racist, anti-Hispanic, and anti-immigrant. It has legally opposed English-only laws and initiatives as well.

National Council of La Raza
1111 19th St., N.W., Suite 1000
Washington, DC 20036
(202) 785–1670
Fax: (202) 776–1792
E-mail: info@nclr.org
http://www.nclr.org

The NCLR is a private, nonprofit, nonpartisan, tax-exempt organization established in 1968 to reduce poverty and discrimination, and improve life opportunities for Hispanic Americans, assisting the development of Hispanic community-based organizations in urban and rural areas nationwide. It conducts applied research, policy analysis, and advocacy, providing a Hispanic perspective on issues such as education, immigration, housing, health, employment and training, and civil rights enforcement, to increase policy-maker and public understanding of Hispanic needs, and to encourage the adoption of programs and policies that equitably serve Hispanics.

Its Policy Analysis Center is a prominent Hispanic "think tank" serving as a voice for Hispanic Americans in Washington, D.C. It works in coalition with other Latino organizations and lobby efforts to reform immigration law in a more humane way.

National Federation of Independent Business
53 Century Blvd., Suite 250
Nashville, TN 37214
(800) NFIB-NOW
E-mail: web_membership@NFIB.org
http://www.nfib.com/cgi-bin/NFIB.dll

The NFIB is the largest advocacy organization representing small and independent businesses in Washington, D.C., and all fifty state capitals. Its Education Foundation promotes the importance of free enterprise and entrepreneurship. Its Research Foundation researches policy-related small business problems and affects public policy debate by making its findings widely available. Its Legal Foundation fights for small business in the courts and seeks to educate small employers on legal issues. It favors the guest-worker proposals of several bills before the Congress and "earned legalization" provisions.

National Immigration Forum
2201 I Street, N.E., Suite 220
Washington, DC 20002–4362
(202) 544–0004
Fax: (202) 544–1905
E-mail: info@immigrationforum.org
http://www.immigrationforum.org

The NIF's stated mission is "to embrace and uphold America's tradition as a nation of immigrants. The Forum advocates and builds public support for public policies that welcome immigrants and refugees and that are fair and supportive to newcomers in our country." The Forum works to unite families torn apart by what it characterizes as unreasonable and arbitrary restrictions. It advocates to secure fair treatment of refugees who have fled persecution; legalize the status of hardworking immigrants caught in legal limbo; promote citizenship as a pathway to full political participation (political incorporation); secure equitable access to social protections; and protect immigrants' fundamental Constitutional rights, no matter their legal or undocumented status. It advocates to promote immigration policies that strengthen the U.S. economy by working with a diverse coalition of allies— immigrant, ethnic, religious, civil rights, labor, business groups, state and local governments, and other organizations—to forge and promote a new vision of immigration policy that is consistent with global realities, fosters economic growth, attracts needed workers to the United States, and protects the rights of workers and families. They work to help settle newcomers into their communities and to climb the socioeconomic ladder of U.S. society; to help localities weave immigrants into the fabric of community life; and to build bonds of mutual understanding between established residents and new immigrants.

National Immigration Law Center
3435 Wilshire Blvd., Suite 2850
Los Angeles, CA 90010
(213) 639–3900
Fax: (213) 639–3911
E-mail: info@nilc.org
http://www.nilc.org

The National Immigration Law Center is a national support center whose mission is to protect and promote the rights and opportunities of low-income immigrants and their family members. Its staff specialize in immigration law and immigrant welfare. It conducts policy analysis and impact litigation and provides publications, technical services, and training to a broad constituency of legal aid agencies, community groups, and pro bono attorneys. It has offices in Los Angeles, Oakland, and Washington, D.C., and operates the Sacramento policy office for the California Immigrant Welfare Collaborative. It lobbies and works in coalition with other organizations favoring legalization and similar approaches to the illegal immigration problem.

National Network for Immigrant and Refugee Rights
310 8th Street, Suite 303
Oakland, CA 94607
(510) 465–1984
Fax: (510) 465–1885
E-mail: nnirr@nnirr.org
http://www.nnirr.org

The NNIRR is a national organization composed of local coalitions and immigrant, refugee, community, religious, civil rights, and labor organizations and activists. It serves as a forum to share information and analysis, to educate communities and the general public, and to develop and coordinate plans of action on important immigrant and refugee issues. It promotes a just immigration and refugee policy in the United States and defending and expanding the rights of all immigrants and refugees, regardless of immigration status. It seeks the enfranchisement of all immigrant and refugee communities in the United States through organizing and advocating for their full labor, environmental, civil, and human rights. It emphasizes the unparalleled change in global, political, and economic structures that has exacerbated regional, national, and international patterns of migration, and the need to build international support and cooperation to strengthen the rights, welfare, and safety of migrants and refugees.

New York Association for New Americans
17 Battery Place
New York, NY 10004–1102
(212) 425–2900
http://www.nyana.org/

The NYANA works to help those new to the United States, and those who have been here for some time, to fashion a roadmap for accomplishing their goals and dreams and to assist refugees and immigrants, their families, their sponsors, and companies that employ them, other institutions that serve them, and the communities in which they live. It serves immigrants without regard to their legal status.

No More Deaths
St. Mark's Presbyterian Church
3809 Third Street
Tucson, AZ 85716
(520) 325–1001
Fax: (520) 495–5567
E-mail: action@nomoredeaths.org
http://www.nomoredeaths.org

No More Deaths is a coalition of diverse individuals, faith communities, and human rights organizers who work for justice in the United States by mobilizing a response to the escalating numbers of deaths among illegal immigrants crossing the borders in the U.S. Southwest. The coalition has established a binational network of immigrant-friendly organizations and people in the Southwest and in northern Mexico who participate in interventions designed to stop migrant deaths, espousing the principle that humanitarian aid is never a crime. They establish movable desert camps, support the maintenance of water stations, and regularly launch what they term "good Samaritan patrols" that search the desert for migrants at risk. A nonprofit organization, they advocate on behalf of migrant-related issues, including promoting public demonstrations such as days of fast in remembrance of the lives claimed along the borders and protesting the policies that cause those deaths. Several of their volunteers have been arrested for giving aid to illegal aliens, and the coalition protests to call on government to drop the charges against its members. They organize clergy and others to contact elected officials, particularly members of Congress, in an attempt to influence immigration reform.

NumbersUSA
1601 N. Kent Street, Suite 1100
Arlington, VA 22209

(703) 816–8820
E-mail: info@numbersusa.com
http://www.numbersusa.com/

NumbersUSA is a nonprofit, nonpartisan, public-policy advocacy organization that seeks an environmentally sustainable and economically just society that protects individual liberties by advocating policies to stop mass illegal immigration. Its stated goals are to examine numerical levels of annual legal and illegal immigration, and to educate the public about the immigration-reduction recommendations from two national commissions of the 1990s: the 1995 Bipartisan U.S. Commission on Immigration Reform (the Barbara Jordan Commission) and the 1996 President's Council on Sustainable Development. It specifically advocates the elimination of chain migration and of the visa lottery. It views the elimination of those two immigration categories as the best way to protect vulnerable U.S. workers and their families. It promotes itself as proenvironment, proworker, proliberty, and proimmigrant. It networks with Americans of all races and includes many immigrants and their spouses, children, and parents. It advocates for illegal immigration reform and against any guest-worker type of program. It seeks to reduce overall legal immigration and advocates the reduction and eventual elimination of all illegal immigration. It advocates stricter border control measures, such as expansion of the Border Patrol and of the fences along the southern border.

**Office of Migration and Refugee Services,
U.S. Conference of Catholic Bishops**
3211 4th Street, N.E.
Washington, DC 20017–1194
(202) 541–3000
http://www.nccbuscc.org/mrs/

Since the turn of the twentieth century, the Catholic Church in the United States has engaged in the resettlement of refugees, advocating on behalf of immigrants and people on the move, and providing pastoral care and services to newcomers from all over the world. Since 1970 alone it has assisted in resettlement of more than 1 million refugees. The MRS is committed to its resettlement, pastoral care, and advocacy roles on behalf of immigrants, migrants, and refugees. It assists the bishops in the development and advocacy of policy positions at the national and international levels, which address the needs and conditions of immigrants, refugees, and other people on the move. It works with the federal government and with local churches in resettling refugees admitted to the United States into caring and supportive communities. It serves its clientele without regard to their legal status and has worked in coalition with other church organizations in the sanctuary movement.

Rights for All People
901 W. 14th Avenue, Suite 7
Denver, CO 80204
(303) 623–3464
E-mail: General@RAP-DPT.org
http://www.rap-dpt.org/

Rights for All People is a recently formed coalition to organize immigrants and their allies to achieve justice, dignity, and human rights for immigrants in Colorado. It formed in response to the passage of anti-immigrant, anti–civil rights initiatives, such as Proposition 187 in California and "Defend Colorado Now." Committed to the struggle for the rights of immigrants, the coalition espouses that the protection of immigrant rights is directly connected to preserving the rights of all people. Their primary strategy is to promote those rights by organizing with immigrants in a broad-based advocacy coalition. They sponsor direct action protests and marshal public opinion against specific legislation— such as the CLEAR Act. They counter by promoting legislation that would allow driver's licenses for undocumented immigrants (backing Colorado Senate bill SB67 in 2002).

Tolstoy Foundation
104 Lake Rd.
Valley Cottage, NY 10989
(845) 268–6722
Fax: (845) 268–6937
E-mail: TFHQ@aol.com
http://www.tolstoyfoundation.org/

The Foundation describes itself as an organization that for more than a half-century has been committed to its founder, Alexandra Tolstoy, whose empathy for the plight of peoples of her homeland

and abhorrence of all forms of oppression and human suffering remain at the heart of the Foundation's charitable activities today. Its stated mission is to promote respect for human dignity, freedom of choice, building of self-reliance through education and practical training, and assistance and relief to the distressed, children, the aged, the sick, and the forgotten at home and abroad. It is dedicated to enhancing the quality of life of its elderly population, providing a home and congenial surroundings to its residents, and caring for their physical, spiritual, and intellectual needs. It seeks to preserve the cultural traditions, the heritage, and the resources of the Russian diaspora, and now has come full circle from its history of assisting new immigrants in their assimilation process, to helping the peoples of Russia and the former Soviet Union acquire the knowledge and skills necessary to achieve self-reliance in their own homeland.

U.S. Chamber of Commerce
1615 H Street, N.W.
Washington, DC 20062–2000
(202) 659–6000
http://www.uschamber.com

Constituting the largest umbrella organization for business in the United States, the U.S. Chamber represents more than 3 million businesses organized into 2,800 state and local chambers and 830 business associations. Its business members are from all sizes and sectors of the economy—from Fortune 500 companies to small, one-person operations. Its staff consists of lobbyists, policy specialists, and lawyers who promote an economic, political, and social system based on individual incentive, initiative, opportunity, and responsibility. The U.S. Chamber founded the Americans for Better Borders coalition. Believing that the borders can and should be a line of defense against international terrorists but also allowing for legitimate commerce and travel, the coalition promotes the efficient allocation of technology, personnel, and infrastructure resources to achieve those goals. The coalition unites regional business organizations, companies, and national trade associations in all sectors of the economy to ensure the efficient flow of exports and tourism across the borders while addressing national security concerns. The Chamber promoted a workable compromise on the Illegal Immigration Reform and Immigrant Responsibility Act of 1996. The Americans for Better Borders

Coalition was founded in 1998. It lobbied the Congress on the establishment of the DHS. It currently endorses and promotes passage of the Kennedy-McCain proposal with its more comprehensive immigration reform provisions and an extensive guest-worker program plan that the U.S. Chamber considers essential to any effective immigration reform.

U.S. Committee for Refugees
1717 Massachusetts Avenue, N.W., Suite 701
Washington, DC 20036
(202) 347-3507
Fax: (202) 347-3418
E-mail: uscr@irsa-uscr.org
http://www.refugees.org/

USCR describes its mission as defending the rights of all uprooted people regardless of their nationality, race, religion, ideology, or social group. They believe that once the consciences of men and women are aroused, great deeds can be accomplished. They base their work on the following principles: (1) refugees have basic human rights, and no person with a well-founded fear of persecution should be forcibly returned to his or her homeland; (2) asylum seekers have the right to a fair and impartial hearing to determine their refugee status; and (3) all uprooted victims of human conflict, regardless of whether they cross a border, have the right to humane treatment as well as adequate protection and assistance.

Immigration Research Centers and Think Tanks

American Assembly
475 Riverside Drive, Suite 456
New York, NY 10115
(212) 870-3500
Fax: (212) 870-3555
http://www.americanassembly.org

The Assembly's major objectives are to focus attention and stimulate information on a range of critical U.S. policy topics, both domestic and international; to provide government officials, community and civic leadership, and the general public with factual background information and the range of policy options on a given issue; and to facilitate communications among decision-makers and the public and private sectors.

Bell Policy Center
1801 Broadway, Suite 280
Denver, CO 80202
(303) 297–0956 or (866) 283–8051
Fax: (303) 297–0460
info@thebell.org
http://www.thebell.org

The Bell Policy Center is a research center located in Colorado and committed to making Colorado a state of opportunity for all. Its stated goal is to reinvigorate the debate on issues affecting the well-being of Coloradoans and to promote policies that open gateways to opportunity. It conducts nonpartisan research on issues of concern, shares its research with policy-makers, uses its staff and a network of supporters and consultants to inform public opinion and to encourage responsible public dialogue and debate, and makes policy recommendations and advocates for changes that will increase opportunities for individuals and families. It has recently issued study briefs on the impact of immigration on Colorado as well as information sheets on immigration bills before the state legislature and the U.S. Congress. It favors a guest-worker program and maintains that immigration drives economic growth in the nation as a whole and in Colorado. Its recent study found that wages and employment of native-born workers were not significantly affected by immigration, that 90 percent of undocumented immigrant men are working, and that immigration adds about $10 billion to the U.S. economy annually.

Brookings Institution,
Center on Urban and Metropolitan Policy
1775 Massachusetts Ave., N.W.
Washington, DC 20036
(202) 797–6000
Fax: (202) 797–6004
E-mail: webmaster@brookings.edu
http://www.brook.edu/about/aboutbi.htm

The Brookings Institution is an independent, nonpartisan organization devoted to research, analysis, education, and publication focused on public policy issues in the areas of economics, foreign policy, and governance. Its stated goal is to improve the performance of U.S. institutions and the quality of public policy by using social science to analyze emerging issues and to offer practical approaches to those issues in language aimed at the general public. It does so through three research programs—Economic Studies, Foreign Policy Studies, and Governance Studies—as well as through the Center for Public Policy Education and the Brookings Institution Press, which publishes about fifty books a year. Its research is conducted to inform the public debate, not to advocate or advance a political agenda. It began in 1927. It is financed largely by endowment and through support by philanthropic foundations, corporations, and private individuals.

Cato Institute
1000 Massachusetts Ave., N.W.
Washington, DC 20001–5403
(202) 842–0200
Fax: (202) 842–3490
E-mail: cato@cato.org
http://www.cato.org

The Cato Institute was founded in 1977 as a public policy research foundation headquartered in Washington, D.C. Named for *Cato's Letters,* a series of libertarian pamphlets that helped lay the philosophical foundation of the American Revolution, the Institute describes its mission as seeking to broaden the parameters of public policy debate to allow consideration of the traditional American principles of limited government, individual liberty, free markets, and peace. To pursue that goal, the Institute strives to achieve greater involvement of the intelligent, concerned lay public in questions of policy and the proper role of government. It is a nonprofit, tax-exempt educational foundation.

Center for Equal Opportunity
14 Pidgeon Hill Drive, Suite 500
Sterling, VA 20165
(703) 421–5443
Fax: (703) 421–6401
http://www.ceousa.org/

The Center is a "think tank" devoted to the promotion of color-blind equal opportunity and racial harmony. It seeks to counter what it holds to be the divisive impact of race-conscious public policies. It focuses on three issues in particular: racial preferences, immigration and assimilation, and multicultural education. The center promotes the assimilation of legal immigrants into society and conducts research on their economic and social impact on the United States. It advocates against bilingual education, holding that such programs promote a racial ideology that risks balkanization of a multiracial society. It was founded and is headed by Linda Chavez.

Center for Human Rights and the Constitutional Law
256 S. Occidental Boulevard
Los Angeles, CA 90057
(213) 388–8693
Fax: (213) 386–9484

The Center runs a homeless youth project that helps homeless twelve to seventeen-year-old inner-city youth find an alternative to life on the streets. Other services provided are case management, job assistance, individual counseling, placement assistance, school placement, legal and medical referrals, life skills training, and aftercare.

Center for Immigration Studies
1522 K Street, N.W., Suite 820
Washington, DC 20005–1202
(202) 466–8185
Fax: (202) 466–8076
E-mail: center@cis.org
http://www.cis.org

The CIS is an independent, nonpartisan, nonprofit research organization founded in 1985. It is the nation's only think tank devoted exclusively to research and policy analysis of the economic, social, demographic, fiscal, and other impacts of immigration on the United States. Its stated mission is to expand the base of knowledge and understanding of the need for an immigration policy that gives first concern to the broad national interest. It is animated by a proimmigrant, low-immigration vision that seeks fewer immigrants but a warmer welcome for those admitted. The center also publishes *Immigration Review.*

Center for Migration Studies
27 Carmine St.
New York, NY 10014
(718) 351–8800
Fax: (718) 667–4598
E-mail: imr@cmsny.org
http://www.cmsny.org

The CMS of New York was founded in 1964. It is one of the premier institutes for migration studies in the United States. Its stated mission is to facilitate the study of sociodemographic, historical, economic, political, legislative, and pastoral aspects of human migration and refugee movements. In 1969 it incorporated as an educational nonprofit institute. It brings an independent perspective to the interdisciplinary study of international migration and refugees without the institutional constraints of government analysts and special interest groups, or the profit considerations of private research firms. It claims to be the only institute in the United States devoted exclusively to understanding and educating the public on the causes and consequences of human mobility at both origin and destination counties. It generates and facilitates the dissemination of new knowledge and the fostering of effective policies. It publishes the leading scholarly journal in the field, the *International Migration Review.*

Immigration History Research Center
University of Minnesota
College of Liberal Arts
311 Andersen Library
222 21st Avenue South
Minneapolis, MN 55455–0439
(612) 625–4800
Fax: (612) 626–0018
http://www1.umn.edu/ihrc

Founded in 1965, the Immigration History Research Center is an international resource on American immigration and ethnic history. The IHRC collects, preserves, and makes available archival and published resources documenting immigration and ethnicity on a national scope and is particularly rich for ethnic groups that originated in Eastern, Central, and Southern Europe and the Near East. It sponsors academic programs and publishes bibliographic and scholarly works.

Manhattan Institute
52 Vanderbilt Ave.
New York, NY 10017
(212) 599–7000
Fax: (212) 599–3494
http://www.manhattan-institute.org

The Manhattan Institute claims to have been an important force shaping American political culture for more than twenty-five years. It supports and publishes research on a host of challenging public policy issues, including welfare, crime, the legal system, urban life, education, and immigration—both legal and illegal. It publishes or supports the research for books, does book reviews and interviews, presents public speeches by its fellows, writes op-ed pieces for major public news outlets, and publishes the quarterly *City Journal.* It sponsors forums and conferences devoted to its research issues.

Migration Policy Institute
1400 16th St., N.W., Suite 300
Washington, DC 20036
(202) 266–1940
Fax: (202) 266–1900
http://www.migrationpolicy.org/about

MPI is an independent, nonpartisan, nonprofit think tank in Washington, D.C., dedicated to the study of the movement of people worldwide. It provides analysis, development, and evaluation of migration and refugee policies at the local, national, and international levels. It aims to meet the rising demand for pragmatic and thoughtful responses to the challenges and opportunities that large-scale migration, whether voluntary or forced, presents to communities and institutions in an increasingly integrated world. Founded in 2001 by Kathleen Newland and Demetrious G. Papademetriou, MPI grew out of the International Migration Policy Program at the Carnegie Endowment for International Peace.

Migrationwatch UK
P.O. Box 765
Guildford, UK
GU2 4XN

Tel.: +4(0) 1869–337007
E-mail: info@migrationwatchUK.org
http://www.migrationwatchuk.org

Established in October 2001, Migrationwatch UK is an independent think tank that has no connections to any political party. Chaired by Sir Andrew Green, a former ambassador to Saudi Arabia, it monitors developments, conducts research, and provides the public with full and accurate facts placed in proper context. In the future it will make policy recommendations. It believes that arguments in favor of the current large-scale immigration are unsound either in fact or in economics or both, and need to be thoroughly examined.

National Immigration Forum
220 I Street, N.E., Suite 220
Washington, DC 20002
E-mail: info@immigrationforum.org
http://www.immigrationforum.org/

The purpose of the NIF is to embrace and uphold America's tradition as a nation of immigrants. The Forum advocates and builds public support for public policies that welcome immigrants and refugees and that are fair and supportive to newcomers in our country.

National Network for Immigrant and Refugee Rights
310 8th Street, Suite 307
Oakland, CA 94607
(510) 465–1984
Fax: (510) 465–1885
E-mail: nnirr@igc.apc.org

A national organization composed of local coalitions and immigrant, refugee, community, religious, civil rights, and labor organizations and activists, the Network serves as a forum to share information and analysis, to educate communities and the general public, and to develop and coordinate plans of action on important immigrant and refugee issues. It works to promote a just immigration and refugee policy in the United States and to defend and expand the rights of all immigrants and refugees, regardless of immigrant status, advocating for their full labor, environmental, civil, and human rights.

Pew Hispanic Center
USC Annenberg School for Communication
1919 M Street, N.W., Suite 460
Washington, DC 20036
(202) 292–3300
Fax: (202) 785–8282
E-mail: info@pewhispanic.org
http://www.pewhispanic.org/

Founded in 2001, the PHC is a nonpartisan research organization supported by the Pew Charitable Trusts. Its mission is to improve understanding of the U.S. Hispanic population and to chronicle Latinos' growing impact on the entire nation. Timeliness, relevance, and scientific rigor characterize the Center's work. The Center does not advocate for or take positions on policy issues. Demography, immigration, and remittances are three of its major research foci that impact on the matter of illegal immigration.

Prejudice Institute
2743 Maryland Ave.
Baltimore, MD 21218
(410) 243–6987
E-mail: prejinst@aol.com
http://www.prejudiceinstitute.org/

The Prejudice Institute describes itself as a resource for activists, lawyers, and social scientists. It is devoted to policy research and education on all dimensions of prejudice, discrimination, and ethnoviolence.

Public Policy Institute of California
500 Washington Street, Suite 800
San Francisco, CA 94111
(415) 291–4400
Fax: (415) 291–4401
http://www.ppic.org/

The PPIC is a private, nonprofit organization dedicated to improving public policy in California through independent, objective, nonpartisan research. It was established in 1994 with an endowment from William R. Hewlett. Its research focuses on three program areas: population, economy, and governance and public finance. Its publications include reports, research briefs, surveys, fact sheets, special papers, and demographic bulletins. It also communicates its research and analysis through conferences, forums, luncheons, and other targeted outreach efforts.

RAND Corporation
1700 Main St., P.O. Box 2138
Santa Monica, CA 90407–2138
(213) 393–0411
http://www.rand/org/about/

RAND (a contraction of the terms "research and development") was the first organization to be called a "think tank." Established in 1946 by the U.S. Air Force, today RAND is a nonprofit institution that helps improve policy and decision-making through research and analysis whose areas of expertise include child policy, civil and criminal justice, community and U.S. regional studies, drug policy, education, health, immigration, infrastructure, international policy, methodology, national security, population and aging, science and technology, and terrorism. On occasion its findings are considered so compelling that it advances specific policy recommendations. In all cases, it serves the public interest by widely disseminating its research findings.

Southern Poverty Law Center
400 Washington Ave.
Montgomery, AL 36104
(334) 956–8200
Fax: (334) 956–8488
http://www.tolerance.org/

Tolerance.org is a web project of the Southern Poverty Law Center, a national civil rights organization. Its stated mission is to create a national community committed to human rights by centralizing e-mail addresses and inviting users to view special features and stories on the website. It promotes and disseminates scholarship on all aspects of prejudice and discrimination, promoting tolerance, exposing hate groups and hate news, providing assistance on litigation and legal matters, and publishing antihate and protolerance tracts such as: "Ten Ways to Fight Hate," "101 Tools for Tolerance," and "Center Information Packet."

Urban Institute
2100 M Street, N.W.
Washington, DC 20037
(202) 833–7200
Fax: (202) 223–3043
E-mail: paffairs@ui.urban.org
http://www.urban.org=hotopics.htm#immigration

One of the oldest of the think tanks, the Urban Institute researches policy matters in which it measures effects, compares options, shows which stakeholders get the most and least, tests conventional wisdom, reveals trends, and makes costs, benefits, and risks explicit on a broad array of public policy issues, employing the right methodologies and quantitative modeling, survey design, and statistical analyses. It publishes an extensive list of books that follow standard academic peer-review procedures for an audience of program administrators, other researchers and university students, the news media, nonprofit organizations, stakeholders in the private sector, and that important segment of the public engaged in policy debates through the media.

8

Selected Print and Nonprint Resources

There are thousands of books, scholarly journal articles, government reports and documents, and nongovernmental agency reports and publications concerning immigration policy, the immigration processes, and its reform. This chapter presents a briefly annotated bibliography of some leading scholarly journals, major reference and scholarly books, government reports, and videos. Web sites of interest are presented, along with the organizations hosting the sites, in Chapter 7. The print and nonprint outlets below cover major sources in the field, so that readers may quickly identify resources most likely to be useful for them. The chapter is divided into print sources, specifying the major scholarly journals in the field, then scholarly and reference volumes. Finally, the chapter identifies pertinent nonprint (video) materials. Although some of the print and nonprint sources identified here reference material that discusses immigration more generally, most of the sources cited are directly related to illegal immigration topics.

Books

Alienkoff, T. Alexander, and Douglas Klusmeyer, eds., 2000. *From Migrants to Citizens: Membership in a Changing World.* Washington, DC: Brookings Institution Press. A scholarly discussion of the incorporation of immigrants with thorough discussion of naturalization law and policy.

————. 2001. *Citizenship Today: Global Perspectives and Practices.* Washington, DC: Brookings Institution Press. A Carnegie Endowment for International Peace book by leading immigration lawyer experts in the subject.

————. 2002. *Citizenship Policies for an Age of Migration.* Washington, DC: Brookings Institution Press. A Carnegie Endowment for International Peace book by two leading immigration lawyers focusing on naturalization policy in a global context.

Andreas, Peter. 2000. *Border Games: Policing the U.S.-Mexico Divide.* Ithaca, NY: Cornell University Press. An extensive study of the difficulty of enacting and implementing policy to control illegal immigration, focusing on the southern border.

Andreas, Peter, and Timothy Snyder, eds. 2000. *The Wall around the West: State Borders and Immigration Controls in North America and Europe.* Lanham, MD: Rowman and Littlefield. A balanced but critical examination of the increasing barriers being enacted to control immigration flows into Canada, the United States, and the major immigration-receiving nations of Europe, particularly the European Union countries.

Arreola, Daniel D., ed. 2004. *Hispanic Spaces, Latino Places: Community and Cultural Diversity in Contemporary America.* Austin: University of Texas Press. A collection of original essays on Hispanic migration to the U.S. Southwest. Numerous scholars examine a panorama of issues and sectors of society affected by the influx, and how those communities affect the incorporation of new Hispanic immigrants.

Baker, Susan Gonzales. 1990. *The Cautious Welcome: The Legalization Program of the Immigration Reform and Control Act.* Santa Monica, CA: Rand Corporation and the Urban Institute Press. A critical examination of IRCA's legalization programs and the difficulties and failures in implementation.

Bean, Frank B., and Stephanie Bell-Rose, eds. 1999. *Immigration and Opportunity: Race, Ethnicity, and Employment in the U.S.* New York: Russell Sage. An extensive collection of essays from leading sociologists and demographers that provides a systematic account of the sundry ways in which immigration impacts the labor market experiences of native-born Americans.

Bean, Frank, Barry Edmonston, and Jeffrey Passell. 1990. *Undocumented Migration to the U.S.* Santa Monica, CA: Rand Corporation and the Urban Institute Press. A thorough and scholarly look at illegal immigration focusing on that across the southern U.S. border.

Bean, Frank D., and Gillian Stevens. 2003. *America's Newcomers: Immigrant Incorporation and the Dynamics of Diversity.* New York: Russell Sage. A demographer and a language specialist examine the factors influencing the gradual incorporation of immigrants and their children and what aspects influence the rate of incorporation.

Bean, Frank, George Vernez, and Charles B. Keely. 1989. *Opening and Closing the Doors.* Santa Monica, CA, and Washington, DC: Rand Corporation and the Urban Institute Press. One of the more important books in a series of excellent books and monographs published as a result of a joint Rand Corporation/Urban Institute major research project examining immigration policy particularly as to the impact of the Immigration Reform and Control Act of 1986 (IRCA).

Beck, Roy H. 1996. *The Case against Immigration.* New York: Norton. A thorough articulation of all the arguments and data that can be marshaled against high levels of immigration.

Boeri, Tito, et al., eds. 2002. *Immigration Policy and the Welfare State.* New York: Oxford University Press. This book draws together and unifies analysis of immigration into the major E.U. countries and the United States, covering the major trends and dramatic developments of the 1990s. It emphasizes the influence of the welfare state on immigration incentives, but examines other influences on both legal and illegal migration and on their market outcomes on these two continents.

Borjas, George. 1997. *Friends and Strangers: The Effects of Immigration on the U.S. Economy.* New York: Basic. A noted scholar examines and critically evaluates the economic impact of high levels of legal and illegal immigration to the United States.

Briggs, Vernon M., Jr., and Stephen Moore. 1994. *Still an Open Door? U.S. Immigration Policy and the American Economy.* Washington, DC: American University Press. Another volume of noted scholars of the economic impact of immigration, stressing the negative effects of large-scale immigration and the negative effects of illegal migration.

Brubaker, William Roger, ed. 1989. *Immigration and the Politics of Citizenship in Europe and North America.* New York: University Press of America and the German Marshall Fund of the United States. An interesting collection of essays on naturalization, citizenship, and the impact of immigration on the politics of the United States and of the European Union nations. Focus is on legal immigration.

Calavita, Kitty. 1992. *Inside the State: The Bracero Program, Immigration, and the INS.* New York: Routledge. One of the best examinations of the Bracero Program, with insights into temporary worker programs and the problems associated with that approach.

Camarota, Steven A. 1999. *Immigrants in the United States–1998: A Snapshot of America's Foreign-Born Population.* Washington, DC: Center for Immigration Studies. An extensive demographic-data look at immigrants in the United States and the degree to which they are assimilating into the socioeconomic structures of society.

Chavez, Leo R. 1992. *Shadowed Lives: Undocumented Immigrants in American Society.* New York: Harcourt Brace Jovanovich. A sharply focused examination of all the problems and negative impacts and discrimination facing undocumented aliens.

Conover, Ted. 1987. *Coyotes: A Journey through the Secret World of America's Illegal Aliens.* New York: Vintage. A reporter's "inside" look at the illegal alien smuggling problem and how it operates and largely avoids border control.

Craig, Richard B. 1971. *The Bracero Program: Interest Groups and Foreign Policy.* Austin: University of Texas Press. One of the early scholarly analyses of the Bracero Program, focusing on interest groups for and against and how they shaped the program and its implementation and relation to foreign policy concerns.

Crane, Keith, et al. 1990. *The Effects of Employer Sanctions on the Flow of Undocumented Immigrants to the United States.* Santa Monica, CA: Rand Corporation and the Urban Institute Press. One of an excellent series of studies by the Rand Corporation and the Urban Institute studying the impact of IRCA and especially the effects of the employer sanctions approach to control illegal immigration.

Crockoff, James D. 1986. *Outlaws in the Promised Land: Mexican Immigrant Workers and America's Future.* New York: Grove. Critical view of the illegal immigration flow, the exploitation of undocumented workers, and the economic effects of illegal immigration on the U.S. economy.

Daniels, Roger. 1990. *Coming to America: A History of Immigration and Ethnicity in American Life.* New York: Harper. A brief but insightful history of immigration and ethnicity and their impact on U.S. society by a noted immigration historian.

Daniels, Roger, and Otis L. Graham. 2003. *Debating American Immigration, 1882–Present.* Lanham, MD: Rowman and Littlefield. Two noted historians of immigration debate the American immigration experience.

Etzioni, Amatai, and Jason H. Marsch, eds. 2003. *Rights v. Public Safety after 9/11: America in the Age of Terrorism.* Lanham, MD: Rowman and Littlefield. A timely scholarly debate on the issues of civil rights, homeland defense, and public safety.

Faist, Thomas. 2000. *The Volume and Dynamics of International Migration and Transnational Social Spaces.* New York: Oxford University Press. This volume offers an innovative theoretical account of the causes, nature, and extent of the movement of international migrants between affluent and poorer countries and provides a conceptual framework for migration decision-making and the dynamics of international movement of peoples.

Ferris, Elizabeth G., ed. 1985. *Refugees and World Politics.* New York: Praeger. A thorough collection of essays on the refugee crisis up to the early 1980s; it is an important source for world refugee numbers to that point in time, and most of the issues and many of the problems remain relevant today.

Fix, Michael, ed. 1991. *The Paper Curtain: Employer Sanctions Implementation, Impact, and Reform.* Washington, DC: Urban Institute. An objective, scholarly examination of the employer sanctions program of IRCA, the problems involved in its implementation, why it largely failed to achieve its aims, and some suggested reform approaches.

Foner, Nancy, Ruben Rumbant, and Steven J. Gold, eds. 2000. *Immigration Research for a New Century: Multidisciplinary Perspectives.* New York: Russell Sage. A thorough examination of current research on the post-1965 wave of immigrants presenting the work of a new generation of immigration scholars from the various social science disciplines.

Francis, Samuel T. 2001. *America Extinguished: Mass Immigration and the Disintegration of American Culture.* Monterey, VA: Americans for Immigration Control. A collection of editorial essays by Samuel Francis of AIC, it presents all of their arguments and perspectives on the cultural wars and reasons to oppose mass immigration. It presents virtually every argument for the dire affects of illegal immigration.

Gerstle, Gary, and John Mollenkopf, eds. 2001. *E Pluribus Unum? Contemporary and Historical Perspectives on Immigrant Political Incorporation.* New York: Russell Sage. A pathbreaking volume that brings together historians and social scientists exploring the dynamics of political incorporation (assimilation) of the twentieth century's two great immigration waves. From political machines to education, transnational loyalties, and racial exclusion, these essays provide insights into the way immigration has and continues to change the United States—both its civic culture and its political life.

Gjerde, Jon, ed. 1998. *Major Problems in American Immigration and Ethnic History.* Boston: Houghton Mifflin. A collection of essays from leading scholars about a wide variety of problems emerging from large-scale immigration flows to the United States.

Glazer, Nathan, ed. 1985. *Clamor at the Gates: The New American Immigration.* San Francisco: ICS Press. One of the most noted scholars of immigration focuses on the "new" wave of post-1965 immigration and examines the demographics of the wave.

Hamermesh, Daniel S., and Frank Bean, eds. 1998. *Help or Hindrance? The Economic Implications of Immigration for African Americans.* New York: Russell Sage. The debate over how, and the degree to which, immigration adversely impacts African Americans is thoroughly examined in this collection of essays edited by two leading scholars/demographers of the U.S. immigration process.

Hammamoto, Darrell Y., and Rodolfo Torres, eds. 1997. *New American Destinies: A Reader in Contemporary Asian and Latino Immigration.* New York: Routledge. A collection of scholarly essays focusing on the changed nature in the flow of immigrants since 1965 and the shift in that flow from Northwestern Europeans to Latin Americans and Asians.

Hero, Rodney, and Christina Wolbrecht, eds. 2005. *The Politics of Democratic Inclusion.* Philadelphia: Temple University Press. A collection of original essays from a variety of scholars on the subject of immigrant incorporation and what aids or hinders the process.

Hirschman, Charles, Joshua DeWind, and Philip Kasinitz, eds. 1999. *The Handbook of International Migration.* New York: Russell Sage. An extensive collection of essays on the basics of international migration flows.

Huddle, Donald. 1993. *The Costs of Immigration.* Washington, DC: Carrying Capacity Network. Huddle's study was among the first careful scholarly attempts to measure the impact of immigration using an economist's cost-benefit analysis approach. Controversial as it was for those interested in measuring immigration's costs, it spurred a host of other studies of the economic impact of immigration over the remainder of the decade.

Information Plus. 2006. *Immigration and Illegal Aliens: Burdens or Blessings?* Farmington Hills, MI: Thomson/Gale. The latest in a series of brief but thorough monographs that examine the "illegal alien issue" from a variety of perspectives and present many graphs, figures, and tables of data that touch upon every aspect of the "illegal alien immigration" issue. Pros and cons of all sides of the issue and a solid historical perspective are included in every volume in the series.

Jones-Correa, Michael, ed. 2001. *Governing American Cities.* New York: Russell Sage. Focusing on the newest wave of immigration, this volume looks at its impact on the nation's major metropolitan areas. The volume provides what is clearly among the best analyses of how immigration has reshaped urban politics in the United States. It covers especially New York, Los Angeles, and Miami. It provides valuable insight into the new American urban melting pot by offering sophisticated theoretical perspectives on intergroup coalitions and conflicts. It provides rich details and analysis of class and generational dynamics as those forces influence the political behavior of diverse immigrant groups.

Kastoryano, Riva. 2000. *Negotiating Identities: States and Immigrants in France and Germany.* Princeton: Princeton University Press. Immigration is even more hotly debated in Europe than in the United States. This pivotal work of action and discourse analysis draws on extensive field interviews with politicians, immigrant leaders, and militants to analyze interactions between the state and immigrants in France and Germany.

Kirstein, Peter N. 1977. *Anglo over Bracero: A History of the Mexican Worker in the United States from Roosevelt to Nixon.* San Francisco: R. and E. Research Associates. A thorough, historical examination of the Bracero Program.

Kiser, George C., and Martha W. Kiser. 1979. *Mexican Workers in the United States.* Albuquerque: University of New Mexico Press. Another thorough and scholarly historical analysis of the Bracero Program.

Klopp, Brett. 2002. *German Multiculturalism: Immigrant Integration and the Transformation of Citizenship.* Westport, CT: Praeger. Migration, asylum, and citizenship have become issues of primary focus in E.U. politics. This volume examines issues of immigration, political incorporation, and multiculturalism as found in Germany, Europe's premier immigrant-receiving nation-state. It examines an emerging multicultural society through perspectives of the immigrants themselves as well as social institutions such as unions, employer associations, schools, and city governments.

Koehn, Peter. 1991. *Refugees from Revolution: U.S. Policy and Third World Migration.* Boulder, CO: Westview. An examination of how U.S. policy responds to refugee flows and immigration waves induced by the political turmoil in "Third World" countries.

Krauss, Erich, and Alex Pacheco. 2004. *On the Line: Inside the U.S. Border Patrol.* New York: Citadel/Kensington. An "insider's" look, journalistic in style, at the Border Patrol, its difficult tasks, resource problems, successes, and shortcomings.

Kraut, Alan. 1994. *Silent Travelers: Germs, Genes and the "Immigrant Menace."* Baltimore, MD: Johns Hopkins University Press. An interesting examination of the problem of mass migration and disease spread, intentional or unintentional, from epidemics to pandemics.

Kyle, David, and Rey Koslowski. 2001. *Global Human Smuggling: Comparative Perspectives.* Baltimore, MD: Johns Hopkins University Press. A careful examination of human smuggling in historical and comparative perspectives; it examines the emergence of international law and of a global moral order of human rights while at the same time exploring the economic and political facets of illegal trafficking in humans. It is a comprehensive examination of illegal immigration and those who profit most from it.

Lamm, R. D., and G. Imhoff. 1985. *The Immigration Time Bomb: The Fragmenting of America.* New York: Truman Tally/E. P. Dutton. Published prior to the enactment of IRCA, this book marshals all the arguments and data to show the cost or detrimental effects of large-scale immigration, particularly those used to promote policy reforms to "control" the illegal immigration flow. The arguments offered here continue to inform former governor Lamm's positions against illegal immigration today.

LeMay, Michael. 1987. *From Open Door to Dutch Door: An Analysis of U.S. Immigration Policy since 1820.* New York: Praeger. A historical overview of immigration policy-making since 1820, it presents the "immigration waves" and distinguishes four phases of immigration policy that dominated historical eras in reaction to preceding waves, employing a "door" analogy to characterize each phase or era of immigration policy.

———. 1994. *Anatomy of a Public Policy: The Reform of Contemporary American Immigration Law.* Westport, CT: Praeger. A detailed "case study" examination of the Immigration Reform and Control Act of 1986 and the Immigration Act of 1990. It examines the political movement to enact IRCA and IMMACT of 1990, using roll-call analysis and interviews with key political actors to explain why the laws were passed and what key provisions each contained.

———. 2004. *U.S. Immigration: A Reference Handbook.* Santa Barbara, CA: ABC-CLIO. A library reference volume examining legal immigration from 1965 to 2004 in the standard format of the Contemporary World Issues series of volumes.

———, ed. 1989. *The Gatekeepers: Comparative Immigration Policies.* New York: Praeger. A collection of six original essays, each examining the immigration policy and the reforms thereof of six leading immigration-receiving nations.

LeMay, Michael, and Elliott Robert Barkan, eds. 1999. *U.S. Immigration and Naturalization Laws and Issues: A Documentary History.* Westport, CT: Greenwood. This unique volume summarizes 150 documents covering all major laws and court cases concerning U.S. immigration and naturalization law from colonial times to 1996.

Light, Paul C. 2002. *Homeland Security Will Be Hard to Manage.* Washington, DC: Brookings Institution. Written just after the enactment of the law establishing the new Department of Homeland Security, this expert in bureaucratic management offers insights and accurate foresight as to the difficulties the new DHS will face as its managers attempt to merge the operations, procedures, and political/bureaucratic cultures of so many diverse agencies into the new mega-department.

Loescher, Gil, and Ann Dull Loescher. 1994. *The Global Refugee Crisis.* Santa Barbara, CA: ABC-CLIO. Another in a series of volumes on contemporary issues viewed in a global perspective, this volume thoroughly examines the current global refugee crisis in the "research handbook" format of the series.

Lutton, Wayne, and John Tanton. 1994. *The Immigration Invasion.* Petosky, MI: Social Contact. An "indictment" of immigration, discussing all of the problems it can be viewed as having caused and marshaling every conceivable argument against it.

Lynch, James P., and Rita J. Simon. 2003. *Immigration the World Over: Statutes, Policies, and Practices.* Lanham, MD: Rowman and Littlefield. A current and thorough, though necessarily somewhat brief, presented of immigration policies and practices of the major immigration-receiving countries of the world presented in a comparative perspective.

Majaridge, Dale. 1996. *The Coming White Minority: California's Eruptions and America's Future.* New York: Random House. A polemical argument for all of the ills that can (will) befall the United States as the rest of the nation experiences California's high level of immigration, both legal and illegal.

Martinez, Oscar J. 1994. *Border People: Life and Society in U.S.-Mexico Borderlands.* Tucson: University of Arizona Press. A sociological examination of life in the borderlands and how the porous flow of people living in and working across the Mexican-U.S. border affects all aspects of their daily lives.

Massey, Douglas, Jorge Durand, and Nolan Malone. 2002. *Beyond Smoke and Mirrors: Mexican Immigration in an Era of Economic Integration.* New York: Russell Sage. The authors provide a fresh perspective of Mexican migration history by systematically tracing the predictable consequences of highly unsystematic policy regimes. They provide an incisive analysis of the current policy dilemma by marshaling new and compelling evidence to expose the flagrant contradiction of allowing the free flow of goods and capital but not people, and they argue for much-needed policy reforms.

Massey, Douglas, et al. 1987. *Return to Aztlan: The Social Process of International Migration from Western Mexico.* Berkeley: University of California Press. A thorough and many-viewed examination of Mexican immigration—both legal and illegal—to the southwestern United States (the mythical Aztlan of the title).

McCarthy, Kevin F., and George Vernez. 1997. *Immigration in a Changing Economy: California's Experience.* Santa Monica, CA: Rand Corporation. Another in a series of volumes and studies that emerged from the massive Rand Corporation study of immigration policy post-IRCA, this volume is an authoritative case study of the impact of immigration on California's economy and politics.

McDowell, Lorraine, and Paul T. Hill. 1990. *Newcomers in America's Schools.* Santa Monica, CA: Rand Corporation. One of the volumes of careful research that the Rand Corporation published on the impact of the new immigration flow; it focuses on the effects of large-scale legal and illegal immigration on California's schools.

Memolovic, Ed O., et al., eds. 1998. *Globalization of Labor Markets: Challenges, Adjustment and Policy Responses in the European Union and the Less Developed Countries.* Dordrecht: Kluwer Academic. An extensive collection of essays that thoroughly examines the globalization of labor markets and how this trend is affecting the major receiving nations in the European Union, variations in their respective policies toward the migration of labor, and the effects on the less developed sending nations.

Mendelbaum, Michael, ed. 2002. *The New European Diasporas: National Minorities and Conflicts in Eastern Europe.* Washington, DC: Brookings Institution. A thorough and interesting collection of essays dealing with the movements of Europeans, east to west, in the recent migrations since the breakup of the former Soviet Union flowing from the ethnic conflicts that resulted from that breakup.

Messina, Anthony, ed. 2002. *West European Immigration and Immigration Policy in the New Century.* Westport, CT: Praeger. This interesting collection of essays analyzes why the major immigrant-receiving nations of Western Europe have historically permitted relatively high levels of migration since World War II.

They assess how governments in Western Europe are currently attempting to control the flow of immigration and manage the resulting domestic social, economic, and political effects induced by such large-scale immigration.

Morris, Milton. 1985. *Immigration: The Beleaguered Bureaucracy.* Washington, DC: Brookings Institution. Then a senior fellow at Brookings, author Morris addresses the concerns over contemporary immigration by focusing on the character and performance of the INS and the State Department's Bureau of Consular Affairs. His focus is on the problems resulting from serious shortcomings in administration: inadequate funding, unclear objectives, and faulty structures and procedures.

Muller, Thomas, and Thomas Espanshade. 1985. *The Fourth Wave.* Washington, DC: Urban Institute, 1985. This groundbreaking book was among the first and most thoroughly analytical examinations of the post-1965 wave of immigrants to the United States. It contributed significantly to renewing the scholarly debate over large-scale immigration and its costs and benefits to the United States.

National Research Council. 1997. *The New Americans: Economic, Demographic, and Fiscal Effects of Immigration.* Washington, DC: NRC/National Academy Press. Continuing to contribute to the now extensive literature examining the new (post-1965) wave of immigration and the degree to which the new immigrants are incorporating into U.S. society socially, politically and economically, it is in many ways *The Fourth Wave* circa 1997.

Nevins, Joseph. 2002. *Operation Gatekeeper: The Rise of "Illegal Aliens" and the Making of the U.S.-Mexican Boundary.* New York: Routledge. A comprehensive look at the illegal immigration problem, flow, and resulting impact of the U.S.- Mexican border sector.

O'Hanlon, Michael E., et al. 2002. *Protecting the American Homeland: A Preliminary Analysis.* Washington, DC: Brookings Institution. The authors offer a four-tier plan for efforts of the Bush administration and Congress; it includes a rationale and recommendations on spending and projected costs to the private sector, and the restructuring of federal agencies associated with establishing a Department of Homeland Security. Its recommendations include the restructuring of the INS and the Border Patrol as well as visa and naturalization activities into the new DHS.

Papademetriou, Demetrios, Alexander Alienkoff, and D. W. Meyers. 1999. *Reorganizing the U.S. Immigration Function: Toward a New Framework for Accountability.* Washington, DC: Carnegie Endowment for International Peace. This volume presents the Carnegie Endowment "plan" for restructuring the INS and reforming immigration policy. Many of its ideas and concerns are reflected in the new DHS approach. Its analysis presents a good picture of "what was wrong" with the INS and with U.S. immigration policy, justifying the concern that it "was broken and needed fixing" in such a way that a major reorganization was necessary rather than the incremental "tinkering" with reform that characterized efforts during the 1990s.

Papademetriou, Demetrious, and Mark Miller, eds. 1984. *The Unavoidable Issue.* Philadelphia: Institute for the Study of Human Issues. This volume is an impressive array of essays discussing all of the major issues of U.S. immigration policy and the need for reforms in policy; it is a particularly good review of the topic for the 1965 to 1980 period.

Passel, Jeffrey. 1994. *Immigrants and Taxes: A Reappraisal of Huddle's "The Cost of Immigration."* Washington, DC: Urban Institute. A major and important "reappraisal" of how to measure the costs of immigration, it rebuts Huddle's approach and finds a considerable difference in such costs, essentially concluding that immigration is a positive benefit rather than a significant cost to the U.S. economy.

Passel, Jeffrey S., and Rebecca L. Clark. 1994. *How Much Do Immigrants Really Cost?* Washington, DC: Urban Institute. Another extensive "rebut" of Huddle's analysis, it helped to fuel the academic debate over how to measure the costs and benefits of immigration, both legal and illegal, that raged during the 1990s as a result of the Huddle thesis.

Perea, Juan F. 1997. *Immigrants Out! The New Nativism and the Anti-Immigrant Impulses in the United States.* New York: New York University Press. A collection of eighteen original and specially commissioned essays by leading immigration scholars, this volume uses interdisciplinary perspectives to examine the current surge in nativism in light of past waves. It takes an unflinchingly critical look at the realities and the rhetoric of the new nativism, and examines the relationship between the races of immigrants and the perception of a national immigration crisis.

Portes, Alejandro, ed. 1996. *The New Second Generation.* New York: Russell Sage. Details the transformation of the postimmigrant generation during the current age of diversity in the United States.

———, ed. 1998. *The Economic Sociology of Immigration.* New York: Russell Sage. A culminating volume presenting the new scholarship on the "incorporation" of the second generation immigrants—politically, socially, and economically.

Portes, Alejandro, and Ruben G. Rumbaut. 2001. *Legacies: The Story of the Immigrant Second Generation.* Berkeley: University of California Press; New York: Russell Sage. This study reports on a series of surveys of immigrant children and their parents conducted between 1992 and 1996 in Miami, Florida, and San Diego, California. It uses interview data and school records to provide an overview of the "New Americans," emphasizes segmented assimilation and its determinants, how to measure "making it" in the United States, immigrants' outlooks on the U.S., language and ethnic identities, the role of schools and education on the psychology of the second generation, and the causes and consequences of school achievement or failure.

———, eds. 2001. *Ethnicities: Children of Immigrants in America.* New York: Russell Sage. These two volumes present the findings of an extensive examination of the "political incorporation" of second-generation immigrants. Whether in the summary volume above or in this collection of essays, the authors detail that while assimilation was in their view in the past a relatively homogeneous linear process, now it is a segmented one.

Pozzetta, George, ed. 1991. *Contemporary Immigration and American Society.* New York: Garland. The volume is the last in a series of twenty relating to immigration history. It is somewhat spotty and varied in its quality and relevance to contemporary society. It covers many groups that one would expect to see: Filipinos, Mexicans, Koreans, Haitians, Hispanics, Cubans, and Vietnamese. Yet some that one might look for are puzzlingly absent: Cambodians, Laotians, Chinese, Indians, Canadians, and Russians. No attention is paid to the influx during the 1980s from Ireland or Eastern Europe. The collection contains twenty-three articles drawn from seventeen journals that provide a useful cross-disciplinary perspective. By selecting sources only from previously published articles rather than original essays, the volume's impact is limited in terms of contributing significantly to the literature. Devoid of any post-IRCA perspective, it is limited too in its contribution toward new methodologies and interpretations relevant to contemporary U.S. society.

Reimers, David. 1985. *Still the Golden Door: The Third World Comes to America.* 2d ed. New York: Columbia University Press. One of the foremost immigrant historians in the United States examines post-1965 and particularly post-1980s immigration, including the impact of IRCA (1986) and IMMACT (1990) and the unforeseen consequences of those laws. Looking at the new "third world coming to America," it assesses these laws as less restrictive in their impact than opponents of the laws suggest.

Russell, James C. 2004. *Breach of Faith: American Churches and the Immigration Crisis.* Raleigh, NC: Representative Government Press. A polemical perspective on the role Christian churches play in the illegal immigration problem, it presents the view of the conservative right on the cultural wars engendered by the process.

Sergeant, Harriet. 2001. *Immigration and Asylum in the U.K.* London: Chameleon. This volume presents the results of a study of the Center for Policy Studies on the issues of immigration and asylum and how they impact the United Kingdom. A scholarly and objective examination of the issue.

Simcox, David. 1985. *Measuring the Fallout: The Cost of the IRCA Amnesty after 10 Years.* Washington, DC: Center for Immigration Studies. An extensive examination of the costs attributable to the legalization program of IRCA, it underscores the CIS's calls for strictly limiting immigration and its opposition to another amnesty.

———. 1997. *U.S. Immigration in the 1980s: Reappraisal and Reform.* Boulder, CO: Westview/Center for Immigration Studies. This collection of sixteen original essays by outstanding immigration scholars from various fields surveys current literature on immigration and its effects on the United States and on the problems or advantages that immigration brings to a rapidly changing society. Its major topics include effects on U.S. workers, national unity, California as the nation's immigrant laboratory, demographics of displacement, and approaches to a more rational, enforceable immigration policy.

Smith, James P., and Barry Edmonston, eds. 1998. *The New Americans: Studies on the Economic, Demographic, and Fiscal Effects of Immigration.* Washington, DC: National Academy Press. Comprehensive and objective analysis of the new immigration, both legal and illegal, and the broad-ranging effects of the issue.

Stedman, Stephen J., and Fred Tanner, eds. 2003. *Refugee Manipulations: War, Politics and the Abuse of Human Suffering.* Washington, DC: Brookings Institution Press. Examines why and the ways in which armed groups manipulate refugees and how and why international actors assist in their manipulation.

Suarez-Orozco, Marcedo, ed. 1998. *Crossings: Mexican Immigration in Interdisciplinary Perspectives.* Cambridge: Harvard University Press. Scholars from numerous disciplines examine the multifaceted effects of Mexican immigrant labor, predominantly undocumented labor, on the United States and on the immigrants themselves.

Tomasi, Lydio, ed. *In Defense of the Alien.* New York: Center for Migration Studies. Annual. These volumes are a series providing the collected essays and papers presented at the Center for Migration Studies' annual National Conference on Immigration Law held in Washington, DC. Each volume presents essays from leading government officials, lawyers, scholars, and immigration policy practitioners focused around the issues and topics discussed at the annual national convention.

Torr, James D. 2004. *Homeland Security.* San Diego: Greenhaven. A highly critical but comprehensive examination of the homeland security issue and its myriad ramifications. Torr is very skeptical as to the effectiveness that can or will be achieved by the "super-agency" approach to the massive new department, focusing on the many and largely unanticipated managerial problems that the huge new department will have.

Ueda, Reed. 1994. *Postwar Immigrant America: A Social History.* Boston: Bedford/St. Martin's. Using an interdisciplinary focus and joining history and several social science perspectives, this volume probes the impact of arriving ethnic groups on the historical foundations of the United States, stressing how the new Asian and Hispanic immigrants revitalized political and civic institutions inherited from the Founders and reshaped the debate over how democracy could encompass ethnic groups with greater inclusiveness and egalitarianism. It uses demographic and quantitative analysis applied to the rise of worldwide immigration as well as sociology and demography to understand the development of group life. Political science and law illuminate the relationship of immigration to U.S. government and its ethnic policies.

Wolfe, Alan. 2002. *One Nation, After All.* New York: Penguin Putnam. A "tour" through what middle-class Americans think about God, country, family, racism, welfare, immigration, homosexuality, the Right, the Left, and each other.

Yang, Philip O. 1995. *Post-1965 Immigration to the United States: Structural Determinants.* Westport, CT: Praeger. Yang examines why countries differ in the scale of legal permanent immigration in the period since 1965 by investigating the structural determinants of cross-national variation during this time. He seeks the integration and development of international migration theories. He discusses the policy implications of how the United States should regulate and control immigration.

Yans-McLaughlin, Virginia, ed. 1990. *Immigration Reconsidered: History, Sociology, and Politics.* New York: Oxford University Press. A collection of eleven original essays by scholars presenting at a conference in New York City in 1986, this volume covers various topics: immigration patterns, ethnicity and social structure, the study of new immigration, and new approaches to the study of immigration and the politics of immigration policy and its reform.

Zhou, Min, and Carl Bankston III. 1999. *Growing Up American: How Vietnamese Children Adapt to Life in the United States.* New York: Russell Sage. This book examines the single largest group of refugee children—the Vietnamese—as they experienced growing up in the United States. Chapters examine such topics as the scattering by the war, resettlement, reconstruction of an ethnic community, social networks, language and adaptation, experiences in adaptation in U.S. schools, bicultural conflicts, gender role changes, and delinquency.

Zimmerman, Klaus F. 2002. *European Migration: What Do We Know?* New York: Oxford University Press. A thorough assessment of the current situation regarding migration in a comprehensive range of European countries. It includes chapters on the United States, Canada, and New Zealand for comparative purposes. Each country "case study" is written by a local expert, and the overall editor is one of Europe's leading scholars on the economics of immigration.

Zolberg, Aristide, Astri Suhrki, and Sergio Aguayo. 1989. *Escape from Violence: Conflict and the Refugee Crisis in the Developing World.* New York: Oxford University Press. A cogent treatment of the causes of refugee flows, emphasizing domestic and international causes and regional differentiations around the globe. Case studies are rich in detail; analysis is systematic and comprehensive.

Zucker, Norman, and Naomi Flink Zucker. 1987. *The Guarded Gate: The Reality of American Refugee Policy.* San Diego: Harcourt Brace, Jovanovich. A critical assessment of U.S. asylum policy, stressing the political elements of the asylum debate. Emphasis is on U.S. government asylum policy rather than refugee policy broadly construed.

Zuniga, Victor, and Ruben Hernandez-Leon, eds. 2005. *New Destinations: Mexican Immigration to the United States.* New York: Russell Sage. An eclectic array of essays on the new Mexican immigration to the United States, it includes both legal and illegal immigration matters. It looks at several U.S. communities where they settle and how they are shaping and shaped by their new areas of settlement. It uses census data to discern the historical evolution of Mexican immigration to the United States, discussing the demographic, economic, and legal factors that led to recent moves to areas beyond where their predecessors had settled, concluding that undocumented aliens did a better job than did their documented peers in integrating into the local culture. It looks at paternalism and xenophobic aspects of local residents toward the new migrants, the strong work ethic of the migrants, and provides hopeful examples of progress. It is the first scholarly assessment of the new settlements and experiences in the Midwest, Northeast, and the deep South, and of America's largest immigrant group enriched by the perspectives from demographers, sociologists, folklorists, anthropologists, and political scientists.

Leading Scholarly Journals

American Demographics
Seema Mayar, Editor
470 Park Avenue South, 8th Floor
New York, NY 10016
(212) 545–3600
Fax (917) 981–2927

Published ten times per year, this peer-reviewed journal is an outlet for multidisciplinary articles dealing with all topics related to demography as well as occasional articles and reflective essays on migration, legal and illegal immigration, and an annual resource guide.

American Journal of Sociology
Andrew Abbott, Editor
University of Chicago Press, Journal Division
1427 East 60th Street
Chicago, IL 60637
E-mail: ajs@src.uchicago.edu
Fax: (773) 753–0811

A scholarly, peer-reviewed quarterly journal of sociology, with frequent articles concerning assimilation and integration, social trends, and policies regarding migration and legal and illegal immigration, it also has book reviews on immigration-related topics.

Citizenship Studies
Engin F. Isin, York University, Canada
Taylor and Francis Group, Carfax Publishing
1185 Avenue of the Americas
New York, NY 10036
E-mail: isin@yorku.ca
http://www.tandf.co.uk/journals

This quarterly journal publishes internationally recognized scholarly work on contemporary issues in citizenship, human rights, and democratic processes from an interdisciplinary perspective covering politics, sociology, history, and cultural studies.

Columbia Law Review
Margaret L. Taylor
435 W. 116th Street
New York, NY 10027
(800) 828–7571

Law review published eight times per year. Frequently has case reviews and analytical articles and original essays dealing with immigration law matters.

Demography
Barbara Entwisle, UNC, Chapel Hill, and
  S. Philip Morgan, Duke University
Editors, Demography
Department of Sociology
Ohio State University
Columbus, OH 43210
(614) 292–2858
E-mail: demography@osu.edu

This peer-reviewed journal of the Population Association of America publishes scholarly research of interest to demographers from a multidisciplinary perspective, with emphasis on social sciences, geography, history, biology, statistics, business, epidemiology, and public health. It publishes specialized research papers and historical and comparative studies.

Ethnic and Racial Studies
John Solomos, South Bank University, UK
Taylor and Francis Group (as above)

A bimonthly journal for the analysis of race, ethnicity, and nationalism in the present global environment. An interdisciplinary forum for research and theoretical analysis, using disciplines of sociology, social policy, anthropology, political science, economics, geography, international relations, history, social psychology, and cultural studies.

Ethnohistory
Neil Whitehead, University of Wisconsin–Madison
905 W. Main Street, 18-B
Durham, NC 27701

A quarterly publication of the *Journal of the American Society for Ethnohistory*, it contains articles of original research, commentaries, review essays, and book reviews.

Ethnology
Leonard Plotnicov
University of Pittsburgh, Department of Anthropology
3H29 Posvar Hall
Pittsburgh, PA 15260
E-mail: ethnology@pitt.edu

This international journal of culture and social anthropology publishes original research articles by scientists of any country regarding cultural anthropology with substantive data. Topics of interest relate to ethnicity, social integration, and migration adaptation.

Foreign Affairs
James F. Hoge Jr., Editor
58 East 68th Street
New York, NY 10021
E-mail: foraff@palmcoastd.com; or ForAff@email.cfr.org
Fax: (212) 434–9859

This bimonthly magazine publishes articles and original essays on topics related to foreign policy, including policy related to both legal and illegal migration, by both scholars and practitioners in the field. It regularly publishes related book reviews.

Georgetown Immigration Law Journal
Georgetown University Law Center
Office of Journal Administration
600 New Jersey Avenue, N.W.
Washington, DC 20001
(202) 662–9635; (800) 828–7571

This quarterly law review is the most specifically related law journal dealing with U.S. immigration law, its current developments, and reform-related matters concerning all three branches of the U.S. government, and frequently focusing on illegal immigration. Contains case reviews, articles, notes and commentaries, and workshop reports devoted to the topic.

Geographical Journal
Andrew Millington
Department of Geography
University of Leicester
University Road, Leicester
LEI 7RH, UK
Tel: +4(0)1865 244083
Fax: +4(0) 1865 381381
E-mail: acm4@le.ac.uk, or jnlinfo@blackwellpublishers.co.uk
http://www.blackwellpublishers.co.uk

The quarterly academic journal of the Royal Geographical Society, publishing research reports and review articles of refereed articles related to all subjects concerning geography, therefore often dealing with international migration matters.

Geographical Review
Paul Starrs, Editor, University of Nevada
American Geographical Society
120 Wall Street, Suite 100
New York, NY 10005
E-mail: starrs@unr.edu
http://www.geography.unr.edu

The quarterly journal of the American Geographical Society, it publishes research on all topics related to geography: hence, occasional ones dealing with legal and illegal migration and immigration reform, and with the incorporation of immigrants. It also publishes related book reviews.

Harvard Law Review
Harvard Law Review, Gannett House
1511 Massachusetts Avenue
Cambridge, MA 02138

This law review is published eight times per year. Contains original articles, case reviews, essays, commentaries, and book reviews occasionally on topics related to U.S immigration law and its reform.

Identities
Jonathan D. Hill, Southern Illinois University,
Taylor and Francis Group (as above)

Identities explores the relationship of racial, ethnic, and national identities and power hierarchies within national and global arenas. Interdisciplinary focus using social, political, and cultural analyses of the processes of domination, struggle, and resistance; class structures and gender relations integral to both maintaining and challenging subordination.

Immigrants and Minorities
Frank Cass, Gainsborough House
11 Gainsborough Road
London Ell 1RS, England

This British quarterly focuses on immigrant minorities in Western societies.

INS Reporter
Immigration and Naturalization Service
425 I Street, N.W.
Washington, DC 20536

A quarterly publication that provides brief surveys of recent developments in U.S. immigration law.

INS Statistical Yearbook
425 I Street, N.W.
Washington, DC 20536

An annual publication giving statistical data in text, graphic, and tabular form. The latest "official" numbers on U.S. immigration.

International Migration
International Organization for Migration
P.O. Box 71
CH-1211 Geneva 19
Switzerland

This quarterly is an intergovernmental publication featuring documents, conference reports, and articles dealing with international migration topics.

International Migration Review
Center for Migration Studies
209 Flagg Place
Staten Island, NY 10304

The leading quarterly journal in the field of migration, *IMR* contains current research articles, book reviews, documents, and bibliographies.

International Organizations
Peter Gourevitch, University of California, San Diego
9500 Gilman Drive
La Jolla, CA 92093–0519
http://www.mitpress.mit.edu/IO

This journal is published quarterly by MIT Press for the World Peace Foundation. It contains articles on all aspects of world politics and international political economy.

International Review of the Red Cross
International Committee of the Red Cross
17 Avenue de la Paix
CH-1211 Geneva
Switzerland

This journal, published six times annually, contains articles on international humanitarian law and policy matters.

International Social Sciences Journal
David Makinson, Editor
108 Cowley Road

Oxford, OX4, JF, UK and
350 Main Street
Malden, MA 02148,
E-mail: jninfo@Blackwellpublishers,co.uk

This quarterly journal is published by Blackwell Publishers for
UNESCO. It regularly contains articles concerning international
migration and its impact on societies and social systems, and
other topics related to UNESCO.

International Studies Quarterly
James M. McCormick, editor
Iowa State University

Another scholarly quarterly journal published by Blackwell Publishers (as above).

International Studies Review
Linda Miller, Brown University, RI

This quarterly journal is another published by Blackwell, with
contact information as listed above. The journal is published for
the International Studies Association. It contains original scholarly articles of research, review essays, book reviews, and an annual special issue on a theme.

Journal of American Studies
Richard Gray, University of Sussex
Cambridge University Press
40 West 20th Street
New York, NY 10011–4211
http://www.cup.cam.ac.uk

Published three times per year, this multidisciplinary, scholarly
refereed journal is multinational with an emphasis on articles on
politics, economics, and geography, and with book reviews that
will often relate to immigration matters.

Journal of Economic History
Jan De Vries, Stanford University
Social Science History Institute, Building 200, Room 3
Stanford, CA 94305–2024

(520) 621–2575
E-mail: sisaac@u.arizona.edu

This journal publishes original scholarship on the study of economic aspects of the human past from a diversity of perspectives, most notably history and economics.

Journal of Economic Issues
Department of Economics
Bucknell University
Lewisburg, PA 89557–0207
E-mail: atkinson@unr.nevada.edu

A scholarly economics journal covering all aspects of economic issues, hence occasional original research on immigration and migration with a focus on economic impact, labor market issues, and so on. Each issue has book reviews of related matters as well.

Journal of Economic Perspectives
Alan Krueger, Princeton University
Hubert Humphrey Institute of Public Affairs
University of Minnesota
301 19th Avenue South
Minneapolis, MN 55455
E-mail: jep@hh.umn.edu

This journal of the American Economic Association publishes occasional symposium issues and, regularly, original scholarly articles, features, and economic analysis on a variety of public policy issues, including both legal and illegal immigration, and reviews of related books.

Journal of Ethnic and Migration Studies
Russell King, University of Sussex, UK
Taylor and Francis Group (as above)

Edited from the Sussex Center for Migration Research at the University of Sussex, the journal publishes quality research on all forms of migration and its consequences, with articles on ethnicity, ethnic relations and ethnic conflict, race and racism, multiculturalism and pluralism, nationalism and transnationalism, citizenship and integration, identity and hybridity, globalization and cosmopolitanism, policy debates, and theoretical papers.

Journal of Intercultural Studies
Pete Lentini and Jan van Bommel, Monash University,
Australia
Taylor and Francis Group (as above)

Presents international research related to intercultural studies across national and disciplinary boundaries. One issue per year is thematic. Examines common issues across a range of disciplinary perspectives. Peer-reviewed research, theoretical papers, and book reviews are included in each issue.

Journal of International Refugee Law
Oxford University Press
Walton Street
Oxford OX2 6DP, UK

This quarterly publishes articles on refugee law and policy matters, including legislation, documentation, and abstracts of recent publications in the field.

Migration
Berlin Institute for Social Research
Postfach 1125
1000 Berlin 30
Germany

This European journal concerns international migration and ethnic relations.

Migration News
http://migration.ucdavis.edu

This monthly newsletter, published by the University of California Davis, concerns all manner of topics related to migration, especially as illegal immigration impacts U.S. society.

Migration World
Center for Migration Studies
209 Flagg Place
Staten Island, NY 10304

This journal publishes articles and information about migration and refugee problems worldwide in a readable and accessible way. It is a good source for school and college reports.

National Identities
Peter Catterall, Queen Mary University of London, UK
Taylor and Francis Group (as above)

Journal published three times annually focusing on identity/ethnicity by examining how they are shaped and changed, and on the transmission/persistence of national identities.

Patterns of Prejudice
David Cesaraini, University of Southampton, UK
Brian Klug, Saint Xavier University, Chicago, IL (U.S. Consulting Editor)
Taylor and Francis Group (as above)

New journal providing a forum for exploring the historical roots and contemporary varieties of demonizations of "the other." Probes language and construction of "race," nation, color, and ethnicity as well as the linkages between these categories. The journal also discusses issues and policy agenda, such as asylum, illegal immigration, hate crimes, Holocaust denial, and citizenship.

Policy Studies Journal
Uday Desai, Southern Illinois University, Carbondale, and
Mark C. Shellby II, Iowa State University
Policy Studies Organization
711 South Ashton Lane
Champaign, IL 61820
(217) 352–7700; Fax: (217) 352–3037

This journal of the Policy Studies Organization is produced at Iowa State University, College of Education. It is published quarterly with articles related to all issues of public policy and has occasional symposium issues and regular book reviews.

Policy Studies Review
Georgia State University, Department of Public
Administration and Urban Studies

As above, this journal is also a product of the Policy Studies Organization.

Political Science Quarterly
Demetrios Caraley, Bernard College, Columbia University
475 Riverside Drive, Suite 1274

New York, NY 10115–1274
(978) 750–8400
http://www.jstor.org

This quarterly scholarly journal discusses public and international affairs. It is nonpartisan, with scholarly reviewed articles devoted to the study and analysis of government, politics, and international affairs, with original articles and essays, review essays, and book reviews.

Race Ethnicity and Education
David Gilborn, University of London, UK
Taylor and Francis Group (as above)

This interdisciplinary refereed journal publishes international scholarship, research, and debate on issues concerning the dynamics of race, racism, and ethnicity in educational policy, theory, and practice, focusing on the interconnections between race, ethnicity, and multiple forms of oppression including class, gender, sexuality, and disability.

Refugee Reports
U.S. Committee for Refugees
1717 Massachusetts Ave, N.W., Suite 701
Washington, DC 20036

This is a monthly report of information and documents concerning refugees and the legislation, policies, and programs affecting them. A year-end statistical issue is published every December.

Refugee Survey Quarterly
Center for the Documentation on Refugees
UNHCR case postale 2500
1211-Geneva 2 Depot, Switzerland

This quarterly lists abstracts of the many publications concerning refugees, including a selection of "country reports" and one on human rights–related legal documents.

Social Identities
Abebe Zegeye, University of South Africa and
David T. Goldberg, University of California, Irvine
Taylor and Francis Group (as above)

This interdisciplinary and international journal focuses on issues addressing social identities in the context of the transforming political economies and cultures of postmodern and postcolonial conditions.

Social Science Quarterly
Robert Lineberry, Department of Political Science
University of Houston
47 PGH
Houston, TX 77204–3011
(713) 743–3935
Fax: (713) 743–3927
E-mail: ssq@mail.uh.edu

Published for the Southwestern Social Science Association by Blackwell Publishing, this interdisciplinary quarterly publishes articles of original research, review essays, book reviews, and occasional symposium issues. It frequently contains articles dealing with U.S. immigration and illegal immigration policy, and with issues related to the incorporation of immigrants and their children into U.S. society.

State of the World Population
UN Population Fund
United Nations Plaza
New York, NY 10017

An annual publication that covers world population growth and problems resulting from it. Includes the latest in official statistics.

Reports and Government Documents

There are innumerable government reports and studies from a variety of agencies that emphasize immigration laws, policies, and their impact. This section lists some exemplary sources.
Center for Immigration Studies (CIS). 2005. "Economy Slowed But Immigration Didn't: The Foreign-born Population, 2000–2004." Washington, DC: CIS, A Steven Camaota study and analysis.

Ewing, Walter A. 2005. "The Economics of Necessity." *Immigration Policy in Focus* 4, no. 3 (May): 8 pgs. An American Immigra-

tion Law Foundation report. Can be found at http://www
.ailf.org/ipc/economicsofnecessityprint.asp. Accessed July 14,
2006.

GAO. 1990. "Immigration Reform: Employer Sanctions and the
Question of Discrimination." Report to Congress. Study measur-
ing, and finding, the increase in discrimination as a result of
IRCA.

INS. *An Immigrant Nation: United States Regulation of Immigration, 1798–1991.* Washington, DC: U.S. Government Printing
Office. A summary report giving the broad outline of the history
of immigration regulation through the 1990 IMMACT.

———. 1995. "Illegal Aliens: National Net Cost Estimates Vary
Widely." Washington, DC: U.S. Government Printing Office. A
summary of all the various studies that found pro and con measures of the net cost effect of immigration on the U.S. economy.

———. 1997. "Illegal Aliens: Extent of Welfare Benefits Received
on Behalf of U.S. Citizen Children." Washington, DC: U.S. Government Printing Office. The GAO's study measuring the extent
of welfare given to the children of illegal aliens.

———. 1998. "Illegal Aliens: Significant Obstacles to Reducing
Unauthorized Alien Employment Exists." Washington, DC: U.S.
Government Printing Office.

———. 1999a. "Illegal Immigration: Status of Southwest Border
Strategy Implementation." Washington, DC: U.S. Government
Printing Office.

———. 1999b. "Welfare Reform: Many States Continued Some
Federal or State Benefits for Immigrants." Washington, DC: U.S.
Government Printing Office.

———. 1999c. "Welfare Reform: Public Assistance Benefits Provided to Recently Naturalized Citizens." Washington, DC: U.S.
Government Printing Office.

———. 2002a. "Alien Smuggling: Management and Operational
Improvements Needed to Address Growing Problem." Washing-

ton, DC: U.S. Government Printing Office. GAO's report on alien smuggling with latest data on estimates of its extent and suggestions to curb the trend.

———. 2000b. "H-1B Foreign Workers: Better Controls Needed to Help Employers and Protect Workers." Washington, DC: U.S. Government Printing Office.

———. 2000c. "Illegal Aliens: Opportunities Exist to Improve the Expedited Removal Process." Washington, DC: U.S. Government Printing Office.

———. 2004. "Overstay Tracking: A Key Component of Homeland Security and a Layered Defense." GAO-04082. Washington, DC: U.S. Government Printing Office.

Pew Hispanic Center. 2003. "Remittance Senders and Receivers: Tracking the Transnational Channels." Washington, DC: Pew Hispanic Center.

Select Commission on Immigration and Refugee Policy (SCIRP). 1981. *Final Report.* Washington, DC. Final report of the SCIRP, which laid the groundwork for what became the Immigration Reform and Control Act of 1986 (IRCA), with its employer sanctions and amnesty provisions as well as expanded seasonal agricultural workers provisions.

Stana, Richard M. 2003. "Homeland Security: Challenges to Implementing the Immigration Interior Enforcement Strategy." GAO-03–660T. Washington, DC: U.S. Government Printing Office.

Suro, Roberto, and Audrey Singer. 2002. "Latino Growth in Metropolitan America: Changing Patterns, New Locations." Survey Series, Census 2000. Washington, DC: Brookings Institution. http://www.brookings.edu/es/urban/publications/surosingerexsum.htm.

Suro, Roberto, and Sonya Tafoya. 2004. "Dispersal and Concentration: Patterns of Latino Residential Settlement." Washington, DC: Pew Hispanic Center.

UN High Commission for Refugees. 2006. "The U.N. Refugee Agency." http://www.unhcr.org/cgi-bin/texis/vtx/home. Accessed February 9, 2006.

U.S. Bureau of the Census. 2001. "The Foreign-Born Population in the United States, March, 2000, Current Population Reports." Washington, DC: U.S. Government Printing Office.

U.S. Department of Health and Human Services. 2000. "Temporary Assistance for Needy Families (TANF) Program: Third Annual Report to Congress." Washington, DC: U.S. Government Printing Office.

U.S. Department of Justice. 2002. "Follow-Up Report on INS Efforts to Improve the Control of Nonimmigrant Overstays." Report No. 1–2002–006. Washington, DC: U.S. Government Printing Office, April.

———. "Undocumented Aliens in the U.S." http://www.usdoj .gov/graphics/aboutinst/statistics/illegal alien/index.htm. Accessed November 14, 2001.

U.S. Department of Labor. 1999. "International Migration to the United States, 1999." Washington, DC: U.S. Government Printing Office.

U.S. Department of State. 1999. "U.S. Refugee Admissions for Fiscal Year 2000." Washington, DC: U.S. Government Printing Office.

———. 2000. "Proposed Refugee Admissions for Fiscal Year 2001: Report to Congress." Washington, DC: U.S. Government Printing Office.

Nonprint Resources

Al Qaeda. 2003. 46 minutes, color.
Insight Media
2162 Broadway

New York, NY 10024
(800) 233–9910: (212) 721–6316
E-mail: elana@insightmedia.com

Covering the period from 9/11 to the start of the Gulf War, this program shows the way in which Al-Qaeda reinvented itself as a high-tech, highly mobile, decentralized terror network. It includes interviews with key specialists and offers footage of jihadist training, U.S. search and destroy missions, and the capture of Islamist militants.

Angel Island: A Story of Chinese Immigration. 2002.
    12 minutes, color.
Films for the Humanities and Sciences
P.O. Box 2053
Princeton, NJ 08543–2053

From 1910 to 1943, Chinese immigrants passed through Angel Island in San Francisco Bay, sometimes called the Ellis Island of the West. They were legally discriminated against, and this program looks at how two women are raising funds and awareness to have the old immigration station restored. Slated for destruction, the station was spared in 1970 when a park ranger discovered, beneath layers of paint, poems written by anxious detainees over their fear of deportation.

The Asianization of America. 2002. 26 minutes, color.
Films for the Humanities and Sciences.

This program examines the role of Asian-Americans half a century after repeal of the Chinese Exclusion Act, seeking to determine what accounts for their success in academia and the extent to which they can, should, or want to blend into the American melting pot.

Biomedical Weapons: A Modern Threat. 2003. 25 minutes, color.
Insight Media.

This program defines biochemical weapons and discusses the manufacture of such weapons as anthrax and mustard gas. It provides simulations of biochemical attack and outlines their psychological affects. It explores the history of biochemical terrorism and addresses the likelihood of a terrorist attack.

Bioterrorism. 2001. 50 minutes, color.
Insight Media.

The anthrax episode in the United States in the wake of 9/11 raised awareness of the possibility of a wide-scale bioterrorism attack in the U.S. In this program, officials from the departments of State and Defense and leading bioterrorism experts including several veterans of the massive Soviet bioweapons program discuss the many obstacles standing in the way of a successful attack.

Caught in the Crossfire: Arab-Americans in Wartime. 2002.
   54 minutes, color.
First Run/Icarus Films
32 Court Street, 21st Floor
Brooklyn, NY 11201
http://www.frif.com. 800–876–1710.

This film covers New York City's Arab population caught in the cross fire of President Bush's War on Terrorism, and the cold welcome they now experience. CNN diplomatic correspondent for the leading independent Arab newspaper, Raghida Dergham, is featured, as are Khader El-Yateem, an Arab-Christian, whose Arabic Lutheran Church serves as a haven for Brooklyn Arabs, Muslim and Christian alike; and Ahmed Nasser, a Yemen-born police officer stationed at Ground Zero after 9/11, who relates how Arab American calls for help when harassed were ignored in his precinct. Film shows how they are torn between their adopted country and their homelands as they wrestle with their place in wartime America.

Chasing the Sleeper Cell. 2003. 60 minutes, color.
Insight Media.

This PBS program features a joint investigation by *Frontline* and the *New York Times* into an ongoing domestic terrorism case involving Al-Qaeda operatives and the U.S. citizens they trained. It discusses FBI and CIA effectiveness in combating sleeper cells.

Conspiracy: The Anthrax Attacks. 2004. 50 minutes, color.
Insight Media.

This program looks at how, less than two weeks after 9/11, news outlets and prominent senators became targets of the first biowarfare attacks in U.S. history. It investigates mysteries surrounding the strain of anthrax used, which had been under the control of the U.S. biodefense industry.

Death on a Friendly Border. 2002. 26 minutes, color.
Filmakers Library
124 East Fortieth Street
No. 901
New York, NY 10016
(212) 808-4980
Fax: (212) 808-4983
E-mail: mailto:info@filmakers.com
http://www.filmakers.com

The border between Tijuana and San Diego is the most militarized border between "friendly" countries anywhere. Since 1994, when the United States began Operation Gatekeeper, on average one person per day dies trying to cross. This film puts a face on that daily tragedy by following the story of a young woman who makes the perilous journey, with its hardships of heat, thirst, and abusive border guards.

The Double Life of Ernesto Gomez. 2001. 54 minutes, color.
Filmakers Library

This film focuses on fifteen-year-old Ernesto Gomez, who has two identities, two families, and three nations: the United States, Mexico, and Puerto Rico. It follows his journey from Mexico to the United States to meet his Puerto Rican birth mother and to learn of his heritage. This award-winning film documents his struggle for identity.

Dying to Get In: Illegal Immigration to the E.U. 2002.
58 minutes, color.
Films for the Humanities and Sciences.

This video surveys the high-tech methods used to secure E.U.'s borders against refugees and asylum seekers. It interviews human smugglers, illegal immigrants, and European immigration bureaucrats who attempt to maintain "fortress Europe" by keeping out as many immigrants as possible.

El Chogui: A Mexican Immigrant Story. 2002. 57 minutes, color.
Filmakers Library

This film follows a young peasant from Oaxaca, Mexico, Louis Miquel, as he tries to lift his family out of poverty by boxing. He immigrates to the United States, as did countless of his compatriots. The film follows his transition over six years, from his tension-filled, illegal border crossing with his sisters, to later when he brings his four brothers to California.

The Electronic Curtain. 1997. 52 minutes, color.
First Run/Icarus Films
32 Court Street
21st Floor
Brooklyn, NY 11201
(800) 876-1710
http://www.frif.com

The program examines the replacement of the former iron curtain with a new, highly sophisticated invisible electronic curtain aimed at curbing illegal immigration from Eastern to Western Europe.

English Only in America. 2002. 25 minutes, color.
Films for the Humanities and Sciences.

When California passed its "English only" law, it set off a storm of legal and social debate that continues to rage. This film interviews persons pro and con the English-only policy from social, legal, and education perspectives.

Escape to the E.U.: Human Rights and Immigration Policy in Conflict. 2002. 58 minutes.
Films for the Humanities and Sciences.

Covers human rights policy of the E.U. since 1960. It examines the processing of refugee/asylum seekers in Sweden and Great Britain, and the UN and E.U. policy on human rights issues. News stories on a Bangladeshi detainee's suicide, Kosivar/Albanian detainees' deportation to near certain death, and Cameroonian political activists are featured. The film looks at xenophobia as a political tool.

Facing Up to Illegal Immigration. 2004. 23 minutes.
Films Media Group
P.O. Box 2053
Princeton, NJ 08543–2053
(800) 257–5126 or Fax: (609) 671–0266
e-mail: custserv@filmsmediagroup.com

Discussion of the issue of whether there is a realistic way to stop illegal immigrants at America's borders. It grapples with the fact that the world's only superpower cannot seem to control its borders; cannot seem to function without illegal immigrants. An ABC News special, it offers a balanced look at the illegal immigration situation in the United States, addressing issues such as the liability of porous borders in a time of terrorism, or the need—like it our not—for illegal aliens in the workforce and whether they really take jobs away from U.S. citizens or are doing work that Americans themselves are unwilling to do.

From a Different Shore: The Japanese-American Experience. 2002.
    50 minutes, color.
Films for the Humanities and Sciences.

Japanese-Americans are often considered a "model minority." This video explores their experiences from the first immigrants, the Issei, through their children, the Nissei, who endured confinement in camps during World War II, to their grandchildren, exploring these through three families whose members span all three generations.

From the Other Side. 2002. 99 minutes, color.
Icarus Films.

With technology developed by the U.S. military, the INS has stemmed the flow of illegal immigrants in San Diego. But for the desperate, there are still the dangerous deserts of Arizona, where renowned filmmaker Chantel Akerman shifts her focus. A multiple-award-winning documentary film.

The Golden Cage: A Story of California's Farmworkers. 1990.
    29 minutes, color.
Filmakers Library

A modern "Grapes of Wrath," this film offers a vivid and moving portrait of contemporary farmworkers using historical footage, interviews, newspaper clippings, and black and white stills. It traces the history of the United Farm Workers union from the 1960s to 1990, showing the tactics used by many companies to evade using union labor. It shows candid interviews with legal and illegal migrant workers, growers, doctors, and others.

Human Contraband: Selling the American Dream. 2002.
  22 minutes, color.
Films for the Humanities and Sciences.

This ABC news program investigates the lucrative trade in smuggling into Mexico desperate human beings from all over the world, who view that country as the back door to the United States. INS officials discuss multilateral efforts to combat illegal entry to the United States.

Illegal Americans. 2002. 45 minutes, color.
Films for the Humanities and Sciences.

This CBS news documentary looks at the hazardous enterprise of immigrants coming to the United States illegally, focusing on their plight. It examines their living conditions in detention centers, the growing strains they place on the U.S. cities who provide assistance to those who manage to evade capture, the sweatshops that exploit them, and the efforts of some who attempt to beat the system via false ID's and marriages of convenience.

Immigration: Who Has Access to the American Dream? 2002.
  28 minutes, color.
Films for the Humanities and Sciences.

Program reviews how new policy directives affect the survival of new immigrants to the United States, covering a variety of questions, such as how many immigrants should be allowed in; who, if anyone, should receive preferential treatment; and how illegal immigrants should be handled. It examines those issues from various perspectives: those seeking entry and organizations who assist them; an immigration judge; an immigrant from Kenya; and a Korean immigrant owner of a New York City deli.

Inside the Terror Network. 2001. 60 minutes, color.
Insight Media.

This PBS video examines three of the 9/11 hijackers for insight into the making of a radical terrorist. It traces their movements in the days, months, and years leading up to the 9/11 attacks and shows how they slipped between the cracks of U.S. law enforcement.

Interpol Investigates: One-Way Ticket. 2004. 60 minutes, color.
Insight Media.

This program examines illegal immigration issues, highlighting the case in which a boat carrying more than 300 illegal Chinese immigrants ran aground in New York harbor. It shows how the case led domestic and international investigators to the gangs of Chinatown and on a seven-year hunt to find the leaders of the smuggling operation.

In the Land of Plenty. 1999. 62 minutes, color.
Filmakers Library.

This video follows Mexican migrant farmworkers, most of whom do not speak English, are undocumented, and lack the means to protect themselves from exploitation, through the strawberry fields of Watsonville, CA. It follows the lives of the workers—their long hours at poor wages, exposure to toxic chemicals, lack of health insurance and child care. It documents how they return far more to the economy than they take from it. Their meager wages are taxed though they have no benefits, yet they are looked upon with hostility by the government as well as by private citizens.

Legacy of Shame: Migrant Labor, an American Institution. 2002.
    52 minutes, color.
Films for the Humanities and Sciences.

This video is a follow-up to the 1960 award-wining "Harvest of Shame." It documents ongoing exploitation of America's migrant labor by highlighting efforts made to protect them. It investigates pesticide risks, uneven enforcement of employment and immigration regulations, and peonage conditions. It covers efforts of rural legal services as advocates for this "silent-minority." A CBS news documentary.

Legal Limbo: The War on Terrorism and the Judicial Process.
　2004. 23 minutes, color.
Films Media Group.

Asks the question, Does the war on terrorism require a fundamental shift in the U.S. judicial process? Highlighting two case studies, the program examines whether the judicial process was sidestepped by the Bush administration in the interest of combating terrorism. Cases examined are those of Zacharias Moussauoui and his role in the attacks of 9/11; and Jose Padilla, a U.S. citizen accused of plans to use a "dirty bomb."

Liberty and Security in an Age of Terrorism. 2003. 23 minutes,
　color.
Films Media Group.

This film grapples with the issues of balance between national security needs of the post-9/11 world and the basic civil liberty values central to our society. Using a hypothetical scenario, a panel of persons confronts the issues and wrestles with the high-stakes questions in discussing the implications of the USA Patriot Act, surveillance of suspects, closed deportation hearings, demands for student information, and just what constitutes an unaligned combatant.

A Nation of Immigrants: The Chinese-American Experience.
　2002. 20 minutes, color.
Films for the Humanities and Sciences.

This video explores the plight of Chinese immigrants, including their hard work for pitifully low wages, racial discrimination, victimization in race riots, and so forth.

Natives: Immigrant Bashing on the Border. 1992. 15 minutes,
　black and white.
Filmakers Library

This video captures the unabashed xenophobia of many Californians living along the U.S.-Mexican border as they react to the influx of illegal aliens who they believe are draining the community's resources and are often criminals. It critiques the nativist position by contrasting their professed love of country with racist and antidemocratic attitudes. One interviewee advocates machine-gunning down a few at the border as a warning to others.

One-Way Ticket to Ghana: Forced Deportation from the E.U.
2002. 58 minutes, color.
Films for Humanities and Sciences.

Video story of a Ugandan, Peter Ulewiri, whose application to the E.U. was denied. He was forcibly deported to Ghana. The film examines the corrupt system in which E.U. police and immigration authorities pay Ghana to act as a transfer point for black deportees whose life in Ghana typically means years of imprisonment and an obscure death. It explores evidence of European racial bias against black Africans.

The Patriot Act under Fire. 2003. 23 minutes, color.
Films Media Group.

For many, worrying about constitutional rights seems like an archaic luxury in an age of international terrorism. The need for tighter security made civil liberties seem less critical when the nation confronted such terrorism by passing urgent measures such as the USA Patriot Act, designed to defend the country. Two years after its passage, ABC News and Ted Koppel take a hard look at the law with representatives from the Justice Department, the ACLU, and others.

Refugees in Our Backyard. 1990. 58 minutes, color.
Icarus Films.

Video focusing on the controversies arising from the arrival of so many undocumented into the U.S. Portions of the film deal with the dangers of the journey, State Department policies contributing to the problem, the hardships of the illegals, the impact of civil strife in Central America, and the enormous obstacles its people face as they attempt to escape to the United States.

Stories from the Mines: How Immigrant Miners Changed America. 2002. 57 minutes, color.
Films for the Humanities and Sciences.

America's rise to superpower status was fueled to a great degree by the social and industrial impact of coal-mining in northeastern Pennsylvania. This meticulously researched program uses location footage, archival film, period photos, dramatizations, and academic commentary to examine U.S. labor. It vividly captures the agitation and the often violent suppression that characterized the times and emphasizes the precedents, including child labor laws, and the right to collective bargaining, set against the stark backdrop of immigrant miners being exploited by industrialists.

Terrorism against Americans. 1996. 50 minutes.
Insight Media.

Until recently, most Americans believed themselves safe from terrorist attacks that occur in other parts of the world. Such incidents as the bombing of the World Trade Center proved that such acts of violence can occur anywhere. The film traces the rise of political terrorism worldwide and the growing threat to the United States.

The Terrorism Alert System. 2003. 23 minutes, color.
Insight Media.

This video explains the now much maligned five-level terrorism alert system developed by the DHS. It provides recommendations to government and the private sector on responses to each level of risk.

Ties that Bind: Immigration Stories. 2002. 58 minutes, color.
Films for Humanities and Sciences.

This film examines the human drama behind the current immigration debate on both sides of the Texas/Mexico border while exploring the root causes of why Mexicans emigrate. Emphasis is on the role of transnational corporations and their social/economic impacts on both Mexicans and North Americans. It explores the increasingly restrictive nature of immigration policies, as well as the strong family values that immigrants bring with them and their positive impact on U.S. culture.

Trafficked: Children as Sexual Slaves. 2004. 52 minutes, color.
Filmakers Library

The trafficking of women and children for the purpose of prostitution is a global problem. The United Nations estimates that more than 1 million children are forced into sexual slavery each year. This documentary follows Chris Payne, a former police officer turned private investigator, as he investigates this shocking crime. It focuses on the case of "Nikkie," a young Thai girl found working in a brothel in Sydney who is hastily deported. Payne examines the circumstances that forced her into a brothel and what became of her after her deportation back to Thailand. His search leads him to Asia and the parents of another Thai "sex slave," whose death in an immigration detention center made the headlines. A powerful documentary, it offers disturbing insight into the international sex trade.

When East Meets East. 2002. 53 minutes, color.
Films for Humanities and Sciences.

This genre-breaking documentary explores the issues of ethnic and cultural identity through interviews with some of today's most prominent Asian film figures.

With Us or Against Us: Afghans in America. 2002. 27 minutes, color.
Filmakers Library

This film explores the experiences of Afghan refugees who fled in the 1970s, many of whom settled in Fremont, California. Post-9/11, they find themselves in a cultural cross fire as their adoptive homeland is at war with their native land. Ironically, in 1996, most of the Fremont community rejected the Taliban.

Glossary

Adjustment to Immigrant Status a procedure whereby a nonimmigrant may apply for a change of status to a lawful permanent resident if an immigrant visa is available for his or her country. The alien is counted as an immigrant as of the date of adjustment.

Alien a person who is not a citizen or a national of a given nation-state.

Amicus Curiae a "friend of the court" legal brief submitted by a state or an interest group that is not a party to a case but that has an interest in the outcome of the case, in which it argues its position on the case.

Amnesty the granting of legal relief or pardon; in IRCA, granting legal temporary resident status to a previously illegal (undocumented) alien.

Asia-Pacific Triangle an area encompassing countries and colonies from Afghanistan to Japan and south to Indonesia and the Pacific Islands. Immigration from the area was severely limited to small quotas established in the McCarran-Walter Act (1952). The Asian-Pacific Triangle replaced the Asiatic Barred Zone.

Asiatic Barred Zone established by the Immigration Act of 1917, it designated a region from which few natives could enter the United States.

Asylee a person in the United States who is unable or unwilling to return to his/her country of origin because of persecution or fear of persecution. The person is eligible to become a permanent resident after one year of continuous residence in the United States.

Asylum the granting of temporary legal entrance to an individual who is an asylee.

Border Card a card allowing a person living within a certain zone of the United States border to legally cross back and forth for employment purposes without a passport or visa.

Border Patrol the law enforcement arm of the Immigration and Naturalization Service.

Bracero Program a temporary farmworker program that allowed migrant farmworkers to come to the United States for up to nine months annually to work in agriculture. The Bracero Program lasted from 1942 to 1964.

Certiorari a writ issued by the U.S. Supreme Court to send up for its review upon appeal the records of a lower court case.

Cuban-Haitian Entrant status accorded Cubans who entered the U.S. illegally between April 15, 1980, and October 10, 1980, and Haitians who entered illegally before January 1, 1981. Those qualified who were in residence continuously for one year were allowed to adjust their status to legal immigrants by the Immigration Reform and Control Act of 1986 (IRCA).

Debarkation leaving a ship or airplane to enter the United States.

Deportation a legal process by which a nation sends individuals back to their country of origin after refusing them legal residence.

Diversity Immigrants a special category of immigrants established by the 1990 IMMACT to allow a certain number of visas to be issued to immigrants from countries that previously had low admission numbers.

Due Process of Law the constitutional limitation on governmental behavior to deal with an individual according to prescribed rules and procedures.

Emigrant an individual who voluntarily leaves his/her country of birth for permanent resettlement elsewhere.

Emigration the act of leaving one's place of origin or birth for permanent resettlement.

Employer Sanctions a restrictive device of IRCA, it imposes penalties (fines or imprisonment, or both) for knowingly hiring an illegal immigrant.

Equal Protection of the Law the constitutionally guaranteed right that all persons be treated the same before the law.

Escapee an individual fleeing persecution from a communist or communist-dominated government usually for racial, religious, ethnic, social organization, or political opinion reasons.

Eugenics a pseudoscientific theory of racial genetics.

EWIs entered without inspection—another term for undocumented or illegal aliens, those who came without proper documentation or a visa.

Excluded Categories a listing in immigration law of those persons specifically denied entrance to the United States for stated reasons for the purpose of permanent settlement.

Exclusion the denial of legal entrance to a sovereign territory.

Exempt an individual or class or category of individuals to whom a certain provision of the law does not apply.

Expulsion the decision of a sovereign nation to legally compel an individual to permanently leave its territory.

Green Card a document issued by the INS that certifies an individual as a legal immigrant entitled to work in the United States.

Guest-worker Program a program enabling the legal importation of workers for temporary labor in specified occupations.

Identity Papers legal documents recognized by government as establishing a person's identity.

Illegal Alien an individual who is in a territory without documentation permitting permanent residence.

Immediate Relatives in recent immigration law, spouses, minor children, parents (of a citizen or resident alien over twenty-one years of age), and brothers or sisters of a U.S. citizen or permanent resident alien.

Immigrant an alien admitted to the United States as a lawful permanent resident.

Investor Immigrant an individual permitted to immigrate based upon a promise to invest $1 million in an urban area or $500,000 in a rural area to create at least ten new jobs.

Legalized Alien an alien lawfully admitted for temporary or permanent residence under the Immigration and Nationality Act of 1965 or under the Immigration Reform and Control Act of 1986 (IRCA).

Literacy Test a device imposed upon immigrants by the 1917 immigration act to restrict immigration to persons able to read and write.

Mortgaging the legal device to "borrow" against future fiscal year immigration quotas to allow entrance of immigrants, for refugee or humanitarian purposes, after their national origin fiscal quota has been filled.

Naturalization the legal act of making an individual a citizen who was not born a citizen.

Net EWIs estimates of the total number from each country who entered without inspection and established residency in the United States, a large majority of whom are from Mexico. Net EWIs are computed by adjusting the count of undernumerated aliens and subtracting the estimated legal resident population and subtracting the estimated number of visa overstays.

NGOs nongovernmental organizations. The term is used to refer to organizations involved in immigration matters, usually advocacy or immigrant assistance, that are not government agencies.

Nonimmigrant an alien seeking temporary entry into the United States for a specific purpose other than permanent settlement—such as a foreign government official, tourist, student, temporary worker, or cultural exchange visitor.

Nonpreference a category of immigrant visas apart from family and employment-based preferences that was available primarily between 1966 and 1978, but eliminated by the Immigration Act of 1990.

Nonquota Immigrant a person allowed entrance for specific reason who is not charged against a nation's annual quota.

Pacific Triangle an area in Southeast Asia from which immigration was specifically excluded during most of the quota era that was ended by a provision of the McCarran-Walter Act (1952).

Parolee an alien, appearing to be inadmissible to the inspecting officer, allowed to enter the United States under urgent humanitarian reasons or when that alien's entry is determined to be for significant public benefit.

Passport a legal identification document issued by a sovereign nation-state attesting to the nationality of an individual for international travel purposes.

Permanent Resident a noncitizen who is allowed to live permanently in the United States and who can travel in and out of the country without a visa and can work without restriction. This person also is permitted to accumulate time toward becoming a citizen.

Preference System a device used in immigration law to establish rules and procedures to determine the order in which annual limits of immigration visas were to be issued.

Preferences specific categories of individuals to be awarded visas for permanent immigration.

Protocol an international agreement governing the understanding and procedures that member states who are parties to a treaty agree upon for a given purpose, as in the UN protocols regarding the status and treatment of refugees.

Pull Factor characteristics of a country that attract immigrants for permanent resettlement.

Push Factor a reason that compels an individual to emigrate from his/her nation of origin and seek permanent resettlement elsewhere.

Quota Immigrant an individual seeking entrance to the United States or coming under the system that fixed an annual number of visas to be awarded to a person from a particular nation or territory.

Refugee-parolee a qualified applicant for conditional entry between 1970 and 1980 whose application for admission could not be approved because of inadequate numbers of seventh-preference visas. The applicant was paroled into the United States under the parole authority granted to the attorney general.

Relocation Camps a number of places established by executive order for holding Japanese aliens or Japanese-American citizens during World War II on their way to the ten permanent internment camps.

Special Agricultural Workers aliens who performed labor in perishable agricultural crop commodities for a specified period of time and were admitted for temporary and then permanent residence under the Immigration Reform and Control Act of 1986.

Transit Alien an alien in immediate and continuous transit through the United States, with or without a visa. Transit aliens are principally aliens and their families serving at the UN headquarters and foreign government officials and their family members.

Unauthorized Alien an individual who is in a territory without documentation—an illegal immigrant.

Undocumented Alien an individual in a sovereign territory without legal authorization to be there—an illegal alien.

Visa a legal document issued by a consular or similar State Department official allowing a person to travel to the United States for either permanent or temporary reasons—such as immigrant, student, tourist, government representative, business, or cultural exchange.

Withdrawal an alien's voluntary removal of an application for admission in lieu of an exclusion hearing before an immigration judge.

Xenophobia an unfounded fear of foreigners.

Index

About the Author

Dr. Michael LeMay is professor emeritus from California State University-San Bernardino, where he served as director of the National Security Studies Program, an interdisciplinary master's degree program, and as chair of the Department of Political Science and assistant dean of the College of Social and Behavioral Sciences. He has frequently written and presented papers at professional conferences on the topics of this book. He has also written numerous journal articles and book reviews. He is published in *The International Migration Review, In Defense of the Alien, Journal of American Ethnic History, Southeastern Political Science Review, Teaching Political Science,* and the *National Civic Review*. Author of a dozen academic volumes, his prior books dealing with immigration policy are *U.S. Immigration: A Reference Handbook* (2004, ABC-CLIO), *U.S. Immigration and Naturalization Laws and Issues: A Documentary History* (with Elliott Barkan, 1999, Greenwood), *Anatomy of a Public Policy: The Reform of Contemporary American Immigration Law* (1994, Praeger), *The Gatekeepers: Comparative Immigration Policy* (1989, Praeger), and *From Open Door to Dutch Door: An Analysis of U.S. Immigration Policy since 1820* (1987, Praeger). Professor LeMay has written two textbooks that have material related to these topics: *Public Administration: Clashing Values in the Administration of Public Policy* (2d ed., 2006, Wadsworth); and *The Perennial Struggle: Race, Ethnicity and Minority Group Relations in the United States* (2d ed., 2005, Prentice-Hall).